International Institute for Labour Studies

NEW APPROACHES TO POVERTY
ANALYSIS AND POLICY – I

The poverty agenda
and the ILO
Issues for research and action

Edited by Gerry Rodgers

A CONTRIBUTION TO THE WORLD SUMMIT FOR SOCIAL DEVELOPMENT

339.46
N532
VOL. 1

ISBN 92-9014-536-6

First published 1995

JL

Copies can be ordered directly from: ILO Publications, International Labour Office, CH-1211 Geneva 22 (Switzerland).

Preface

Fifty years ago the ILO adopted its Declaration of Philadelphia which was to serve as its postwar charter. The Declaration affirmed that poverty anywhere constitutes a danger to prosperity everywhere; that labour is not a commodity; and that freedom of expression and of association are essential to sustained progress. The task for the international community was to carry on the "war against want", both within nations and by concerted international effort.

The fight against poverty and for social justice lies at the heart of all the ILO's concerns. It runs through the ILO's work in such areas as employment, social security, minimum legal provisions for the conditions of work and for relationships within the world of work; and in the broader governance of civil society itself.

The attempt to integrate normative social policies with macro-economic strategies and with institutional change is the essential hallmark of ILO action against poverty. The ILO's approach has three characteristics. First, poverty is not viewed as merely residual or incidental, but as related to the structure and functioning of economic and social institutions. Poverty cannot be understood solely in terms of jobs, but in terms of the social context in which such jobs are embedded. Secondly, the poor have always been viewed as potential social actors rather than as targets for policy. The emphasis on the organization of social actors and their participation in development reflects the tripartite dynamic of the ILO. Thirdly, domestic anti-poverty action has always been set within the external environment. The ILO's concern in the 1950s and 1960s with growth and balance of payments constraints, and in the 1980s with economic stabilization and structural adjustment, are examples of this perspective. It is challenged by the process of globalization at the beginning of the new millenium.

In the last 50 years, per capita income has tripled, but income disparities have doubled. Seven hundred and fifty million people in developing countries are either unemployed or under-employed, a good proportion of them living in conditions of absolute poverty. In the developed economies, 35 million people are unemployed, and the share of precarious, low-quality jobs is continuing to grow. Growth has not led to the automatic eradication of poverty; neither is poverty afflicting solely those without work. The social dilemmas of transition in Eastern and Central Europe, and the problems of Africa, have all served to bring the issue of poverty to the forefront of global agendas.

On the occasion of the 50th anniversary of the Declaration of Philadelphia, the International Institute for Labour Studies reviewed the ILO's experience in this field, to identify options for future strategies. The symposium on "Poverty: New approaches to analysis and policy", organized by the Institute on 22-24 November 1993, brought contributions from a broad spectrum of opinion, including academic researchers, ILO staff, members of the ILO's constituencies and those concerned with the formulation of anti-poverty policies. The intention was to explore innovations, both in the analysis of the problem and in the design of policy, and to bring researchers together with practitioners in identifying promising avenues for future ILO work.

The symposium reviewed past and current ILO research and policy approaches to poverty, and examined recent trends and new options which have emerged in the theoretical and empirical literature. It analysed different aspects of anti-poverty policies: macro-economic and sectoral policies; labour market policies; policies to promote social coherence including social security and other forms of social protection; and the organization and representation of the poor.

The main contributions to this symposium are being published in three monographs. Monograph I comprises a critical review of ILO's action against poverty, including a broad analysis of research issues, a bibliography of ILO publications, and a summary of discussions in the symposium. Monograph II includes papers on the relationship between labour market policies and poverty. It evaluates in particular the potential impact of minimum wages, training, and labour market regulation on the incidence of poverty. Monograph III examines macro-economic and structural adjustment policies in terms of their contribution to poverty eradication in different parts of the world.

Many at the ILO and at the Institute have contributed to this work. Their names appear in each monograph, and their contribution is gratefully acknowledged. I would, however, like to make particular mention of my former colleague, Mr. Gerry Rodgers, whose vision and commitment made the symposium possible.

January 1995

Padmanabha Gopinath
Director of the International Institute
for Labour Studies

Contents

Acknowledgements

Many people were involved in the production of this monograph. First, we should like to thank the authors and particularly those who contributed to the ILO framework paper. We should also like to thank participants of the Symposium, especially those who intervened early in the meeting, setting the standards of the debates, as well as those who made fruitful comments.

We have been greatly assisted in the preparation of this monograph by a number of colleagues and friends, in particular: Gowrie Ponniah, who undertook substantive and difficult editing work on the basis of the transcripts of the debates of the Symposium; Maryse Gaudier, who compiled a most appropriate bibliographical selection; Carmen Ruppert, who corrected and did the initial formatting of many of the contributions; Hazel Cecconi, who copy edited, formatted and proof-read the papers. We hope you will enjoy reading this volume and that it will raise issues of relevance to other institutions concerned with poverty.

1 The framework of ILO action against poverty[1]

I. Introduction

"Poverty anywhere constitutes a danger to prosperity everywhere". Everyone who works with or for the ILO knows this phrase, one of the most powerful statements of the 1944 Declaration of Philadelphia [ILO, 1944]. But 50 years later, both prosperity and poverty have increased. Is this statement just empty rhetoric, or is it really true? And if it is true, what does this mean for the ILO and its work? For translating a concern with poverty into effective action against poverty is a task which history has demonstrated to be difficult, and certainly beyond the capabilities of a single organization.

This paper seeks to review the ways poverty and attempts to reduce poverty have been reflected in the policies and work of the ILO. Although authored by a group coming from different sectors of the organization, it inevitably reflects personal views and experiences, and so cannot be taken as an official statement of an ILO position. Nevertheless, the objective is a broad one of capturing the diversity of elements and policy instruments with which the ILO is concerned, and assessing their contribution to action against poverty. Do these elements add up to an "ILO approach" to poverty? The following pages suggest that, in so far as such an approach can be identified, it consists of a number of lines of attack which are only loosely linked. But there is one fundamental notion that recurs in ILO work. It is that poverty is not a marginal or incidental phenomenon, but is structurally related to the way economic and social systems function. That is, systems of production, labour use and distribution have embedded

[1] Prepared by an ILO Working Group consisting of the following: Jean-Paul Arlès, Roger Beattie, José Burle de Figueiredo, Amanda Carrizo, Maryse Gaudier, Colin Gillion, Wouter van Ginneken, Rolph van der Hoeven, Eddy Lee, Gowrie Ponniah, Samir Radwan, Gerry Rodgers. Additional contributions were provided by M. Ali Ibrahim, Azita Berar, Vali Jamal, Carlos Maldonado and Zafar Shaheed. The bulk of the writing is due to Messrs. Gillion, van Ginneken, van der Hoeven, Lee, Radwan and Rodgers.

within them mechanisms which lead to poverty, for a variety of reasons: because of the low productivity or poor mobilization of labour, because of the ways in which the benefits of production are shared, and because of institutions or patterns of organization of production which limit access or marginalize groups which lack certain characteristics or abilities. It follows that to tackle poverty it is necessary to start with an understanding of these underlying social and economic relations, and to modify them through a range of economic, institutional and legislative interventions. This perspective has led to considerable emphasis on strategic issues of economic development and macro-economic policy in action against poverty. Section II takes up this notion and explores the main issues which have been addressed.

But it is also necessary to consider more specific instruments. Many of the policy areas within the mandate of the ILO have a bearing on or contribute to more general strategies against poverty, and need to be examined in these terms. This is the subject of Section III.

Finally, an attempt is made in Section IV to outline the options for future strategy, in the light of past successes and failures, and of the changes under way in global political and economic structures.

1. The extent and characteristics of poverty

According to World Bank estimates (Table 1), around 30 per cent of the population in developing countries lived in poverty in 1990, on the basis of an absolute poverty line of $31 per person per month and an estimate of household income distribution within and across regions of the world. Close to one-half of the population was in poverty in South Asia and sub-Saharan Africa, compared with a quarter in Latin America and the Caribbean, one-third in the Middle East and North Africa, and a little over one-tenth in East Asia. The global incidence of poverty remained almost unchanged between the two years quoted in the table — 1985 and 1990 — although the absolute numbers in poverty increased because of population growth. Asia, with its rapid income growth, continued to be the most successful at alleviating poverty. But poverty increased in Africa, the Middle East and Latin America. These figures are, of course, only indicative; there is a great deal of subjectivity in poverty estimates. But they illustrate the persistence and enormous scale of the problem. The poor tend to be concentrated in rural areas, where average real incomes are much lower than in urban areas; but there is also much extreme poverty in the cities, where the poor typically live in slums or squatter settlements, and often have to contend with overcrowding, bad sanitation and contaminated

Table 1: Poverty in the developing world, 1985-1990

Region	Percentage of population below the poverty line		Number of poor persons (millions)	
	1985	1990	1985	1990
All developing countries	30.5	29.7	1,051	1,133
South Asia	51.8	49.0	532	562
East Asia	13.2	11.3	182	169
Sub-Saharan Africa	47.6	47.8	184	216
Middle East & North Africa	30.6	33.1	60	73
Latin America & Caribbean	22.4	25.5	87	108

Source: World Bank, *World Development Report*, 1992.

water. In recent years, civil wars and the breakdown of law and order have also resulted in much extreme deprivation, sometimes associated with large-scale movements of refugees.

In the longer term, there have been significant changes in the nature of poverty and poverty processes in developing countries. Major structural transformations have occurred since the 1960s, involving the relocation of vast numbers of rural people to the urban areas. In most Latin American countries, over two-thirds of the population now lives in the cities compared with only one-third 30 years ago. In sub-Saharan Africa, urbanization has proceeded at annual rates of 6 to 8 per cent and one-third of the population is now urban, compared with only 10 per cent or so at the start of the 1960s. The rural population is already a minority in most of the Asian NICs. But whereas urbanization in the newly-industrializing countries (NICs) has increased in line with employment opportunities, in most other developing countries rural-urban migration has occurred at much higher rates than warranted by the absorptive capacity of the formal sector. Unemployment and underemployment have grown, with the informal sector having to bear the brunt of urban labour absorption. In the rural areas, too, significant changes have occurred. Because of land shortage or changes in land-holding patterns, landlessness has increased and the new entrants to the rural labour force are increasingly forced into wage labour. The number of net buyers of food has begun to rival the surplus producers and the self-sufficient, even in Africa.

The long-term trends towards urbanization and landlessness have been exacerbated by the now two-decade-long crisis in Latin America and Africa and the ensuing structural adjustment programmes. The Asian region has been somewhat protected from these two trends, although some of the impacts are discernible even there. While the crisis originated in the tradeables sector — effectively the agricultural sector — because of declining commodity prices, it had its most visible impact in the urban areas in terms of declines in real wages: a fall of 30-50 per cent was common in the sub-Saharan countries and similar situations occurred in many countries of Latin America. The structural adjustment programmes, with their emphasis on wage restraint and de-subsidization of staple foods, contributed to the fall in real wages. Combined with a decline in the numbers in formal, wage employment, this has sometimes meant a total eclipse of wage incomes in urban areas, notably in Africa. It is in this dual sense that the African countries have become "informalized": not only has the urban wage class been reduced to a minority, but so have wages compared to informal sector incomes. Similar tendencies are present in Latin America, but this is less true of East Asia where rapid economic expansion has in fact resulted in the contraction of informal activities.

In the rural areas, the impact of the crisis and adjustment programmes has varied. The hardest-hit have been wage workers, whose wages have fallen along with those of their urban counterparts, and for similar reasons — the rescinding or decline of minimum wages and the freeing of food prices. Export crop producers were less affected, as declines in world prices were often offset by devaluation.

The declining incomes in both rural and urban areas have resulted in a great blurring of economic roles, with most families increasing their outreach over several sectors to make ends meet. The changes have been most noticeable in the urban areas where families have resorted to straddling strategies, including even urban farming. This fusion of economic roles has rendered the identification of poverty groups difficult. The usual "indicators" of poverty, such as wages and farm prices, can no longer be taken as guides to family income since the composition of family income varies between groups and over time. By and large the vulnerable groups are to be found among the smallholders, the farm workers, the urban wage earners, and the informal sector workers but, because of the diversity of strategies, this characterization may well be too imprecise for the design of effective policy.

Several other factors have led to changes in the characteristics of poverty, notably a series of structural changes in the world economy. One such change is increasing polarization in the labour market. As enterprises attempt to reduce costs in the face of increasingly fierce global competition, the number of jobs with higher incomes and employment security declines. These advantages are restricted to a core group of workers who possess human capital acquired both from formal education and from on-the-job acquisition of skills. Around them is a larger group of "secondary" workers who are often employed under fixed-term or temporary contracts.

Finally, there is an army of subcontracted informal workers and small enterprises where employment conditions are much less generous. This process of differentiation can be observed in developed and developing countries alike.

The breakdown of the extended — and often even the nuclear — family is another factor explaining the changing composition of poverty. As a result of education and migration, the bonds of the extended family are loosening. One result is that more households are headed by women, who often command lower wages than men. The ageing of the population is also likely to shape the composition of poverty in the future. In the developed countries, old people are protected by private pensions, social insurance and social assistance. But in the developing countries such provisions are hardly available so that, without countervailing policies, poverty is likely to worsen among old people.

Poverty is by no means confined to the developing countries included in Table 1. The nature of poverty in industrialized countries is different — relatively few people are totally unable to obtain subsistence in high income societies, if only because of officially sanctioned safety nets, or sometimes due to the existence of private charities. But deprivation and relative poverty persist and in many countries have been growing in the face of the rise of individualistic ideologies ("poverty is the fault of the poor") and the decreasing capacity of states to maintain full-scale welfare systems. Failure to deal with such problems, which could, in principle at least, be solved with the allocation of relatively small proportions of national product in rich countries, is an indictment of the functioning of many industrialized societies, and one which threatens stability and economic progress. In this case, the rhetoric of the Declaration of Philadelphia may well still be justified. The recent growth in poverty in Central and Eastern Europe following the collapse of socialist systems of public provisioning surely poses an equal threat to economic reconstruction.

The poor usually lack assets as well as income, including the "human capital" embodied in skills and knowledge. Vulnerability to ill-health is common as cause or consequence of poverty, often associated with malnutrition. Poor women are particularly badly off, discriminated against in the labour market and subject to particular vulnerabilities because of motherhood. All this undermines the capacity for work of the poor — so diminishing their main or only asset.

But the poor remain a very heterogeneous group. Poverty may have many causes and it affects many different groups. It is possible to identify characteristics such as cultural, social and ethnic background, family situation, or the area and housing that people live in, which help to identify and locate the poor. But, even if all these characteristics were the same for all families with the same income or the same pattern of deprivation, it is quite possible that they would adopt different strategies to overcome their situation. And in reality the economic and social situations of the poor are very diverse. Too simple a notion of poverty is therefore likely to lead to inappropriate policy.

2.   Notions of poverty

As Amartya Sen has commented, in an ILO-supported publication on poverty and famines [Sen, 1981], "much about poverty is obvious enough". But there are very different views of what poverty means, and they affect the design of action against poverty. At the simplest level, individuals or families are considered poor when their level of living, measured in terms of income or consumption, is below a particular standard. The most widespread approach is to define a minimum standard or poverty line in absolute terms. Minimum food requirements are usually determined on the basis of recommended calorie intake, to which is added a special allowance for non-food needs, consistent with the spending pattern of the poor or with perceptions of their needs. Account may be taken of access to government services such as education, health and other infrastructure. Such "absolute" poverty lines implicitly contain elements of relative poverty, since they are defined at higher levels in countries with higher average standards of living, but poverty may also be explicitly defined in relative terms, as when it refers to position in relation to average income or consumption in a particular country or region.

When viewed in these terms, poverty is a static concept: it measures the level of living at a particular moment of time. But an important element in the concept of poverty is insecurity. If people are temporarily poor, but are likely to escape from poverty after some time, their situation is less serious than that of the permanently poor. The security provided by assets — a house or a piece of land — may be significant here. Social or economic rights may also be important in providing security: citizenship rights, for instance, which may qualify individuals for government help through social security or food stamps, or informal, social rights based on family or community solidarity.

Social exclusion and marginalization provide further sets of concepts closely related to poverty. Individuals or groups may be marginalized through a variety of economic and social processes, and it is not uncommon for such groups to internalize the stigma of not being part of "normal" or "modern" society. This provides one important mechanism whereby poverty is transmitted from one generation to the other. Much work on poverty has also been built around concepts of deprivation — failure to obtain the goods, services, rights and activities which, in any given society, form the basis of normal social and economic behaviour. Multiple deprivation is a broader notion than poverty, and one which is essentially relative in character, because deprivation is defined in relation to social standards and norms. Another, alternative, approach is to see poverty in terms of exclusion — not only exclusion from participation in society in a general sense as in the notion of marginalization but more specifically in terms of lack of access to jobs, lack of social protection, lack of possibility for self-development or organization and many other particular dimensions. These different visions of the problems make it clear that breaking out of the vicious circle of poverty is more than an economic issue. It also means changing the values and structure of society as well as the perception that the poor have of themselves.

All these different views of poverty have informed ILO work at one time or another. In an ILO policy context, the basic conceptual problem is one of linking poverty with labour. The most powerful idea has been one of satisfying minimum needs through productive employment, and this idea has recurred, notably in the promotion of minimum wages, in the Director-General's report of 1970 [ILO, 1970a] devoted to minimum needs, and particularly in the World Employment Conference in 1976 which explicitly focused on how to achieve the satisfaction of an absolute level of basic needs [see ILO, 1976]. Two fundamental issues have emerged: first, how to link such "developmental" objectives with the rights and standards promoted within various ILO programmes; and second, how to clarify the relationships between employment, unemployment and labour underutilization on the one hand, and different aspects or notions of poverty on the other.

The first of these issues derives from the normative nature of much of the ILO's work. But poverty cannot at first sight be approached through a normative route. Freedom from poverty may indeed be regarded as a right, but it is necessary to distinguish two classes of rights: those which are "actor-impeded", and those which are "structure-impeded".[2] Rights which are actor-impeded are those which result from relationships between human beings; they refer to domains such as freedom of association,

---

[2] For a development of this argument, see Galtung & Wirak [1977]. See also Dasgupta [1989].

discrimination or working conditions. Legislative interventions may contribute directly to achieving such rights. Rights which are structure-impeded depend on social and economic resources and factors which require interventions of a different order. A second important distinction is that between material and non-material needs and rights. Non-material needs may include the need for identity or for liberty of expression. In these terms, the right to freedom from poverty has mainly been conceptualized as falling within the category "material, structure-impeded". But clearly, rights in different categories may reinforce or undermine each other, and they need to be addressed together, so action against poverty has to be linked to action in favour of non-material needs and other rights. As the following pages will show, this issue has not been fully resolved in the work of the ILO.

The second issue, on the conceptual relationships between work, employment and poverty, has received more attention. One approach is to consider that poverty is mainly caused by labour force underutilization, either through unemployment, or through the absorption of surplus labour in low productivity jobs. Initially, the concept of *labour force under-utilization* [ILO, 1971a] was associated with that of labour surplus in agriculture, i.e. that part of the agricultural labour force that could theoretically be removed without reducing the total amount of agricultural output. However, this approach suffers from various theoretical problems, as well as from the important practical disadvantage that it produces one global figure of labour force underutilization that cannot be attributed to specific categories of workers. Subsequent work attempted to deal with this issue of categorization, notably through the distinction between unemployment, and visible and invisible underemployment, as laid down by the Thirteenth International Conference of Labour Statisticians [ILO, 1982]. While the unemployed were defined as those "without work", "currently available for work", and "seeking work", the visibly under-employed are those who involuntarily work less than the normal duration of work determined for the activity, and who are seeking more work. On the other hand, the concept of invisible underemployment is a more subtle construct. It reflects a misallocation between labour and other factors of production and might be characterized by low income, underutilization of skill and low productivity. Invisible unemployment is difficult to measure and, in practice, people were often considered invisibly underemployed when their labour income (either from self-employment or wage employ-ment) was below the minimum wage level or the poverty line; in other words, invisible unemployment has often been equated with poverty. An equally important and closely related concept is that of the so-called *working poor*. They are the workers in the urban informal and rural sectors who may work long hours, but do not earn enough to lift their families out of poverty. Poverty may therefore be associated with "overemployment", as well as with underemployment.

In all these cases, an important issue has to be addressed: welfare (and poverty) are most appropriately measured at the level of the household or income-sharing unit, whereas (except in some household enterprises) earnings, work and unemployment refer to individuals. The characteristics of jobs are therefore only one of the determinants of poverty, for the sharing mechanisms within households or communities are equally important. Within households, for instance, the consumption of income-earners may considerably exceed that of dependents. This has an important effect on the poverty status of women, of child workers and of other groups. There are conceptual and measurement difficulties here which have not been fully resolved.

3. ILO action before and after the Second World War

Between the First and Second World Wars the idea of social justice guided much of ILO's action on poverty. Vulnerable groups such as children and migrants worked under inhuman conditions. And most workers did not have income protection when, because of disease, old-age or other misfortune, they were not able to earn a living. The greatest "misfortune" occurred during the Depression of the early 1930s when millions of workers lost their jobs without having any income protection.

During this period, legislation and social security schemes were considered the main instruments for workers' protection. Hence the ILO adopted a range of Conventions on vulnerable groups (mainly children and migrants), social security and working conditions (hours of work and safety and health). During the crisis years, the ILO also adopted Conventions on employment agencies and unemployment provisions. These Conventions were mainly applied and ratified in the advanced countries of Europe and the Americas.

In 1944, the International Labour Conference in Philadelphia recognized that widespread unemployment and poverty had been among the root causes of the two World Wars, and placed concern with these issues at the centre of the work of the organization. The years after the Second World War also saw the establishment of the United Nations and the formulation of the two human rights covenants: one on civil and political rights and one on economic, social and cultural rights. Similarly, in the immediate post-war years the ILO adopted a series of basic labour rights Conventions such as those on freedom of association (1948), collective bargaining (1949), minimum wages and equal remuneration (1951), social security (1952), forced labour (1957) and discrimination (1958).

When many African and Asian countries became independent after the Second World War their governments embarked on a process of modernization and industrial development which they hoped would solve the problem of underdevelopment and poverty. The ILO's contribution was to develop technical cooperation programmes and policies designed to support social development, stressing the provision of productive employment as one of the key policies to lift people out of poverty. To provide advice on these matters to member countries, the ILO decided in 1969 — on its 50th anniversary — to set up the World Employment Programme (WEP), which became the most important single programme of the ILO with respect to poverty alleviation.

A part of the ILO's work on Conventions attempts to formulate more specific human rights standards in the welfare area. Signatories of the Employment Convention (No. 122), for example, declare that they will "pursue, as a major goal, an active policy designed to promote full, productive and freely chosen employment". The accompanying Recommendation (No. 122) indicates what policies governments can adopt to achieve full employment. The Convention on Social Security (No. 102) establishes minimum standards for social security, while signatories of the Convention on Minimum Wage-Fixing (No. 131) "undertake to establish a system of minimum wages which covers all groups of wage earners whose terms of employment are such that coverage would be appropriate". The Social Policy (Basic Aims and Standards) Convention (No. 117) considers the "improvement of standards of living" as the "principal objective in the planning of economic development".

In the ILO's philosophy, these welfare rights can only be achieved in a context of equality, freedom and collaboration. Workers should be free to organize so as to defend their own interests. And the social partners should be willing to collaborate with each other so as to create a socio-economic environment in which unemployment and poverty can be eliminated. But, most importantly, governments must develop new and comprehensive economic and social policies to support such objectives.

4.   The ILO's work on poverty within the international system

Many of the bodies of the United Nations system deal with aspects of poverty. Specialized agencies either deal with specific production sectors (industry, agriculture), with special groups (children), or with particular social sectors (health, education). While these agencies, in particular the FAO and UNICEF, have paid considerable attention to poverty, the central concern with employment and labour issues at ILO appears to provide this organization with one of the strongest mandates for work on poverty among the specialized agencies of the UN system. Beyond the specialized agencies, the UN proper, and especially UNDP, has taken a lead in developing broader development strategies, notably involving the concept of human development, which are highly complementary to the mandate of ILO. But within the United Nations system, the organization which has worked most on poverty in recent years is clearly the World Bank. The Bank has the advantage of a broader focus than the specialized agencies, and has a considerably greater resource base. But its vision of labour, as for most other issues, has been coloured in the past by the fact that it is a bank, so that its projects have to meet financial objectives even when their primary purpose is social. Work on labour and employment in the Bank also tends to stress market relationships to a much greater degree than work at ILO. There are differences of philosophy here which remain to be reconciled.

What marks out the work of the ILO is that it directly focuses on labour use in production systems, and so arguably goes to the core of the relationships of production from which poverty and wealth emerge, and where poverty can be combated. In so doing, the ILO places importance on equity issues and normative action, establishing standards to regulate the terms and conditions of employment. Its tripartite structure, while not necessarily facilitating work on poverty directly, also provides a window to non-governmental bodies which other UN agencies do not have.

II. Poverty, employment and growth: Strategic options

1. Economic patterns and the perception of poverty

During the first half of the twentieth century, action against poverty and inequality was on the whole not integrated into broader economic policy in the economically advanced countries and their colonies. This is not to say that concern for poor people and special measures to take care of the poor were absent.[3] Action against poverty, dominated by charitable

---

[3] Indeed, Alfred Marshall wrote "I have devoted myself for the last 20 years to the problem of poverty... Very little of my work has been devoted to any inquiry which does not bear on that" [*Official Papers*, 1893].

"poor relief" and workhouses in the nineteenth century, was greatly influenced by the studies of Rowntree at the turn of the century [Rowntree, 1909]. Rowntree emphasized the income and consumption patterns of poor households, and how they could be used to determine poverty thresholds. His work was a powerful input to the design of income support and social insurance policies, and greatly influenced awareness of poverty. Action against poverty also received increasing attention from local administrations and, after the First World War, from the gradually developing welfare agencies. The Constitution of the ILO bears witness to this, with its stress on hardship and privation among workers, and on the need to improve working conditions. But poverty was, on the whole, not treated as an inherent outcome of the pattern of economic growth. Whole societies could be poor because of low productivity. But in high productivity economies, poverty was either a marginal phenomenon, because particular groups failed for one reason or another to join the economic mainstream, or a temporary one, linked to problems of unemployment in the economic cycle, or a social or labour issue which could be treated separately from economic policy. Even Keynes' solution to the Great Depression and the New Deal movement was not really concerned with structural poverty issues. For example, the index of the *General theory of employment, interest and money* [Keynes, 1936] does not have an entry on poverty, only on "employment in poor community", where Keynes refers to the consumption patterns of the poor [p. 31] and discusses what will happen if a poor community catches up with the rich [p. 219].

At the time of the Declaration of Philadelphia attention was already shifting towards the growth path of the world economy in the post-war period, and the complexity of the relationship between economic growth and the elimination of poverty was clearly recognized. But the stress in the immediate post-war period in the economically advanced countries was on the development of systems of social insurance. The belief was that a comprehensive safety-net, including unemployment insurance, income support, universal old-age pensions and access to public services for health and education would compensate for any tendency for poverty to persist; and economic growth would provide the resources to pay the bill. While poverty has, of course, not disappeared in the advanced industrialized countries, and has in some ways and at some times grown, this vision remains the reference point for action against poverty in Western Europe at least. And where, as in the United States, general systems of social provisioning proved more difficult to establish, concern with poverty focused on the disadvantages of specific groups, rather than on any deficiencies in the growth path itself.

But attention to poverty as an integral part of economic analysis did come to the fore in a different context in the 1950s and early 1960s, when a generation of experienced economists became concerned about the pattern of economic growth in what were then known as the underdeveloped countries. This coincided with the process of decolonization and the creation of new nations whose populations were expecting rapid progress and a rapid decline in poverty, and looked to the freshly-created independent states to promote this.

The most influential view of development during this period linked poverty to the dualistic structure of the economies concerned. Development was seen as a process of modernization and industrialization, but traditional and modern sectors co-existed in the process of modernization. Poverty, then, was to be found in traditional sectors, and modernization with labour protection was its cure. ILO thinking reflected this. Many ILO standards were implicitly or explicitly linked to, indeed formed part of, the process of modernization, which generally involved the spread of wage labour. The traditional sectors were a sponge, absorbing excess labour, a means of sharing poverty. While at first "traditional" tended to be equated with rural and "modern" with urban, the obvious importance of non-modern economic activities in urban areas led in time to a perception of dualism within the urban economy as well. A corollary of this view of the development process was that certain changes in the patterns of inequality over time could be expected. The work of Kuznets, in particular, suggested that most countries developed from a situation of relative equality (shared poverty in traditional activities) through a stage of increased inequality (as a small, modern, high-income sector developed) to a stage of lower inequality in mature, modern economies. ILO work [Paukert, 1973] documented the existence of such a pattern in the 1960s, at least in cross-section. It followed that during some phases of the development process, growth would not necessarily reduce absolute poverty and relative poverty would increase. If inequality increased and if growth were sluggish in relation to population growth, poverty might increase both relatively and absolutely.

The recognition that poverty could be structural, and its elimination through development a very long-term process, led to increased attention to (a) the mechanisms through which growth may lead to poverty alleviation — the beginnings of the debate about "trickle-down"; and (b) the analysis of whether interventions to reduce income inequality promote or hinder growth. Clear differences emerged in the literature between those who considered the priority lay in accelerated growth, even if poverty persisted, and those who saw a need for a structurally different development path which could reduce poverty rapidly. While the debate has since moved on from earlier simple conceptions of dualism, what remains is a belief in the importance of structure. Economic outcomes in general, and poverty in particular, have structural explanations in terms of differing rules, institutions and opportunities in different economic and social environments. Successful intervention implies either attempting to modify these structures, or adapting to the realities which they reflect.

The international aspects of poverty formed an integral part of the development debate from the outset. The structural factors underlying poverty were seen as international as much as they were national, and poverty arose from an unfavourable position in the world trading system as much as from adverse national structures. Several "grand" development strategies were, in effect, built around changing the links between national and international economies, so as to permit countries to escape a low-income-cum-poverty-equilibrium trap. For example, the Prebisch-Singer notion of import-substitution-led growth was designed to overcome endemic poverty due to declining terms of trade for primary commodity exports. Development was seen as a process of catching up with the industrialized world (e.g. in the UN's First Development Decade), and it was considered that international aid flows and appropriate development planning could avoid the perpetuation of poverty in this process.

ILO's involvement in debates in the 1970s on the international dimensions of poverty emphasized the importance of comparative advantage and of the removal of trade barriers so that countries could benefit from their comparative advantage, and highlighted much more than is common today the need for adjustment in both industrialized and developing countries [Lydall, 1975; Mukherhee, 1979; Renshaw, 1980]. This work stressed employment creation more than poverty reduction and, partly as a result, export promotion received increasing attention. But the question was also raised whether increased trade, in economies with an unequal asset distribution and low levels of education and training, might not widen inequality and worsen poverty. Some writers suggested that countries should aim to provide for the satisfaction of essential needs, an upgrading of educational standards and a fair distribution of land and other assets, before launching themselves into a strategy of shifting from import substitution towards active export promotion [see Griffin & Khan, 1978; Adelman, 1978]. This would be a prerequisite for linking integration in the international economy with decreasing poverty. Others suggested possible scenarios for poverty reduction through international capital and aid flows [Hopkins & van der Hoeven, 1982; Hopkins & Norbye, 1978] and argued for policy changes in both developing and industrialized countries and in international markets. Such analyses might have provided a useful point of reference for ILO policy in the 1980s. However, the changing international mood made it difficult to promote an approach which linked together domestic and international policies with an explicit focus on poverty. We return to this point below.

2. Development strategies, poverty and the ILO

The link between development strategies and poverty constituted the dominant *problematique* in the work of the World Employment Programme (WEP) in the 1970s. This link is still a key element in recent thinking on poverty in developing countries, even though the ILO itself has largely retreated from this area of inquiry.

The underlying premise of this work is that changes in the level of poverty are powerfully influenced by the total set of economic policies adopted by a country in pursuit of its development objectives. These include its macro-economic policies, its trade and industrialization regime, policies influencing the distribution of income and the pattern of demand, its incentive structure influencing the choice of industrial structure, product mix and technique of production, and its choice of economic system (role of the state in production and degree of intervention in, and regulation of, markets). Various configurations of policy mixes can be categorized as constituting different "development strategies" (e.g. export led or import substituting, free market or mixed economy, etc.). The choice of development strategy is held to determine the rate and pattern of growth which, mediated through different initial conditions (in terms of economic structure, degree of equality in asset distribution, competitiveness or degree of distortion in markets, etc.), in turn affects the level of poverty, favourably or negatively.

The choice of development strategy is considered to be the dominant influence on the fate of the poor because the rate of growth determines overall income prospects while the pattern of growth, mediated through economic structures and institutions, determines the primary distribution of income amongst different groups. The impact on levels of income and its distribution, and hence on poverty, is thus all-pervasive. This is why so much attention has been directed at this link between development strategies and poverty. If development strategies can be influenced in a poverty-reducing direction this would be the most powerful lever for eradicating mass poverty, dwarfing the impact of any number of direct poverty-alleviation programmes which deal with specific symptoms rather than underlying causes.

The ILO's Comprehensive Employment Strategy Missions (CESMs) to a series of developing countries in the initial years of WEP addressed this large issue of the link between development strategies and poverty (albeit at a slight remove since they focused on the development strategy and employment nexus). They were inspired by the growing empirical evidence at the time that there was a persistent or growing problem of unemployment and underemployment in developing countries in spite of steady growth in GDP. Growth per se was seen to be insufficient for solving the employment and congruent poverty problem in developing countries. GDP growth had to be dethroned from its position as the paramount objective and yardstick of economic development. Employment and other social indicators had to be included among the explicit objectives of development. The CESMs explored possibilities for structural change in the development path in the light of these new perspectives, although certain CESMs were clearly more "structuralist" than others and it was not always clear whether official ILO policy was really premised upon the need for substantial structural changes or rather aimed mainly to limit the inegalitarian aspects of development.

The CESMs undertook comprehensive reviews of development strategies in order to recommend reforms which would lead to levels and patterns of growth that maximized the rate of productive employment creation. These recommendations were truly comprehensive in that they covered the sectoral allocation of investments, changes in exchange rates and commercial policy, choice of technology, and reforms in capital and labour markets. The basic thrust of these recommendations was the need to remove policy and institutional biases against the labour-intensive pattern of growth that was warranted by the factor endowments and comparative advantage of labour-abundant economies. The recommendations covered issues such as the capital intensity of investments; changes in exchange rates, trade and industrialization strategy, and relative factor prices that were required to promote more labour-intensive growth; investment, fiscal and other policies to stimulate the growth of competitive labour-intensive activities; and redistributive policies to promote a more equitable pattern of growth.

This comprehensive framework developed by the CESMs led to programmes of research centred around key aspects of development strategies in WEP's work. These included (i) technology and employment, which focused on economic and technology policies for promoting the adoption of more labour-intensive techniques of production; (ii) income distribution policies for promoting equitable growth; (iii) rural employment policies for countering growing rural poverty and landlessness, and; (iv) policies for promoting increased productive labour absorption in the urban informal sector.

All this work fed into a major synthesis in the form of the Basic Needs Strategy which was presented to the World Employment Conference in 1976. WEP research had highlighted the need to widen the development strategy beyond employment objectives towards a broad-based anti-poverty strategy, which would affect a much larger part of the population. The notion of poverty which emerged, however, went beyond income and consumption to encompass other important and essential elements of well-being, notably those that are usually provided partly or completely outside the market mechanism (education, health, water supply, housing). These factors were built, along with others, into a broad concept of *basic needs*. The basic needs strategy which was adopted is perhaps the clearest recent example of the ILO attempting to set the terms of the debate around poverty and its alleviation; in its simplest terms, the proposition was to reorient development strategy towards the satisfaction of the basic needs of the population as a whole, through the orientation of the economic system towards the production of basic needs goods, through public provision, and through the widening of participation in the production process.

Some important elements of the basic needs strategy were the identification of and the specific attention to target groups in the planning process, the use of corrective measures by the government (through asset redistribution or through factor rewards) if the development process failed to reach the target groups sufficiently, and the use of the government budget to deliver non-marketable needs to the target and other groups. Another important element was a concern to promote the participation of all members of the society, not only in formulating targets for themselves, but also in finding creative solutions as to how to reach these targets.

On the whole, the basic needs strategy met with relatively little success. Conceived at a time of rapid economic growth and growing public resources, it was promoted in the unfriendly economic atmosphere of the late 1970s, in the face of declining resources for investment and public action. The structural changes in economic systems required to meet basic needs appeared to be widely politically unviable, the approach did not have sufficient backing from the ILO's constituency. The political influence of the beneficiaries was weak, and leaders of many low-income countries objected to the idea that *basic* goods and services were good enough for them, arguing (apparently with some merit in view of the subsequent performance of the "Newly Industrializing Countries") that successful growth required advanced technology and sophisticated and competitive production systems. Elements of the basic needs strategy were subsequently promoted by the World Bank, with its focus on redistribution with growth, and much later as part of the UNDP's work on human development, but at ILO this approach was effectively abandoned.

Work on the larger issues of development strategy continued in ILO in the aftermath of the World Employment Conference to the end of the 1970s, extending into the early 1980s in the case of some Regional Employment Teams. Notable examples of work on the broad theme of development strategies were: (i) ARTEP's work on labour absorption in agriculture which sought to identify the policy and institutional factors that explained the substantially higher levels of labour absorption in East Asian agriculture (at comparable levels of development) as compared to South Asia; (ii) ARTEP's work on export-led industrialization and on export processing zones which examined the policies responsible for the successful employment-intensive growth observed in East and South-East Asian economies and the replicability of this experience; (iii) various country mission and studies by PREALC, JASPA and ARTEP which undertook comprehensive diagnoses of the employment problem and recommended changes in development strategy in order to raise the rate of productive employment creation; (iv) PREALC and JASPA work on policies for promoting productive labour absorption in the urban informal sector; (v) JASPA studies on the dynamics of rural-urban income distribution.

The momentum of such work began petering out in the 1980s for a combination of reasons. One was the feeling that the ILO had over-extended itself through the work on general development policies. This arose from a perception that there was an unacceptable radical and *dirigiste* tone to parts of this work and from doubts over whether the ILO, with its given mandate and constituency, could really be an influential actor in bringing about changes in overall development strategies. These internal doubts were reinforced by changes in attitudes and policies among donors who for over a decade had provided significant support to WEP research in both Geneva and the regions. These donors, who were increasingly turning towards technical cooperation, began to question the practical impact of such research. They could find few countries which had fully adopted the comprehensive policy recommendations emerging from WEP research. They had expected tangible results in terms of improved employment outcomes and they were disappointed. They advocated more practical action and this led to a marked shift towards the development and implementation of technical cooperation projects in the work of WEP. Much of this work was inspired by a "direct, targeted action" approach to poverty alleviation, rather than an attempt to induce structural change. There was a proliferation of income generation projects for target groups (especially rural women), of informal sector and cottage industry promotion projects and of labour-intensive public works projects.

Changes in the economic circumstances of developing countries and in the intellectual climate which occurred in the 1980s also helped to erode the basis for WEP's work on development strategies. The dramatic onset of a developing country debt crisis at the beginning of the 1980s shifted the attention of the international community towards short-run problems of macro-economic stabilization and accompanying reforms in economic policies.

The ILO's work on development strategies, focusing as it did on essentially long-term issues of the dynamics of growth, distribution and employment generation, appeared incongruous in the context of the endemic economic retrogression and crises of the 1980s. Although the ILO did undertake a number of studies on the social effects of adjustment and stabilization, they remained isolated, never synthesized into an "ILO view". As a result, the ILO had relatively little influence in the international debates over stabilization and structural adjustment, dominated by the Bretton Woods institutions from the mid-1980s onwards.

ILO research in this period nevertheless explored the impact of adjustment on poverty and unemployment [van der Hoeven, 1987; ILO, 1987; ARTEP, 1987; PREALC, 1987]. ILO work in Africa [Jamal & Weeks, 1987; Jamal, 1988; JASPA, 1982] figured in the debate in both academic and UN circles. It questioned the premises of adjustment programmes, showing that the presumed model of "urban bias" no longer applied because of the massive declines in urban wages and the consequent narrowing of the rural-urban gap. The impact on income distribution was adverse since export crop producers, who were set to gain, were not among the "poorest of the poor" and since the wage-earners who were likely to lose were no longer the "aristocracy" they had long been claimed to be. The much desired impact on growth had not transpired because of the lack of action on the non-price constraints facing the agricultural sector. In Latin America, ILO work stressed the increased informalization of the economies and the growing precariousness of jobs, which added to the poverty problem. PREALC studies showed that the informal sector grew counter-cyclically to GDP, implying that it had a dynamic pattern of its own. An innovation was to point to the growing "social debt", i.e. the share of the national product needed to lift the population out of poverty [PREALC, 1988]. Work in Asia demonstrated that it was those outside the modern or organized labour markets who suffered the most during the adjustment process. In many countries, youth, women and migrants from depressed rural areas were unable to find jobs in the organized or formal sectors and increasingly had to resort to insecure and low-paid employment. But where economic growth remained sluggish, modern sector wage employees were also exposed to a decline in real income and increasing poverty [ARTEP, 1987]. A general conclusion of this work in all three continents was that, because alleviation of poverty was clearly not an objective of the adjustment policies, poverty worsened, when a socially aware development strategy could have protected the poor from the burden of adjustment.

Reiterated concern over the social effects of adjustment, expressed by the ILO among other bodies, started to have an impact on the design of macro-economic policy in the later 1980s and early 1990s. While the primary aim of adjustment programmes remains the restoration of financial health, there has been an evolution from mere stabilization to adjustment, to structural adjustment with growth, to structural adjustment with growth accompanied by social funds or compensatory programmes. The inter-national financial agencies have clearly become more sensitive to social questions and the poverty issue. Initial compensatory programmes in Bolivia (the Emergency Social Fund) and Ghana have found many followers in other countries. The major purpose of these programmes is to provide rapidly disbursed funds to "mitigate" the consequences of the adjustment policies. The outcomes of such programmes have, however, been rather mixed. Some additional resources did indeed become available for social policy purposes, but often with a narrow range of beneficiaries and a fairly limited effect on poverty [van der Hoeven, 1993].

The ILO's earlier work on development strategies, along with the more recent work of other UN agencies such as UNDP with its concentra-tion on human development, and UNICEF with its stress on protecting the vulnerable in adjustment, suggests that if poverty is to be overcome the following are important:

(a) enabling poor households to have access to productive assets and employment opportunities, and to receive adequate prices and wages;

(b) increasing the productivity of the labour and assets of poor households through access to capital, education and skills;

(c) providing adequate access to a range of basic services, such as agricultural extension services and other types of infrastructure;

(d) providing systems of protection against abuse and exploitation of the economically or socially weak;

(e) providing safety nets for households and individuals who cannot produce enough to survive or escape from absolute poverty;

(f) enabling poor households to live in a situation of law and order and be protected against violence.

Structural adjustment programmes, especially the so-called compensatory programmes, have been fairly forthcoming on safety nets *(e)* and to some extent also on access to basic services *(c)*, but much less so on political stability and protection *(d)* and *(f)* and hardly at all on enabling poor households to produce more and more productively *(a)* and *(b)*. In other words, structural adjustment has not addressed the structural factors underlying poverty.

The foregoing suggests that the important question is not whether adjustment policies have caused more poverty or not; it is rather, to what extent do the institutional and other policy changes, which usually make up a structural adjustment package, also promote whatever structural changes are needed to decrease poverty permanently? This implies the need for a wide-ranging, integrated view. It makes little sense to break down the various adjustment policies into distinct policy instruments and argue the merits of these instruments separately, using arguments such as "less regulation will decrease rent-seeking and help the poor", "less public ownership will free resources for education and help the poor", or "a better incentive structure will make everybody better off in the long run", propositions which are encountered all too often but which fail to take account of the interactions between different instruments. The question is much more one of balance and mutual reinforcement between different components of policy within a comprehensive approach, so that a change in one area (e.g. privatization) can be made to promote the interests of the poor, by simultaneously introducing other changes (regulation of capital or labour markets, incomes policy, redistribution of assets, etc.). It is this integrated approach which often seems to be lacking. Yet it was precisely this broad-based vision of development strategy which characterized the earlier work of the World Employment Programme.

3. Poverty and work: Analytical and strategic concerns

Behind the macro-framework of development strategy lies a set of issues at the heart of the ILO's traditional mandate. Most ILO policy analysis concerns jobs, directly or indirectly: creating employment; promoting the development of income opportunities in self-employment; regulating the conditions under which jobs are undertaken; intervening in labour markets to increase information and reduce discrimination; promoting systems of social insurance for the unemployed; supporting the institutions for representation of workers and employers, etc. Some of these, such as employment creation, have been perceived as more closely related to poverty than others, such as representation or labour market information. The compartmentalized structure of the ILO did not lend itself to the integration of these different elements in a coherent strategy against poverty. But the real problem was not so much bureaucratic as conceptual. Different forms of ILO intervention have a different conceptual and sometimes philosophical basis, and it is worth trying to explore some of the implications of this for work on poverty.

A. Employment and unemployment

While employment has not been the only instrument addressed by the ILO in its work on poverty, it has been central to much of the ILO's work in the field. At its simplest level, the relationship between poverty and employment lies in the extent to which income generated from employment permits workers and their dependents to obtain the minimum needs expressed in a poverty line. But even this level implies a duality in the approach to poverty within the ILO: first there is a question of the level of employment, or, inversely, the extent of unemployment or underemployment; and second there is the income derived from work.

The notion of a "job", in the sense of regular, full-time work, underlay the ILO's approach to employment and labour underutilization for many years. The growth of the industrial workforce in the industrialized countries steered the conceptualization of employment issues towards a dichotomy of "in work" (meaning in a regular, full-time, wage-paid job) and "unemployed". The effectiveness of action to protect the conditions of work of the employed meant that poverty was concentrated among the unemployed — so that social insurance to protect the living standards of the unemployed was a necessary complement to long-term job creation programmes, and a primary instrument against poverty.

The increasing stress on the employment and poverty problems of low-income countries in the 1960s and 1970s led to a reformulation of these concerns. The regular, full-time wage job characterized only a small fraction of the workforce of most developing countries. Open unemployment in the classic sense was only a relatively small component of labour underutilization, which was concentrated in underemployment in agriculture or in low productivity services. What is more, the relatively small numbers of unemployed were perceived to be reasonably well off — the

Ceylon Employment Strategy Mission [ILO, 1971b] drew particular attention to the "educated unemployed"; their problem was not seen as poverty, for they came from relatively high-income households on which they could rely for income support while they searched for jobs, but rather one of a mismatch between aspirations and the jobs on offer in the labour market. The poor, on the other hand, have no choice but to work in order to survive, and so would undertake any available economic activities, regardless of productivity; their vulnerability would show up in under-employment and low income rather than unemployment.

Instead of stressing unemployment in addressing poverty, then, the ILO's World Employment Programme turned towards the generation of income through productive employment. This, as outlined in the previous section, involved not only creating regular jobs, but also generating opportunities for increased labour use and higher productivity in self-employment, and the creation of employment in temporary programmes. The aim was not so much to reduce open unemployment as to provide income opportunities, but employment was either the means — income was generated through increased production generated by higher levels of labour utilization — or the legitimation — transfer payments to bring people above the poverty line were socially acceptable only if they had the appearance of a wage, as in employment-creating public works program-mes which often failed to create durable infrastructure.

Experience has shown, however, that too simplified a notion of employment can lead to inappropriate policies. WEP research suggested that one can usefully separate *income, production* and *recognition* aspects of employment [Sen, 1975]. The income aspect has been emphasized most in the analysis of poverty, and this has led to the conclusion that it may not matter very much if income is earned through employment or obtained through transfer payments. But this has serious long-term implications, not only for the fiscal situation of the public authorities, but also for the integration of the poor in the social and economic system, as cutting the link between income and employment may promote the development of an "underclass" alienated from the mainstream of society and condemned to permanent dependence. This awareness of the recognition aspects of employment led to the inclusion of employment as a human need in its own right in some formulations of the basic needs strategy. But probably the most crucial issue has been the productivity of employment, which is important — in different ways — in both development strategy and poverty alleviation. "Trickle-down" models suggest that the benefits of growth filter through to the population at large through the creation of productive jobs. But the evidence suggests that trickle-down mechanisms are weak, although the ILO has not succeeded in demonstrating the general viability of the reverse causation, in which the creation of high productivity employment becomes the motor of growth. Part of the problem may lie in an excessive focus on "employment creation". The more successful cases where employment opportunities and real wages have increased are not in those countries where employment was meticulously planned, but where opportunities and incentives were given for communities or enterprises to develop productive activities autonomously, but in socially desirable directions (agriculture and village industries in China, manufacturing in some of the NICs).

A reorientation of employment policy towards growth strategy, however, risks shifting the focus away from poverty. If poverty-reducing development strategies are to emerge, it is all the more important to identify the characteristics of the poor and their points of insertion in the economy. Work in this direction has suggested that the earlier abandonment of concern with open unemployment in relation to poverty was a mistake. Recent empirical work suggests that — at least in urban areas, which account for a large and rapidly growing share of the workforce — the unemployed are heterogeneous, most are poor and only a small fraction fall in the "well-off job seeker" category. Poor urban households are continually faced with irregular job access, as periods of work and of unemployment succeed each other, while discrimination against specific groups, or disabilities which limit labour market capabilities, lead to a coincidence of long term unemployment and severe deprivation. Such issues can only be tackled through a restructuring of labour demand or a comprehensive social security system. At the same time, underemployment, in its various forms, is also an important determinant of poverty.

B.   The structure of the labour market

Labour market analysis within the ILO has covered a wide range of issues: minimum wage-fixing; discrimination in employment; labour market information and skill matching, and associated employment and placement services; and international labour mobility. However, poverty has not figured prominently in this work. The main exception concerns wage determination, especially minimum wage-fixing. Work on discrimination, relevant in principle, has in practice been only incidentally concerned with poverty. Although there was always considerable attention paid to training, skills and qualifications, this tended to concentrate on the formal economy. More recently work on enterprise development has paid increasing attention to skill, but poverty is again a secondary rather than a primary focus.

For historical reasons, work on wages and work on employment have been carried out in different departments of the ILO. While this has not prevented integrated analysis of the effects of both wages and employment on incomes and poverty, it has probably led to less attention being paid to the interactions between wages and employment than the subject merits. There are some exceptions to this rule. Some of the Comprehensive Employment Strategy Missions, for instance, explicitly tackled this issue. The Colombia mission report argued that "big increases in employment can be attained more easily (provided that action is taken along the lines recommended in the other sections of the report) if large increases in wages are avoided" [ILO, 1970b, p. 186]. The qualification in parentheses is important, because it linked action on wages to action in other domains. PREALC work in Latin America [e.g. PREALC, 1983] suggested that there was little relationship between average wages and the overall employment level — the latter was determined by aggregate demand and other macro-economic factors, so that dramatic real wage declines in many Latin American countries had little or no positive effect on employment. Similar conclusions can be derived from African experiences. But, on the whole, notions of fair wages or target living standards have predominated in ILO normative action on wages; while ILO research on employment and poverty has been rather reluctant to tackle the possible trade-offs between wages and employment. Nevertheless it is apparent that poverty is most widespread in situations outside the effective control of minimum wage legislation or other forms of regulation, and that patterns of wage inequality are important determinants of both absolute and relative poverty.

But work on employment issues suggested that more attention should be paid to the structure of labour markets. Poverty arises in part because access to jobs is unequally distributed, or because particular types of jobs are insecure or ill-paid. This is not just a question of labour market efficiency or labour market information, but is an outcome of the way labour markets are structured. Increasing attention was then paid in ILO work to the structural reasons which might lead to the persistence and growth of "bad" jobs — casual, irregular, unprotected, low-productivity jobs which would often be found associated with poverty. Identifying and conceptualizing these categories of jobs was also important, because the conventional classifications in terms of industry, occupation or work status were very blunt instruments for locating the vulnerable.

Several theoretical perspectives have been developed to address these issues. Notions of labour market segmentation have been particularly important in PREALC work in Latin America, where they constituted an extension of the formal/informal dichotomy. There are considerable differences in rewards to labour in different labour market segments. Some of these reflect productivity differences, and can be traced back to questions of capital, both human and physical, or to the organization of production. But labour markets tend to be organized in such a way that access to the "good" jobs is limited and controlled, and this prevents wages from equalizing (upwards or downwards) even if market forces would tend to promote this. As a result, poverty is concentrated in those segments of the labour market where access to jobs is easier, but returns to labour are low because of overcrowding. But the capacity of such segments to absorb labour is limited, and in practice there is a considerable spillover into open unemployment, especially in times of recession. Much of this unemployment is short term and interspersed with casual work. Recent research suggests that it is strongly linked with poverty. Work on labour market flexibility, while not directly concerned with poverty, has also highlighted processes of casualization of formerly regular jobs, and the growth of inequality between core and peripheral workers, both associated with a deterioration in the security and living conditions of particular groups among the poor.

This broad view of the labour market encompasses much that has in the past been treated separately under the "informal sector" heading. The notion of the informal sector originally emerged from theories of dualism in economic development which were discussed above, but it represented a qualitative shift in thinking. "Traditional" activities were now seen as potentially dynamic and productive, and not simply as a sponge absorbing surplus labour. So dualism no longer mapped cleanly onto poverty, and solutions to poverty lay also within the informal sector itself, for there was potential for growth in productive employment. Also, other factors lay behind dualism — differentials in technology, or in the organization of firms, or in access to markets or to capital. Such factors led to low productivity and so to poverty, but solutions could be found. On the other hand, the informal sector was heterogenous: a low-productivity fringe of street vendors and personal service workers also formed part of the sector. There was therefore an important distinction between survival activities and activities with growth potential. Ever since these ideas were first systematically developed in the Kenya CESM [ILO, 1972], poverty reduction has been an important rationale for ILO attempts to intervene in the informal sector.

Alongside work on the informal sector as such, increasing attention has been paid to the other aspects of informality in production relations and labour market mechanisms. Informality, in this sense, refers to a lack of formal regulation (legal, administrative) or of formal institutions (organizations of workers, training institutions). Much informal activity occurs in environments where, in theory, formal rules apply, so there is not a clear distinction but rather a continuum between the formal and the informal, depending how clearly the rules are specified and how vigorously they are applied; informality is in many cases specifically designed to escape control and regulation, and the growth of casual and unprotected jobs in many countries during the 1980s is an illustration of how this may result in a process of informalization. ILO actions through standards are necessarily formal; but if they are to contribute to action against poverty they must reach situations which are unregulated. There is therefore a contradiction between the objective of setting and enforcing standards for workers — including for levels of living and hence for poverty — and the informality of much employment. The resolution of this contradiction would appear to involve formalizing the informal, but this is easier said than done [Tokman, 1992; see also ILO, 1990a].

The more general issue here is one of labour market regulation and deregulation. The development of the orthodoxy of the market in the 1980s put pressure on the traditional ILO approach of standard-setting and intervention to promote dialogue and protect workers. But deregulation was always a chimera; regulation is always present, whether in the sense of formal rules and the legislative framework, or in the sense of the patterns of behaviour — cooperation or conflict — of the actors concerned and the power relations between them. There is always an institutional framework underlying the economic relationships, so that both social effectiveness and economic efficiency have to be considered; attempting to maximize the latter may well undermine the former. Poverty is one outcome of the interaction between economic and social mechanisms in the labour market — either because of the position of particular actors, or because the processes exclude particular groups from access to incomes or protection. But the impact on poverty of differing forms of regulation and of different institutional structures has not received much attention in past ILO work.

C. Security

Several approaches to security have been deployed in ILO work, among which formal systems of social insurance have predominated. When poverty was conceived mainly as the result of unemployment or specific disadvantages in relatively wealthy countries, the link between social security issues and poverty was clear. A Beveridge-type model of security, linking together different forms of social provision — unemployment insurance, state-guaranteed old-age pensions, access to public services, income assistance for those falling outside the unemployment insurance net — provided a coherent framework for dealing with poverty. But while this model has underpinned much work on social security in the ILO, those concerned with poverty in developing countries have mostly regarded this type of social security system as either inappropriate or inconceivable. The Kenya and Colombia CESM [ILO, 1972; 1970b] reports, for instance, are totally silent on the issue. The report of the Director-General of 1970 on poverty and minimum living standards [ILO, 1970a] suggested that for urban, industrial and plantation workers at least there was some scope for social security in developing countries, but commented that "social security schemes in those countries have as yet had a relatively small impact on poverty". The situation has not changed qualitatively since, for in so far as schemes have expanded it is generally the better-off who are better protected.

The underlying issue here is the notion of security itself, and the way it is linked to poverty. First, insecurity can be seen as part of the concept of poverty: one dimension of poverty may involve economic insecurity, in the sense of uncertainty about or lack of control over continued access to income or basic consumption goods. This may arise out of the lack of assets or income reserves, a lack of information, a lack of influence. Second, insecurity (irregularity in employment, uncertainty of income) leads to vulnerability to poverty, which may be temporary or permanent. Third, the poor lack insurance against ill-fortune (sickness, death of income earner), or against the vagaries of the life cycle (dependency, old age). These ideas are related to the concept of entitlements, which was explored in the World Employment Programme at the end of the 1970s. An entitlement, seen as a right to or a claim on social and economic resources, implies a corresponding degree of social or economic security; poverty could be seen as an absence of entitlement and hence insecurity. A particular example which was examined was vulnerability in the case of famine. "Exchange entitlements" referred to the rules, whether socially or market determined, by which individuals and groups obtained rights over and access to the goods and services they needed. This concept of entitlements thus included not only the ownership of factors of production, such as land, capital, etc., but also decent prices for products and labour. Sen [1981] argued that development policies should aim to increase entitlements, especially for the poorer parts of the population, in order for these groups to increase their capabilities. In general, however, the entitlement approach received rather a mixed reception from policy-makers, partly because it did not provide a clear cut set of policy prescriptions, partly because the adverse economic climate of the late 1970s and early 1980 led to a dwindling interest in distributional issues.

Instead, other routes towards providing security have been examined. "Traditional" protection systems (i.e. transfers and mutual help within kin and community groups on the basis of informal principles) are widespread. Examples are given in the 1993 *World Labour Report* [ILO, 1993], where it is also commented that the long-term trend is for such systems to break down because of population pressure or the intrusion of market relationships. Food security — through subsidies and rationing schemes — provides another option, focusing on the aspect of security which is most closely connected with poverty. Employment guarantee schemes provide a counter to employment insecurity, and asset redistribution may provide income security. But on the whole it must be said that rather little attention has been paid to the design or analysis of comprehensive systems to provide security in low-income countries; it has simply been assumed that these countries cannot aspire to such security because average levels of income and productivity are too low to bear the cost. Yet many of the specific interventions against poverty can be seen to make much more sense as part of a comprehensive system than they do on their own, and in such a system the means by which security is attained will be crucial.

D. The quality of jobs

More general questions of security against misfortune apart, many of the foregoing points can be reduced to a general concern with the quality of jobs. At the simplest level, one may distinguish good jobs and bad jobs. Good jobs provide a degree of security, a decent income, acceptable working conditions, the possibility to develop and apply skills. They are protected by law or by collective organization. Bad jobs are insecure, low-skilled and low-paid, and are subject to little state regulation. This is a caricature, but a useful one, because it offers two quite different employment strategies. The first, the high road, attempts to increase the fraction of good jobs in the economy; the second, the low road, attempts to make the bad jobs less bad.

The high road, then, involves the definition of a core of rights which it is believed should be attached to jobs or to workers — the right to a minimum wage, to protection from unfair dismissal, the right to organize... In other words there is a set of labour standards. These are established at levels which are regarded as legitimate aspirations — but in the short term at least, not everyone succeeds in obtaining them, especially in low-income settings. In other words, the attainment of some or all of these rights is in practice to some degree subordinate to economic constraints. But even in low-income countries, in the public sector and large-scale private establishments, not only can they be attained immediately, but also to grant them is a political (and perhaps also economic) imperative. The strategy is then one of gradually increasing the fraction of the labour market where these rights are obtained, directly through state action, or indirectly through encouraging agreements to this effect among the actors involved. This approach has characterized much of the ILO's work.

The low road, at the other extreme, focuses on the standards of living and working of the labour force as a whole. Underlying this vision is a notion of aggregate well-being rather than of rights. The aim is to create the conditions for improved incomes and employment opportunities among those working in sectors or labour market segments where legislation and public action to enforce standards is ineffective or partial. The types of policy interventions involved include attempts to generate broad-based increases in levels of economic activity and employment, or more specific policies designed to sustain the levels of living of vulnerable groups. From this perspective, it is sometimes argued that the creation of enough jobs for the population as a whole requires labour costs to be kept low, so as to maintain competitiveness, and inferred that the advantages of the protected workers in public sector and organized sector jobs should be undermined.

This levelling-down argument is frequently heard as part of a liberalization package, as a way of achieving competitiveness and promoting growth. However, there is little evidence that reducing labour costs and conditions promotes growth, and reason to believe the opposite. The idea that reducing the advantages of one fraction of the workforce will have any positive effect on the others seems both unlikely and empirically quite unsupported. On the contrary, there is a respectable argument that high labour standards are important as a way of generating motivation, of supporting skill development, and of providing the institutional framework for effective commitment by labour to, say, productivity goals. But this virtuous circle is apparently not open to all: there are many sectors and economic activities where the constraints on productivity lie elsewhere — in inadequate technology or limited access to capital, in low skill levels or in systems of exploitation. Where the potential for positive economic reinforcement exists, the design of the supporting institutions is crucial.

These alternatives are important for the analysis of poverty, for the high road has moral force and provides crucial legitimation, but may contribute little to poverty alleviation in the short term; while the gains offered by the low road may insidiously undermine longer-term objectives. In this debate the ILO has sometimes appeared schizophrenic, promoting both routes in different aspects of its work without always carefully analysing the complementarities and contradictions. But there is clearly a need for a differentiated approach; the problems of the working poor are different from those of the unemployed, and among the working poor the mechanisms behind poverty vary: the clearest difference is between wage and self-employment, but there are many others. The work of the ILO has attempted to tackle these mechanisms at a number of levels, and we look at some of them again in discussing policy issues in the Section III.

4. Development strategy and poverty in the mid-1990s

The 1980s saw a growing ascendency of neo-classical influences on development thinking, and notions of development planning and strategy fell out of fashion. Even before the fall of communism there was growing scepticism over the usefulness of the role of the state and economic planning in determining development strategies. State interventions in the setting of investment priorities, in fixing trade and industrialization strategy and in regulating markets were increasingly perceived to be the cause of economic inefficiency and slower growth rather than as solutions to the problem of inequitable development. The same scepticism applied to state ownership and to collective or communal forms of economic organization. The primary aim of development policy came to be seen as permitting the market to function efficiently by providing stability, order and an appropriate legal framework. The dominant approach to dealing with poverty, given this theoretical background, is best expressed in the World Bank's *World Development Report, 1990*. It is based upon the notion that the best road to poverty alleviation is rapid growth of national income and of employment, achieved through investment and improvements in human capital as well as through removing obstacles to market functioning in the form of government regulation, with concomitant attention to those households which fall below the poverty line through income transfers and public services.

This new "classicism", although hailed as a change of thinking by some, has surprisingly few new theoretical aspects to offer. Those which are offered were mostly developed in the 1970s. The fact that the new "classicism" is based upon rather old theories is not a cause for criticism. However, its emphasis on a modified trickle-down approach with income transfers is one which needs to be closely scrutinized, for it fails to take account of the relation between poverty and the structural and qualitative aspects of growth. As a result, very little attention is paid to institutions, agents of development and the non-monetary aspects of poverty.

The ILO reaction to these changes was largely a defensive one. It developed work on social safety nets in countries undergoing structural adjustment, a topic which had not received much attention in its earlier work on poverty. It is beginning to place greater emphasis on active labour market policies and other direct measures for alleviating existing unemployment. It also became more assertive about core ILO means of action such as the promotion of labour standards and tripartism, but without engaging in any substantive debate with neo-liberal critics who have highlighted what they believe to be the distortionary effects of labour market regulation. In this process, work on the larger issue of the relationship between general economic policies and employment and poverty has fallen by the wayside.

This is unfortunate for several reasons. First, the political and economic failure of centrally-planned economic systems has removed one option from the range of possible development strategies but has by no means eliminated all choice; paradoxically, because there is no longer polarization between centrally-planned and market economies, the range of options may have increased, because the social and institutional differences between different variants of the market economy have become more apparent. So while there is now a near-total consensus that the market economy is the most efficient route for ensuring economic progress, this by no means spells the end of development strategy. Both the international and national economies are characterized by serious systemic failures such as slow growth, high unemployment and growing inequalities. Solutions to these problems will not emerge automatically as a result of the universal conversion to market economics; they require institutional interventions to mould market forces in the direction of social objectives. For many developing countries there is now the vital challenge of defining development strategies which can counter the growing threat of their marginalization from the global economy. New technological developments have eroded their traditional comparative advantage based on natural resource endowments and cheap labour. The revolution in materials science has reduced demand for many raw materials produced by developing countries while developments in production technology give an absolute advantage to production techniques relying exclusively on highly-skilled labour, even in low-tech and previously labour-intensive industries. The consequence of these developments for poor countries could well be declining inflows of direct foreign investment and greater difficulty in finding export markets. In such an increasingly competitive international economic environment poor countries will face increasing pressure to define development strategies which can mobilize their human and other resources to generate growth. Finding a space for national policy in a world increasingly dominated by international and global forces is a major challenge, but a vital one. The role of the state, and the policies and institutional framework that can ensure the most effective mobilization of resources to increase the competitiveness of an economy, will be thus a central issue. But equally important will be issues relating to how best equity can be maintained, and poverty alleviated, within a chosen development strategy.

Secondly, it is more important than ever that the ILO should focus on the underlying economic causes of labour and social problems. A major wave of economic reform is under way in developing and transition economies and the ILO should have an interest in influencing the shape of reforms since this will impact strongly on labour and social outcomes. If this opportunity is not seized then the ILO will be largely relegated to the role of a minor actor purveying "quick fixes" for the social consequences of reform and injunctions on labour standards and tripartism. An exclusive focus on direct programmes will not be sufficient for attaining ILO objectives, such as the promotion of employment, alleviating poverty and reducing the social costs of transition or structural adjustment. Such a focus on direct programmes must be supplemented by a parallel concern with influencing economic policies which determine the structure of production, factor use, and the primary distribution of income.

Thirdly, there is a growing shift away from the view that *laissez-faire*, moderated by safety nets for the destitute, is the best and unique prescription for eradicating poverty. Even with universal acceptance of the ideal of a market economy, there remain vast differences in economic structures, in the distribution of assets and in the level of development of market institutions across countries. Given these differences, there can be no unique prescription in terms of development strategy since outcomes will differ across different economies. There is thus a clear need for work on appropriate packages of economic and social policies for particular countries if a serious dent is to be made in the alleviation of poverty.

III. Policies for poverty eradication

1. Introduction

The perspectives reviewed in the last section have led to an emphasis on poverty reduction in a significant part of the ILO's work. Much attention has been devoted to the measurement and monitoring of poverty, to research on particular aspects of poverty and to the development of policy prescriptions. But there is great diversity in this work, and it is very difficult to speak of a single ILO policy approach towards poverty reduction in the sense of a systematic and coherent policy stance.

One fundamental distinction should be noted: that between intervention aimed at structural change in economic organization, and policies aimed at directly improving specific situations. Both types of approaches can be found in ILO work. The remodelling of the development path which was promoted by WEP in the 1970s is a good example of the former, but the latter is much more widespread, including action to alleviate poverty among women, to provide jobs for the disabled, to raise the productivity of informal sector workers, and so on. Advocates of broad redistributive measures are often dismissive of the possibility of solving the poverty problem through direct poverty alleviation programmes. They argue that, without basic changes in development policies and asset distribution, direct programmes are an exercise in futility since they can never be large enough to abate the fundamental economic forces generating poverty. Advocates of direct programmes, on the other hand, tend to be sceptical of the political and economic feasibility and desirability of implementing a redistributive development strategy. They fear that attempts to implement "grand schemes" of social engineering will cause economic and social disruption which, compounded by the inefficiencies engendered by extensive state intervention, is likely to leave everyone, including the poor, worse off. Advocates of direct programmes therefore feel that theirs is the safer and surer road to poverty alleviation.

In spite of these differences in attitude, the two approaches are, in principle, complementary. Direct programmes can provide interim support to the poor while the full effects of a redistributive development strategy are being worked through; they can constitute part of the support mechanisms required by the poor even in a post-reform situation; and they help to bring about necessary enhancements of the capabilities of the poor. Similarly major policy and institutional reforms are often required in order to ensure that direct programmes achieve their objectives fully. Programmes to promote new economic activities among the poor and to raise productivity in existing activities have the best chance of success when they are accompanied by changes which ensure a supportive institutional and policy environment. The choice between the two approaches is thus not an "either or" one but relates instead to the balance between the two types of interventions.

This implies that there is no contradiction in promoting both routes simultaneously and, indeed, the ILO has done so. But because there has not been much emphasis on linkage between action at these two levels, it is difficult to pinpoint a unique ILO approach. On the other hand, we can identify a number of policy *orientations* which recur in ILO work, and which emphasize the importance of one or the other of the main instruments within the organization's mandate — normative or regulatory action, various forms of technical cooperation, advice on national policy development. At least five such orientations can be distinguished: policies related to asset redistribution; policies aimed at restructuring production systems, notably in order to create employment; policies to improve access to jobs and reduce the vulnerability of particular population groups; policies to transfer income, goods or services directly to the poor; and policies concerned with the organization of the poor. These are the subjects of the next five sections.

The deep roots of poverty in the economic, social and political structure of society depend heavily on the distribution of the basic factors of production — land, capital and labour. The first group of anti-poverty policies to be reviewed, therefore, covers access to assets such as land, and the development of "human capital". This is the subject of Section III.2.

The principal asset of the poor is not capital or land, but labour. The next policy issue is therefore how to change the process of economic development so as to create the maximum amount of remunerative employment. In addition to the macro-economic policies reviewed above, a host of sectoral policies play an important part, and these are discussed in Section III.3. They include policies for developing the small-scale and informal sectors in urban areas, attempts to restructure rural production and the promotion of labour-based public works designed to create durable assets.

A third group of anti-poverty policies, examined in Section III.4, aims at changing labour market outcomes such as access to employment and the remuneration of labour. This may involve either protecting the interests of particular vulnerable groups of workers, such as women, children and the disabled, or modifying labour market institutions and regulations in favour of the poor.

Most of the foregoing aims at changing the primary income distribution. But redistribution of income through direct transfers remains necessary as well. Particularly important programmes, discussed in Section III.5, include social expenditures and pricing policies designed to ensure that the poor have access to public provisioning and promote the satisfaction of basic needs. The section also includes a discussion on the impact on poverty of income transfers through social security and social assistance, areas in which the ILO has been active for many years.

Attempting to change the income distribution in favour of the poor inevitably has adverse effects on the interests of powerful social groups. In a democratic society it is therefore necessary to mobilize popular support for such strategies. One important way in which this can be achieved is through improved organization of the poor and of particular vulnerable groups, an issue examined in Section III.6.

2. Changing the distribution of assets

A. Land and physical capital

An important strand of ILO work on poverty has stressed the importance of asset redistribution. The main rationale for this approach has been that the distribution of asset ownership is a major determinant of income distribution in developing countries. The vast majority of the economically-active population in these countries works in the rural and informal sectors where self-employment predominates. The returns to self-employment are largely determined by the productive assets available to the self-employed, whether they are engaged in peasant farming, non-farm rural activity, or the urban informal sector. As a consequence, there is a strong correlation between poverty and asset deprivation. The rural poor are mostly landless or have farms too small to yield an adequate income, while many of the urban poor are struggling to subsist in the informal sector from what they can produce from makeshift and improvised bits of productive equipment.

Agrarian reform has therefore been frequently advocated in ILO work as an effective and efficient policy instrument in dealing with rural poverty, especially in Asia and Latin America. It was argued that unequal distribution of land ownership and archaic land tenure arrangements were direct causes of poverty. The access by the poor to other inputs, especially credit, was also curtailed by their lack of access to land. Moreover, land reform may lead to an increase in productivity since there is an inverse correlation between farm size and output per unit of land, so the advocacy of land reform was also based on efficiency grounds.

A second strand in the rationale for the focus on asset distribution was also related to efficiency. This was based on the observation that the secondary effects of an unequal distribution of assets reinforce the poverty directly caused by the inadequacy of productive assets. In the rural economy, unequal land distribution results in a concentration of economic and political power which impacts negatively on the poor. Monopsonistic power in rural labour markets, derived from concentrated land ownership, lowers the earnings for rural wage labour while raising rents in land markets. This is reinforced by interlocked power over production and consumption loans in credit markets as well as by extra-economic control derived from the congruence between economic and political power. This interlocking hold of the rich blocks most escape routes from poverty and also encourages growing marginalization in the context of growing demographic pressure on limited land. In the urban economy, there is a similar set of problems. Increasing the incomes of the self-employed poor in the informal sector depends on giving them improved access to possibilities for expanding and upgrading their asset base. However, this is blocked by an interlocking set of systematic biases: trade and industrialization strategy tilt incentives in favour of large modern-sector enterprises; credit markets are biased against small informal-sector producers; economic regulation creates barriers to entry into self-employment activities; concentration of capital and market power threaten the survival of small enterprises; and unequal access to education and training block the acquisition by poor producers of the improved information, skills and production techniques required to raise their productivity.

WEP's work in the late 1970s paid significant attention to the issue of asset distribution. For example the study on *Poverty and landlessness in rural Asia* [ILO, 1977a] argued that, because of unequal agrarian structure, rural poverty increased in spite of economic growth. A redistribution of assets (land and tenancy reform) was therefore necessary. This challenged the orthodox "trickle-down" view that the promotion of agricultural growth through land augmenting policies (new seeds, irrigation investments, small farmer programmes) would lead to an automatic decline in the incidence of rural poverty. Subsequent work on agrarian systems pursued this idea that asset redistribution was a key element in development strategies by evaluating the functioning of different modes of organizing land ownership and rural development. It contrasted agrarian systems based on a highly concentrated pattern of land ownership with post-reform systems such as egalitarian peasant farming and various forms of communal agriculture. Its *broad* conclusion was that agrarian reform was potentially a powerful means for ensuring equitable growth and poverty alleviation and that these post-reform models were viable in both socialist and market economies.

This broad conclusion needs, however, to be tempered by other considerations. For instance, research has shown that in many countries land reform was not a panacea: it was a necessary, but not a sufficient, instrument for poverty reduction. In densely populated economies, land was often too scarce to make a meaningful distribution possible. In such situations, a first round of land redistribution may have produced some positive results, but such gains were soon eroded, particularly through population growth. Moreover land reform by itself was not sufficient to bring about an increase in productivity. The provision of inputs and the adoption of correct pricing policies were perhaps as important as land reform in determining returns to land and labour. Finally, surveys of countries that undertook land reform [Radwan, 1977; Collier & Radwan, 1986] have shown that, while the distribution of assets explains about half of the variation in poverty incidence, the other half is determined by the skill endowment of the household or its access to remittances from migrant members. Such results point to the need for complementary policies to deal with the lack of access by the poor to such factors as credit and skills and to enhance their bargaining power in the labour markets. In the light of this, but even more so in the light of the strength of the interests opposed to asset redistribution, the effective contribution to poverty reduction of policies in this field has remained limited in most countries despite their theoretical importance.

B.   Human capital

Investments in education and training are a potentially powerful instrument for reducing inequality in the size distribution of income and for raising the productivity and earnings of the poor. Improving the human capital base of the poor through the spread of literacy and basic education enhances their capabilities in several ways. In the rural economy, improved educational levels have been shown to raise productivity in peasant agriculture through enhancing the willingness to innovate and the capacity to absorb information on new techniques of production. More generally, it also enhances the capacity to respond to market opportunities in both farm and non-farm rural activities, and offers an access route to training and, through this, to better jobs. In the urban economy, improved access to further education and training for the poor is a key escape route from poverty to more skilled and better paying jobs. Training is also an important component of support services provided to raise productivity and incomes in the informal sector.

The above view of the role of human resource development in poverty alleviation suggests that policy interventions are required at several levels. At the macro level policies are required to ensure that adequate provisions are made for expenditures in education and training and that these are allocated equitably. It is particularly important to ensure universal access to good basic education since this is most beneficial from the standpoint of poverty alleviation. At the meso level, policy interventions are required to ensure that school fees and other cost-recovery measures do not prevent access by the poor to education and training. Positive measures to promote greater school enrolment and attendance by the poor will also often be required. At the same time, labour market interventions may often be required to remove barriers to the access of the poor to training opportunities. Finally, direct interventions at the micro level will also be required to provide training to upgrade production among the poor in peasant agriculture and the urban informal sector. Such targeted interventions also serve to promote new income-generating activities among the poor.

The ILO's mandate in human resource development is largely confined to vocational training outside the regular school system. Within the UN system, responsibility for primary and higher levels of education, and well as for technical and vocational education within schools, rests with UNESCO. As a consequence, the ILO's work has rarely touched on the broader questions of the impact of the level and allocation of educational expenditures on the alleviation of poverty. There was some work on education as a basic need in the aftermath of the World Employment Conference but this remained a minor part of the ILO's overall work on basic needs.

The main thrust of ILO work on training since the early 1960s has been the provision of technical assistance to developing countries in expanding and improving formal systems for providing pre-employment vocational training. The rationale for this arose from the analyses of the 1960s which identified the shortage of skilled labour as a principal constraint on industrialization and economic development. A large technical assistance programme was developed, aimed at assisting developing countries in designing training institutions, developing curricula, training trainers and procuring appropriate equipment. However, this work had very few links with the issue of poverty alleviation, apart from the possible indirect link through its impact on labour productivity and growth in the economy. Since the late 1970s new operational activities have been developed in the area of targeted training programmes for poor or disadvantaged groups. These have included the skills development for self-reliance (SDSR) and TRUGA (Training for Rural Gainful Activities) programmes which have been directed at training and complementary support for promoting rural income-generating activities. A programme for promoting income-generating activities for women was also developed. From 1986 onwards the issue of training for the informal sector also began to be addressed in ILO research. This highlighted the problem that pre-employment training in formal institutions benefited only a relatively small proportion of the labour force who were being prepared for skilled employment in the formal sector. A serious issue of equity was involved since public expenditures on training provided hardly any benefits to the large numbers already in, or having to enter, informal-sector employment. Among the issues addressed in this work were the possibilities for promoting greater outreach by training institutions to the informal sector, the need to give greater emphasis to training for self-employment and the means through which traditional apprenticeship systems in the informal sector could be upgraded and rendered more effective.

These new areas of work represent a welcome shift towards greater sensitivity for poverty and equity issues, but they face problems of cost-effectiveness and replicability. There is also a need to link training interventions per se with other support measures since it is rarely the case that training on its own can succeed in raising the incomes of the poor. Recently, more attention has been given to the promotion and application of ILO standards on human resources development and training — Convention No. 142 on Human Resources Development, 1975, and the corresponding Recommendation No. 150. These standards emphasize equality of access and other equity issues and provide a clear mandate for action at the macro policy and other levels that are more closely linked to issues of poverty alleviation.

3. Restructuring production at the sectoral level

A. Promoting production and employment in the informal and small-scale sectors

Since its initial conceptualization, popularized by the ILO's Employment Strategy Mission to Kenya in 1972, the "informal sector" has been looked upon as a large source of employment potential. One of the mission's main findings was that the main employment problem was not unemployment, but the existence of large numbers of the "working poor", involved in the production of goods and services, whose activities were not recognized, recorded, protected or regulated. Many such workers are self-employed, and research on the sources of their poverty shows that it can in large part be traced to inadequate access to productive assets, an issue discussed above. Two distinct poverty situations can be identified — those where poverty persists despite long working hours either because of low productivity or exploitative or coercive external economic relationships; and those where there is involuntary underemployment. In the former case, much self-employment in low-income settings, both urban and rural, has been found to hide relationships of dependency (on suppliers of assets, inputs or credit, or on purchasers of output) which raise issues of protection identical to those which arise for wage labour. Homeworkers are an obvious but by no means the only case.

Clearly, this is a major target group for action against poverty, but systematic policy design has been inhibited by several factors: the haziness of the concept of the informal sector and the heterogeneity of the activities which it encompasses; the lack of organization of informal sector workers and producers and their lack of direct representation in the ILO; the difficulty of applying universal labour standards, both because of the difficulty of enforcement and because of the inability of many informal producers to comply; and the very real difficulties faced by formal organizations such as the ILO and its constituents in dealing with non-formalized situations. While the ultimate objective of ILO action regarding the informal sector is seen as being its progressive integration into the formal economy, together with the application of the protective measures articulated in international labour standards, it is clear that its employment-creating potential must be maintained.[4] Analysis of the constraints imposed upon the informal sector by existing institutional, legal and regulatory structures suggest that, while it is important to provide basic social protection to informal sector producers and workers, it would be unrealistic to try to immediately apply to them all the existing labour legislation. Most informal sector producers are unable to comply with such regulatory structures, and such a move would only cause them to retreat further into the hidden economy, thus depriving the labour market of a vital source of employment. However, if action in the informal sector is to contribute to reducing poverty it is essential to ensure that at least minimum levels of income and protection be attained.

---

[4] This has been explicitly referred to in the Employment Policy (Supplementary Provisions) Recommendation No. 169, 1984.

To achieve these goals, access to skills, capital and markets are clearly crucial. In ILO work, promotion of informal sector productivity has been undertaken through targeted programmes of support to small producers, designed to strengthen their capacity to provide increased employment and income opportunities. Areas of support have included improving access to credit and technology; provision of technical training; and information relating to marketing of products. The support programmes are based on the concept of participatory development, which contains three guiding principles: attaining autonomy by including the target groups' own resources (financial, technical and human); building organizational structures to ensure the effective participation of the beneficiaries; and empowerment, by installing the institutional capacity to overcome economic and social constraints.

A number of examples can be cited of how these notions have been applied in practice, and their impact on poverty. In Benin, an ILO programme aimed to create mutual savings and loan associations for small producers belonging to the most deprived population groups, both from the capital and from three smaller cities. The target group of 1,600 craftsmen, organized in 60 associations, created small-scale production units for food processing, mechanical repairs and construction, dressmaking and carpentry. The outcomes included not only employment opportunities for the most deprived in the labour force, but also increased social integration. Another component of that programme helped younger unemployed women with training and financial support for investment in urban micro-firms dealing with the agricultural sector. The resulting food processing, catering and commercialization activities had important backward linkages with rural areas, where the majority of the poor are located, as well as providing better quality and cheaper food to the urban population. Another interesting programme started in 1982 in Mali, Rwanda and Togo. The aim was to create different types of associations designed to give support to the more disadvantaged small-scale producers, in areas such as training, financial assistance, work organization and negotiation. Considerable increases in incomes were observed in these associations, and visible underemployment dropped. This was due not only to a larger number of hours worked but also to an increase in hourly income and productivity, indicating that people's working capabilities had improved. Apart from its direct positive impacts on poverty, through the provision of new jobs and income growth for the more deprived groups of the labour force, this programme also had important qualitative side effects in the form of mobility of workers to better jobs, improvement of labour standards and greater stability and regularity in activity and income over the year. In similar work in Latin America it was also found that the growth of the more successful informal sector firms resulted in improved living standards for their employees. The importance of organization is illustrated by the finding that where artisans are involved in the definition of their own priorities, strategies and organization, the result has been improved productivity, increased employment and higher quality of output. Industrial homeworkers, the overwhelming majority of whom are women, have been an important target group for ILO informal sector activities in South-east Asia (Philippines, Indonesia, Thailand). Programmes in these countries have combined employment promotion and the raising of productivity with selective and gradual extension of social protection measures, alongside the organization of homeworkers with a view to strengthening their bargaining position vis-à-vis employers and the State. The question remains, however, whether positive experiences such as these can be replicated on a sufficiently large scale to have a significant impact on overall levels of poverty.

B. Employment creation in the rural economy

The ILO has confronted the issue of rural job creation at two levels: maximizing employment intensity in agriculture through land augmenting technology; and labour absorption in the non-farm sectors. The potential for increasing employment in agriculture through technological change and agrarian reform is considerable, as East Asian experiences in particular have shown. But even under the most optimistic scenarios, it seems unlikely that developing countries' agriculture will be able to absorb the growing numbers of entrants to the labour market. The result may be an increasing stream of rural-urban migration, swelling the ranks of the urban informal sector or the urban unemployed, or an intensification of rural underemployment and deprivation. To deal with this situation, the ILO [1988] proposed a "rural-focused, employment-oriented strategy of development". The main thrust of such a strategy would be to increase labour absorption in the rural areas through the promotion of growth linkages between a dynamic non-farm rural economy and an agricultural sector experiencing rapid productivity growth due to the adoption of innovative and appropriate technology.

Evidence from recent research on the experience of some developing countries suggests that such a strategy is feasible. The basic objective of the strategy is to create conditions for the maximization of labour absorption in the rural economy through three basic features. First, agricultural growth must be accelerated through land-augmenting technological progress. The experience of the "green revolution" has suggested that technological innovation can increase agricultural employment and productivity provided that the technology and the credit system are scale-neutral, i.e. they do not favour large farms at the expense of small ones, and provided the institutions are not too strongly biased towards the interests of the larger producers. The situation in sub-Saharan Africa is particularly suited to such actions since the poor performance of the agricultural and food sectors can mainly be ascribed to the lack of technological progress. Secondly, the growth of agriculture/non-agriculture linkages should be fostered by the increase of effective demand from agriculture for the products of the non-agricultural enterprises, especially those located in the rural areas. There is solid evidence that agricultural growth, through production and consumption linkages, provides a major impetus to the growth of incomes and employment in the non-farm economy. An essential requirement for the success of this strategy is that agriculture's demand for the output of the non-farm sector should be for a wide range of goods and services with a high employment content. Thirdly, the domestic demand for agricultural output must grow rapidly. This can only occur through accelerated growth in employment in the non-farm sector, facilitated in turn by the indirect effects of agricultural growth.

In implementing such a strategy, certain considerations have to be borne in mind. First, it is not a universal recipe for all countries at all times, and the role of agriculture in employment creation varies considerably between regions.

Secondly, in the long run a shift out of agriculture towards industry and services is inevitable, for agricultural growth by itself cannot solve the problem of employment in the economy as a whole. A coherent long-run strategy needs to take this into account.

Thirdly, the pitfalls of the green revolution experience should be kept in mind, especially the bias against small farmers and the high cost of using chemical inputs. Even when research produces scale-neutral technologies, these acquire a scale bias in actual practice. This is because the benefits of credit and extension services tend to be distributed in the same manner as landholding, often quite independently of the intentions of the governments. In addition, since the adoption of new technologies requires as preconditions both the acquisition of knowledge and the capacity to invest, the relatively larger farmers with better access to credit and extension are better able to benefit.

Fourthly, supplementary policies are needed to encourage the labour-intensive, non-farm economy. On the demand side, raising the incomes of the rural poor will tend to increase effective demand for locally-produced goods and services, and so support the growth of rural non-farm production. But supply side policies are also crucial, including the provision of credit and marketing facilities and the improvement of skills through appropriate training and investment in human capital. Credit is particularly important, but the formal financial system often fails to support the smallest and most disadvantaged enterprises, especially in rural areas. There is therefore a need to direct finance towards those with a specific "credit need" which cannot be satisfied by the formal financial institutions. While some would question the wisdom of attempting to distort market forces by introducing social concerns through direct intervention into the financial system through quotas, subsidies and lending targets, the market often gives the wrong signals as far as poverty alleviation is concerned.

The extent to which the promotion of this approach by the ILO has effectively reduced poverty is difficult to judge. Its success relies heavily on its broad approach to the twin objectives of growth and equity, and this also depends on asset redistribution issues discussed above. The vulnerability of the rural poor may be partially reduced through an increase in agricultural productivity and returns to labour, but greater stress would also be needed on the promotion of the rural non-farm economy. The ILO has for many years supported a comprehensive programme of assistance to small enterprise development [Levitsky, 1993], and there is perhaps scope for extending this in rural areas beyond the usual informal sector activities. In addition, the increase in the collective power of the poor through participatory organizations, including trade unions and cooperatives, is a prerequisite for success, an issue to which we return in Section III.6.

C.   Public works and food-for-work schemes

Another manifestation of the targeted approach to poverty reduction is found in labour-based public works and the advocacy of food-for-work.[5] This approach is based on the observation that the most abundant asset of the poor is their labour, so that their entitlement to income can be enhanced by increasing demand for their labour in building up badly-needed infrastructure, particularly in the rural areas. Food-for-work programmes have been widely promoted by the ILO, especially in Asia and Africa, to provide such employment. Since the late 1970s, these projects

---

[5] For an overview of this approach, see the special issue of the *International Labour Review*, Vol. 131, No. 1, 1992.

have aimed at poverty alleviation through providing poorer population groups with employment and access to basic infrastructure and services. Labour-intensive investment policies were particularly relevant to a growing number of developing countries adopting structural adjustment programmes.

There is no doubt that this approach has been effective in creating employment opportunities in the rural areas, particularly during slack agricultural seasons, and some urban public works programmes have also had a significant employment impact. However these programmes also have limitations. In particular, their scale is usually small in relation to the overall magnitude of the problem of poverty and underemployment. Where this is not the case, the budgetary implications make it difficult to maintain programmes over long periods of time. The approach is most appropriate in situations where it is cost-effective and sustainable in the longer term and where the technology mix of labour and equipment can be flexibly adapted to relative factor cost and labour availability. For instance, the Maharashtra Employment Guarantee scheme in India appears to have satisfied these requirements. But success requires a positive policy environment in public agencies and necessitates the creation of new technical and managerial capacities in public and private sector agencies and firms to cope with such new tasks.

Some public works programmes have been used to improve food security of the poorest people, whereby wages were paid in food instead of cash and were often financed by food aid. Food payments have often been seen as an incentive to encourage poor and undernourished populations to participate in self-help projects. In an increasing number of cases, however, food has become a wage good with a greater appeal to workers than cash. In such situations, the resale of foodstuffs in local markets to meet essential non-food needs is inevitable. The long-term effects of food-for-work programmes financed by food aid have been questioned on the grounds that they lower the prices for domestic food producers, create price uncertainty, the supply of food aid is erratic, and it encourages consumption habits (for example of wheat in the tropics) or types of agro-industries which domestic producers cannot supply.

The balance of past experience indicates that public works programmes have considerable potential for poverty alleviation, although this potential is not always realized. Evaluations that have been made show that everything depends on the programme design, on decentralized planning and on the early involvement of local populations. In this context, it is significant that the assets created by the poor are not usually controlled by them, and this sharply reduces their share of the benefits. But the fact that many labour-intensive infrastructure works do not live up to expectations is not an argument against them as such, but rather an argument for devising and implementing programmes likely to successfully reach the poor. Labour-intensive investment policies have already proved to be a successful employment creation instrument, particularly when compared with the efforts and resources needed to design and implement alternative policies with a similar impact on the poor.

4. Labour market access and vulnerability

In Section II it is argued that the structuring of the labour market is an important source of poverty. This applies as much to rural as to urban labour markets, for in many parts of the world there is a rapid growth in the numbers of rural landless labourers, and labour market outcomes are not usually favourable to the rural poor in view of their disadvantaged position and weak bargaining power [Radwan, 1989]. A central question, then, is how to improve the outcomes of both urban and rural labour markets, especially in terms of returns to labour, and particularly for the poor. Four broad and overlapping areas of labour market policy may be identified. First, an area which has received considerable attention in ILO work concerns labour market information. But the impact on poverty of policy in this area is limited — the poor require not only information but also access. So employment services generally cannot tackle the structural barriers preventing poor groups from obtaining decent jobs. A second area on which traditionally the ILO has had a great deal to say concerns the regulation of contractual relations in employment. This may involve outlawing some types of coercive labour contract (e.g. bonded labour), or limiting the conditions of work, the way in which the employment contract is defined, and the right to negotiate terms and conditions. Again, much of this is not directly concerned with poverty (because application is mainly in the formal sector where poverty is less), but some aspects of the employment relationship are potentially important in action against poverty. This is particularly true of the regulation of wage-setting, especially policy on wage inequality and minimum wage legislation. Third, there are direct implications for poverty of policies to strengthen the labour market position of groups which are vulnerable to discrimination, exploitation or exclusion. A fourth area concerns policy interventions designed to promote the bargaining power of low income groups in the labour market. The first of these is of relatively less interest, and the last we return to in Section III.6. We consider the remaining two areas in a little more detail below.

A. Labour market regulation against poverty: Minimum wages and other interventions

The relationship between minimum wages and poverty is less clear than might be imagined [Starr, 1981]; among other reasons, the impact on poverty of the wages of individual workers depends on the pattern of economic activity of different household members and the level of dependency. Nevertheless, minimum wages are a potentially important labour market policy instrument for reducing poverty, an aim which is implicit in the ILO Convention on the subject (No. 131, 1970) and explicit in ILO Recommendation No. 135. Whether this potential is realized depends on several factors: the extent of coverage; the extent of compliance; the level of the minimum wages; the indirect effects on labour demand, which may increase unemployment or underemployment; the indirect effects on consumption demand of those receiving the minimum wage; effects on labour productivity; and the effects of minimum wages on wage demands of those in the higher strata of the wage hierarchy. The net outcome is far from obvious. Neoclassical economists assume that the effects of minimum wages are bound to be adverse, but PREALC work [Garcia, 1993], for instance, suggests that minimum wage policy has been important in several Latin American countries in preventing the burden of structural adjustment from falling on the poor.

An example of a safety-net minimum that has evolved over time, and has followed the general state of the economy, is provided by the statutory minimum wage in Thailand [ARTEP, 1981]. The first prescribed minimum wage, introduced in 1973, was about half the average wage of unskilled workers in the non-agricultural sector, covering all economic activities except for agriculture and the civil service. It was so low because of considerable opposition to the very notion of a minimum wage by employers at the time, and constituted a compromise and a beginning of minimum wage-fixing. Since then, with the Thai economy growing robustly, the minimum wage, through annual adjustments, has been substantially increased in both real terms and relative to average wages, so that by the beginning of the 1980s, the minimum wage was enough to meet the basic needs of a three-member family. Recently however, there is growing concern among some circles that annual adjustments might be leading to unsustainable wage increases, and a review of the minimum wage-fixing system is currently under consideration.

A general problem in assessing the effects of minimum wages or other forms of labour market regulation on poverty is the extent of compliance. A minimum wage which reaches, say, 20 per cent of workers will have little effect on poverty, and may simply reduce labour absorption in large-scale industry. For minimum wages to be effective in action against poverty, they have to be widely applied, and too often governments are content with the appearance of action which unenforced minimum wage legislation provides. Such attitudes are facilitated by the difficulty of assessing and documenting compliance.

Broadly similar concerns can be expressed with respect to other forms of labour market regulation, such as employment security legislation. Casual, unprotected, irregular work is important as a cause of poverty, and carefully designed legislation to outlaw exploitative practices and precarious employment statuses can certainly contribute to action against poverty, provided they extend to the labour market as a whole. But there are preconditions, in terms of labour market institutions and economics, before legislation is likely to be effective (see, for instance, Siddiqui [1990]). Similar comments can be made about the abolition of bonded or forced labour. In this area the mutual reinforcement of economic policy and legislation would be important, and the subject merits more attention from the ILO than it has received in the past.

B. Reducing labour market vulnerability

ILO attempts to reach specific target groups in poverty programmes are often linked to perceived labour market vulnerability. Much vulnerability is related to age, gender, ethnic group or household status. In the labour market, children and the elderly are both subject to (different) types of disadvantage, in both cases leading to vicious circles of intensifying deprivation. If the elderly are forced to work for lack of alternative income sources, they face both discrimination and vulnerability to ill health, which simultaneously undermine their productivity and increase their need to work. Understanding these interactions is crucial if the pattern is to be broken, a simple intervention to, say, ban child labour, is unlikely to work if the logic of child labour is not understood and alternatives provided. The importance of labour market vulnerability lies not only in the poverty of those thereby trapped in low income, low productivity jobs, but also in its contribution to structuring jobs and segmenting the labour market.

These issues are particularly well illustrated by the position of women in the labour market, which has distinct implications for poverty. Until recent years these were not much stressed in ILO work, but it is now generally admitted that a "gender-blind" approach to labour market or other policy in practice has a negative bias against women. Because women often start from disadvantaged positions — lack of direct control over assets, lack of access to training, discrimination in the labour market, lack of organization, competing domestic and labour market demands on time, cultural and normative constraints — policy which does not specifically discriminate in favour of women ends up reinforcing gender inequality. This is notably true of many of the mechanisms which underlie poverty. While figures are difficult to come by, it is almost certain that a significantly higher percentage of women are poor than of men. Women tend to be clustered in relatively low-income occupations, and within these occupations earn less than men. In the informal sector, women tend to obtain low returns to self-employment because of their lack of access to traditional skills (except those which are regarded as in some sense female), to credit or to land. This sort of mechanism is crucial to explain the high incidence of poverty in female-headed households.

The particular labour market situations of women in poor households arise from a combination of the general mechanisms creating labour market vulnerability and the particular handicaps and disadvantages of women. Labour market segmentation, for instance, widely follows gender lines. Access to the labour market may depend on informal mechanisms where cultural constraints and attitudes tend to reinforce discrimination against women; or it may require formal educational qualifications, where investment in girls' education is seen as offering lower returns than investment in boys'. Home-based work is a particularly feminized labour market category, often subject to very low pay and sometimes intense exploitation without this being visible to the outside world. Women's domestic roles in any case interfere with career progression in regular wage work.

Growing attention has been paid by the ILO to women workers, though only a fraction of this work has stressed the linkage with poverty. A number of international instruments have been adopted to promote equal employment opportunities for women and protect their rights as workers: Equal Remuneration Convention, 1951 (No. 100); Discrimination (Employment and Occupation) Convention, 1958 (No. 111); Human Resources Development Convention, 1975 (No. 142); Workers with Family Responsibility Convention, 1981 (No. 156). The adoption of these instruments, however, does not necessarily guarantee their implementation, and the number of countries that have actually ratified certain Conventions is disappointing.

One programme which has focused on the links between women's work and poverty is the WEP Programme on Rural Women [Berar, 1988]. This work has combined in an integrated approach policy advice, analytical work, technical cooperation and promotion of standards. The main activities in the labour market area have consisted in assisting in the formulation and implementation of programmes and projects concerned with self-employment and credit schemes for poor women and female-headed households, and social protection of vulnerable groups such as home-based piece-rate workers. Much work in the late 1970s and 1980s focused on the survival strategies of poor women, bringing to light the multiple, diverse and rapidly-changing nature of poor women's portfolios of activities in various socio-economic contexts. In the late 1980s and early 1990s, the emphasis shifted to analysing the impact of economic restructuring on patterns of poverty and employment amongst women, both in terms of new opportunities created as well as new forms of discrimination and exploitation emerging from these processes.

The ILO recently initiated a gender-focused review of poverty alleviation strategies promoted over the last 25 years by national and international bodies. Some of the findings of the review could be summed up as follows:

(a) In spite of criticism of the limitations of such programmes, especially in terms of scale and sustainability, there continues to be strong demand for expansion of these interventions. This is a reflection of the observation that women continue to share a large burden of poverty, of an increasing recognition of their needs and their role in poverty alleviation and of the fact that no viable alternative strategies have been found.

(b) Many programmes have had a positive impact on the income levels and income security of poor working women and therefore contributed to the survival of the poorest households. However, the majority of schemes have failed to get beyond the survival stage and did not lead to a permanent escape from poverty. While this could be partly explained by the fact that most poverty alleviation programmes have emphasized support to low productivity and relatively high risk self-employment activities, more analysis of the reasons for stagnation is required.

(c) Beyond direct and immediate economic gains, two important achievements of these interventions are worth noting. Firstly, they have contributed to developing and testing successful strategies and approaches. There has been a rich experience gained in the identification of appropriate approaches for effectively reaching poor women in different contexts. We know "how" to do it. The unresolved challenge ahead is that of replicating these approaches on a much larger and more meaningful scale. Secondly, the importance has

been demonstrated of the broader context of empowerment, especially where the sum of a multitude of national and international interventions fosters a social movement which can influence the policy environment.

Many of the issues which are relevant with respect to women's vulnerability in the labour market are relevant, *mutatis mutandis*, for other vulnerable groups. Child labour is case in point. Whatever form it takes, child labour is an extreme manifestation of poverty, since the poorest families have to use their children's labour to survive; but it also results in a perpetuation of poverty, since child labour prevents children from acquiring the necessary skills and education that would equip them for gainful employment. The ILO's general legal instrument on the subject is the Minimum Age Convention (No. 138), 1973. This aims at the elimination of child labour, but attempts also to provide for the protection of working children, and — attempting to break the vicious circle of poverty — for the provision of welfare and educational facilities.

Another example concerns migrants. ILO work has not identified any general tendency for migration, either internal or international, to aggravate poverty — indeed the predominant pattern is probably the reverse. But some migrants are clearly vulnerable to poverty and exploitation (especially when they form an ethnically distinct group) and migration might increase inequality and relative poverty in destination areas (by swelling the low-wage, low-skill population which does not have access to the high-income jobs). An investigation of the impact of discrimination on migrant workers and second-generation migrants in industrialized countries, for instance, has identified the continuing existence of an underclass of migrants, who are excluded from equitable participation in working life. Conventions No. 97, 1949 and 143, 1975, provide a legal basis for action against discrimination in these circumstances, although it is obvious that abuse continues to be widespread.

How effective is labour market policy in these different circumstances? There is evidence that affirmative action policies can have positive effects, but they need to be systematically and vigorously enforced. This involves using not only administrative controls and inspections, but also the mobilization of the groups affected, public opinion and non-government organizations; even so, success is unlikely to be total. Likewise, labour market regulation is unlikely to be a primary instrument in reducing poverty, for it is liable to be ineffective in the situations where poverty is most extreme, though it may be an important supporting policy where broader economic strategy to reduce poverty is given high priority.

Labour market policies against poverty seem to make sense as part of a package, not as an independent, self-contained approach.

5. Social transfers

Measures to improve the position of the poor through altering the distribution of assets, restructuring systems of production or increasing the access of the poor to jobs imply fundamental changes in economic relationships. Such measures may take a very long time to become effective and, even when they do, political, cultural and other factors may impede a generalized improvement in the position of the poor. A more direct approach, and one which promises more immediate results, is to undertake measures and policies aimed at a redistribution of existing income and wealth. Such measures include direct transfers of income, financed out of general revenues or earmarked social security contributions; the direct provision in kind of basic commodities or the subsidization of their cost; or modifications of general economic policies in ways which directly affect material standards of living at low income levels.

Such approaches are not without their problems. In the first place, they depend critically on the willingness of the non-poor to undertake such transfers, implicit or explicit. This may not be forthcoming, particularly if the non-poor in poor countries have before them models of the higher living standards achievable in the advanced economies and simultaneously possess the economic and political power to block or limit such transfers in their own country. Second, such transfers rely on the administrative capacity of governments to regulate, monitor and implement measures which impose a significant degree of solidarity within the economic structure. An absence of solidarity among the poor themselves may represent a difficulty: labour market regulations or agreements on burden-sharing may be ineffectual and avoided by both employers and employees if it is to their joint advantage. Similar remarks apply to enforcing compliance within social security schemes or to controlling the application of means-tested social assistance schemes. In a number of countries, corruption can be a major problem. Finally, in modifying the rules of the game and undertaking commitments to essentially public transfers, governments may be acting counter to current directions of economic reform, particularly those associated with structural adjustment programmes.

The following sections amplify some of these issues. First, we look at social provisioning, both directly and through subsidy and price policies. The following section looks in more detail at social security and social assistance.

A. Supporting social consumption and provisioning

Meeting basic needs through social expenditures and transfers

The ILO basic needs strategy of the 1970s, *qua* strategy, is discussed in Section II. This perspective on development emerged after a series of studies had attempted to measure the incidence of poverty and establish profiles of the poor in the rural and urban areas of developing countries in the mid-1970s. This work suggested that targeted transfers were the most efficient way of reaching the poor in the short run, while at the same time fostering programmes for structural change which would put productive assets in the hands of the poor. It was argued then that poverty reflected lack of satisfaction of basic needs (food, shelter, health services, etc.), and therefore an anti-poverty strategy should aim at meeting such basic needs, in the first instance through a redirection of public expenditure [ILO, 1977b; Ghai et al., 1977]. Various attempts were made to measure the shortfall in basic needs satisfaction, and to estimate the cost of providing the poor with the goods and services required. But there were two quite different conceptions of a basic needs strategy, one based on a "hand-out" approach, where the state primarily takes charge of providing basic needs, the other treating the satisfaction of basic needs as an integral part of economic development strategy. It was the former vision which rapidly gained the upper hand, at both national and international level, as national policy applications and the recommendations of international organizations were mainly built around the redirection of social expenditure, and so implicitly adopted a restrictive interpretation of the basic needs approach.

The factors which led to the demise of the basic needs strategy, both the more comprehensive approach involving structural change in the production system, and the more restrictive approach based mainly on a redirection of government expenditure, are evoked in Section II. Among them, the one which is most critical for the viability of direct transfers as a means of eliminating poverty was the erosion of the ability of most States in poor countries to fulfil their obligation to satisfy basic needs. A programme of transfers sufficient to satisfy basic needs was simply beyond the resource capacities of the States where it was most needed.

Nevertheless, in most countries social expenditure continues, mostly in less ambitious ways, to aim at providing services and public goods to the poor. Social expenditure as a share of total public expenditure varies considerably among developing countries. According to the Human Development Report [UNDP, 1991], it ranges from as low as 13 per cent in Indonesia to 50 per cent in Chile and Costa Rica. The allocation of these resources among the social sectors is equally diverse. Moreover, the lack of statistical information makes it difficult to obtain indicators for an assessment of the impacts which such expenditures have on the poorer sections of society. Studies on a limited number of Latin American countries [Infante, 1993] have nonetheless produced some evidence on this issue. For example, some programmes directed towards the poor — such as the "Social Investment Funds" which focus on nutritional assistance and on investment in the construction of social infrastructure — have been shown to have had positive (albeit smaller than expected) effects in Honduras, Bolivia and Costa Rica. Special surveys carried out during the 1980s in Chile, Costa Rica and Uruguay have indicated that social expenditures had an income redistribution role, as well as contributing in a non-negligible way to the living standards of the most deprived (lowest quintile) population groups. But, on the whole, in only a few cases — Colombia, Chile and Costa Rica — have such expenditures managed to compensate, and only partially, for the reduction in household income during economic adjustment; and it remains unclear how far successful cases can be replicated.

Although the ILO has maintained a relatively low profile in recent years on this issue, it is clearly central. If economic systems cannot be transformed in directions which lead to the eradication of poverty, resources have to be mobilized for social expenditure, and more attention clearly needs to be paid to the circumstances under which this is possible, and the nature of the expenditures which are most effective.

Subsidies and price policies

At least in principle, subsidies and price policies appear to offer a cheaper way of transferring resources to the poor, in that the state does not bear the full cost. Instead, incentive systems are modified so that private producers behave in line with the objectives of social policy.

Most of ILO's work in this area has focused on the effect of incentive policies (prices and subsidies) on agricultural production, with little attention given to the effects of these policies on urban areas, in particular the role of consumer subsidies in urban poverty alleviation. In so doing, the ILO was responding to the debate on "price distortions" and their effect on growth and equity. This is a recurrent theme in the debate on development and structural adjustment concerning the alleged inappropriateness of the price policies pursued by the State in developing countries.[6] It was widely held that in the past market intervention by the State kept the relative price of agricultural products low in relation to manufactured goods. It was also argued that, in some cases, even within agriculture, the price of export crops relative to food crops was unfavourable to the export crops. These policies, it was believed, were to a significant extent responsible for the slow growth of agricultural output (and hence growth of employment) and the persistence of rural poverty.

ILO research on these issues suggests that in practice there is no straightforward relationship between relative prices on the one hand and agricultural output and rural poverty on the other. Many factors affect the relative profitability of agricultural production, including procurement prices, subsidies on inputs and credit, taxes on exports, subsidies on imported food, exchange rates and the pattern of technological change. Which factors dominate varies from country to country. In Pakistan and India, State-controlled low prices for foodgrains, aimed at benefiting urban consumers and promoting industrialization (by reducing wage costs), have been consistent with the attainment of self-sufficiency in grain production despite growing populations. In Latin America, similar policies appear to have been associated with growing food imports. Price policy does not seem to provide an adequate explanation of the success or failure of agricultural growth in sub-Saharan Africa either [Ghai & Smith, 1987; Ghai, 1987]. Most African farmers remain subsistence-oriented in the sense that they have very little surplus to sell, and hence to them changes in relative prices are of little significance. On the other hand, there is growing evidence of increasing reliance on the market for purchasing staple foods, so changes in food prices do have important implications for welfare in rural areas [Jamal, 1988, 1993]. In effect what this means is that we can no longer assume a priori that increasing relative prices in favour of the agricultural sector is equity-enhancing. The farmers who have a surplus to sell on the market benefit the most and they are, of course, those at the upper end of the income scale. As for the growth impact, while in general there is evidence to show that the price of one crop relative to another does influence the cropping pattern, there is no evidence to show that the relative prices of agricultural products vis-à-vis manufactures influence aggregate agricultural production [Ghose, 1987a]. Finally, the equity impact of movements in relative prices depends on the

---

[6] The basis of the argument is succinctly presented in the World Bank's influential document, *Accelerated development in sub-Saharan Africa: An agenda for action* (Washington, DC, World Bank, 1981). For a critique of the price-first argument see, in particular, Green & Allison [1986].

structure of landholding. Evidence from India confirms that rising relative prices of agricultural products benefit large farmers more than the small farmers and usually hurt the rural wage labourers — the poorest segment of the rural population [Ghose, 1987b].

This appears to be an area in which much more could be done, especially on the consumption side — how can market outcomes be influenced in such a way as to either reduce the prices paid by the poor, or increase the prices they receive for the goods they produce? But it has not received priority in recent ILO work.

B. Social security and social assistance.

Attempts to reduce poverty through transfers of income basically rest on two broad types of programmes: social assistance programmes, which are generally directed to individuals according to their need, are most frequently means-tested, and are usually funded out of tax or general revenues; and social security programmes which represent a mechanism by which all members of society, and to a very large extent the non-poor, can provide against the income needs of old age and against the risk of certain contingencies such as disability, sickness or unemployment. Social security programmes are, in almost all countries, financed by earnings-related contributions from employers and/or employees, and benefits are also usually earnings-related. While benefits bear some relation to contributions, social security schemes frequently contain significant solidarity between income and social groups, as well as between generations. As for schemes financed out of general revenues, these include not only social assistance but also benefits, such as child allowances, and health-care services which are frequently available on a universal basis — although in developing countries sometimes at a minimal level.

From an economic point of view, the two approaches present a strong contrast. Means-tested systems aim to prevent or minimize any leakage of benefits to the non-poor, and also aim to focus limited resources where they are most needed. But expenditure under such systems is usually quite limited. Social security programmes, on the other hand, are a response to the demand for economic security on the part of the population as a whole — here the only limit to expenditure is the level of compulsory contributions that society will accept to pay, and this varies over time and between countries.

The means-tested approach is customarily thought to be an efficient way of dealing with poverty, in the sense that a high proportion of expenditure actually goes to the poor. But even the efficiency of the means-tested approach is subject to some qualification. In the first place, means-tested benefits are relatively complex and expensive to administer. Secondly, a certain amount of benefit will be received by the non-poor, either as a result of fraud and abuse or simply because of administrative error. Thirdly, means tests adversely affect incentives facing actual and potential benefit recipients, in particular the incentives to work and to save, e.g. they tend to place beneficiaries in a poverty trap, so that earning more leads to little or no increase in net income. But perhaps the most important feature is that, in almost all means-tested schemes, a large proportion of those eligible fail to apply for the benefit to which they are entitled. This is not just the result of ignorance. Reluctance to claim means-tested benefits often results from the stigmatizing nature of schemes which cater only for the poor. In addition, the more the State focuses its system of social protection on the poor, the more the general population's demands for economic security will have to be met by private schemes which tend to favour the better-off groups of the population and which lack the elements of solidarity characteristic of social measures.

As far as social insurance and citizenship benefits are concerned, their effectiveness in preventing poverty depends on how comprehensive the system is in terms of the contingencies covered and of the population protected and, of course, on the level of the benefits. In industrialized countries, the proportion of the population covered by social insurance is generally high, and social security transfers have met with great success in reducing the incidence of poverty in old age, of providing income maintenance during sickness and disability, and ensuring (almost) universal access to quality health care. They have been less successful in providing income protection during long-term unemployment. Other contingencies for which protection tends to be inadequate are single parenthood and long-term care for the elderly and disabled (often excluded or inadequately covered by health insurance). In circumstances like these, people often have to fall back on means-tested benefits of one kind or another.

The level of social insurance benefits may also be insufficient to keep the beneficiary and his or her dependants out of poverty, either because income replacements rates are low, or because the individual has not built up adequate entitlements. To help deal with the latter type of problem, a minimum benefit is often provided to those whose earnings during their working life have been exceptionally low. Social insurance underpinned by flat-rate benefits has been found by a number of countries to be a particularly effective way of preventing poverty, more effective than the means-tested approach, primarily because it has succeeded in mobilizing far more resources. As an earlier ILO report put it, "people are much

more willing to contribute to a fund from which they derive benefit than
to a fund going exclusively to the poor" [ILO, 1984, p. 23]. However,
even the best systems of social insurance and of citizenship benefits tend
to have shortcomings which necessitate a national minimum income or
safety net. Thus means-tested benefits will still have some residual role to
play.

It must be stressed that no system of social protection can operate
satisfactorily unless certain economic preconditions are fulfilled. Social
security presupposes that income from work will normally provide sufficient income to live on, and that most people will be in regular work, and
aims to replace such income when people are not able (or expected) to
work and to supplement it when they face the extra costs of supporting
children. In developing countries these conditions are often not met. As a
result, in terms of social protection, the developing countries offer a stark
contrast to the industrialized world. A relatively small proportion of the
population is covered by any kind of social security scheme. Social
insurance constitutes the bulk of existing provision: it is limited essentially
by the fact that relatively few of the population are engaged in forms of
employment or self-employment of a sufficiently formal character to
facilitate the collection of contributions. The only citizenship benefit of
much importance is the public health service, though for many people this
benefit is more theoretical than real and the quality of the service tends to
be low.

The coverage of social insurance systems has been extended significantly in a number of developing countries, particularly in Latin America
and in parts of Asia with a relatively large formal sector. Such schemes are
frequently criticized as being a privilege for a section of the community
that is already much better off than most of the population. But if statutory
social insurance schemes were not established, private schemes would no
doubt be set up, probably favouring long-serving employees and those in
top positions, and so more unequal still in their impact, so the argument
against state-run schemes is unconvincing. However, it is clear that for
many years to come it will be impossible to provide social protection in
this way for the majority of the population in many developing countries,
especially in Africa. Other methods, such as means-tested or citizenship
benefits, must be used to provide a minimum of protection to those at
present most prone to poverty. As this will need to be financed from
general government revenue, and thus will be competing with other forms
of public expenditure, the best that can be hoped for is that modest benefits
can be gradually introduced for the most vulnerable categories of the
population.

Individual social benefits for poor people in developing countries are still very rare. What help they get from the authorities tends to be in the form of projects directed at the local community as a whole, i.e. development promotion rather than social protection. It has been argued that much more could be done to extend protective measures to the unorganized poor (those outside sectors covered by existing social protection schemes), along the lines of the social assistance schemes operating in the Indian State of Tamil Nadu [Guhan, 1992]. Under this particular proposal, a basic package comprising a (small) pension for the elderly and disabled, a lump-sum survivor's benefit, and a maternity benefit would be provided, all on a means-tested basis, initially with the aim of covering 50 per cent of those below the poverty line, i.e. those who are not merely poor but destitute. The package is estimated in the Indian context to cost between 0.3 and 0.5 per cent of GDP, which puts it within the range of feasible options even in societies with low incomes and constrained budgets.

The main thrust of the ILO's work in the developing countries has been to establish, strengthen and, wherever possible, extend the coverage of social insurance schemes.[7] The aim has been to extend protection in geographical terms, as many schemes initially covered employees in urban areas only, to bring into coverage workers in small enterprises, also often excluded in the early stages, and to accord some type of protection to the self-employed. To date, the schemes proposed by the ILO have been mainly of a contributory character. This reflects the concern of most governments in the developing world not to commit themselves to higher public expenditure. Nevertheless, the need for some form of national solidarity has been underlined by the ILO, in order to help finance benefits for those of the self-employed with the lowest capacity to pay contributions. The needs of the self-employed, in so far as they can be ascertained from observation and from social surveys, have been found to differ to some extent from those of employees, as also does their capacity and readiness to pay contributions. Accordingly, in its technical cooperation projects in Africa, for example, the ILO has proposed more modest forms of protection for the self-employed. In the case of the Cameroon, the initial priority was identified as health insurance and, resources permitting, a grant towards expenses of pupils at the beginning of the school year [ILO, 1989].

---

[7] The relevant Convention is the Social Security (Minimum Standards) Convention, No. 102, 1952.

Certain governments have been prepared to contemplate a more significant use of public funds in order to extend some basic form of social protection to the most vulnerable sections of the population. Thus, in Gabon, the indigent were granted health care coverage, family allowances and certain maternity benefits, within the framework of the Social Guarantee Scheme introduced in 1982. The cost of these benefits was, inter alia, to be covered in principle by a government subsidy. Schemes which are financed out of public funds tend to be vulnerable, whenever public expenditure is restricted for economic or political reasons. The case of Gabon proved to be no exception. In 1987 and 1988, the scheme did not receive the amounts which were due from the Ministry of Finance. This illustrates how the scope for the ILO to promote social protection for the most vulnerable groups of the population has been and continues to be severely restricted by the restrictive public expenditure stance of most governments in the developing world, and by the very low priority they generally accord to this particular objective.

The value of informal social protection mechanisms has also been acknowledged for many years and taken into account by the ILO in its technical cooperation activities. For example, in some cases, informal mechanisms have been found to suffice in providing subsistence for people in their old age in traditional African communities, so priority has been given to the development of health insurance. The question may be asked, however, whether the ILO should not be undertaking more work on the question of informal social protection mechanisms. In terms of research, more could be done to understand the scope and the limitations of existing informal mechanisms: but practical implementation remains an intractable problem, both for the ILO and the governments concerned.

There should be no underestimating the political will that must exist if any effective schemes of social protection — formal or informal, social assistance or social security — are to be implemented and further developed. Even in industrialized countries, where the poor are probably in a better position to express their needs, there is a constant tendency for them to lose out whenever governments are facing financial difficulties. For this reason, social assistance measures should not be seen as the ultimate goal, but rather as a stop-gap solution until the categories of the population concerned can be integrated into universal or social insurance schemes. This will probably not happen until they are also fully integrated into the mainstream formal labour force. Finally, in developing all schemes of social protection, policy-makers must adapt them to the contingencies which represent the biggest threat to the livelihood of the population, bearing in mind that these may not necessarily be the same as in the industrialized world or even as in other developing countries.

Over the years there has been surprisingly little work done within the framework of the ILO social security programme which has focused explicitly on poverty. Consequently, the ILO has not been able to speak authoritatively about the scope for reducing poverty through social protection (and about the limitations of such an approach). Nor has it been involved in assessing either the effectiveness or the efficiency of existing systems of social protection in reducing poverty. As governments are increasingly trying to set priorities and to restrict whatever is seen as unnecessary expenditure, it is crucial for the ILO to come to grips with this issue. Furthermore, other international organizations have become increasingly active in the field of social protection: their major concern has tended to be to contain rising public expenditure and their policy prescriptions have not always taken adequate account of the wider range of objectives considered to be important by the ILO's constituents. Recently a start has been made in giving the ILO's work on social security a broader focus, but much remains to be done.

6. The organization of the poor

The foregoing sections notwithstanding, progress in reducing rural and urban poverty remains to a large extent dependent on the degree to which various groups among the poor are organized in bodies of their own choosing and on the effectiveness of those organizations in furthering and defending the interests of their members.

In their struggle for survival, poor households rely first and foremost on their own labour to make ends meet. But their individual efforts can be amplified when they organize themselves. Their main interest is obviously to increase their incomes, but they may also wish to strengthen their cultural identity, raise their status in society, establish social rights or have a political impact. "The great masses (of Chileans) have no organization", said Frei in 1966, "and without organization no power, and without power no representation in the life of the country".

The organization of the poor starts at the grass-roots — local — level. The poor are often so involved in their daily struggle for survival that they have neither time nor energy left for organized contact with the outside world. Moreover, there may be simply a lack of awareness that they can actively change their life situation. Often, they will need a catalyst or outside animator who helps them analyse their position in society and mobilize their initiative and creativity to improve their living conditions.

In view of this, in 1977 the ILO launched a programme concerned with "Participatory Organizations of the Rural Poor" [Rahman, 1984]. In this programme, participation was viewed as an organized activity of the rural poor, who take their own initiatives, and control the content, pace and directions of those initiatives. A participatory research methodology was used, in which it was, in fact, the poor who undertook their own research, in dialogue with the external researcher who provided the initial stimulus for the investigation and acted as a rapporteur of the results. In principle, the task of the external agent or animator is to withdraw as soon as possible, when a group seems to have acquired sufficient momentum and confidence to continue with its initiative, so as to avoid the development of either a dependent relationship or one where the animator becomes the group leader [Tilakaratna, 1987; Rahman, 1983].

In the urban informal sector, too, there is a need for workers to organize themselves in order to secure lasting improvements in their situations. This has been supported, in the ILO, by the adaptation of the participatory strategy to sustain initiatives for self-help taken by informal sector producers. In gradually developing group strategies, a new institutional actor is created with growing resources of its own, able to defend the interests of its members and to act as a pressure group for social and economic change [Maldonado, 1993].

Since the beginning of the 1980s, the ILO has also been involved in promoting the organization of women, in both the rural and the urban informal sectors. Such organizations may provide a legal basis for access to land; enhance bargaining power vis-à-vis the local government and the State; foster assertiveness and self-confidence in dealings with power holders; and enable women to identify their own needs and priorities and to set up their own projects. To achieve these objectives it is often important to obtain legal recognition. This aim is more often achieved in Asia than in Africa, where the organizational setting is more informal. Another benefit is the exchange of information and experience between women's organizations, not only within but also between countries. This international exchange has led, for example, to the replication of local-level grass-roots organizations developed along the lines of SEWA, the Self-Employed Women's Association, and the Working Women's Forum in India.

Cooperatives may provide an additional mechanism for the organization of the poor if certain preconditions are met, such as access to capital and assets. Within the ILO, the role of cooperatives in poverty alleviation through the promotion of employment and income was reiterated in the 1992 Report of the Director-General, entitled *Democratization and the ILO*

[ILO, 1992], which argued that cooperatives offered a special advantage — in terms of enterprise and job creation — to developing countries undertaking structural adjustment programmes and to countries that had rejected centralized economic planning. Traditional cooperative structures can be adapted to fashion new organizational forms of self-help, particularly in the rural and urban informal sectors, and to create self-employment and income for vulnerable groups and the poor. This is reflected, for example, in the development and promotion of self-help, participatory and sustainable methods of finance and investment through savings and credit cooperatives. But cooperatives may also operate exclusively in the interests of the rich: a careful and critical approach is needed.

The philosophy behind most of these activities is that, through organization, the poor can increase their negotiating power. But, as is brought out by the Convention on Rural Workers' Organisations (No. 141, 1975), it is clear that the scope of these activities and the groups involved go well beyond the territory of the traditional labour relations between wage workers and employers. The negotiating parties may be wage-earners, the self-employed or female homeworkers on the one hand and employers, landowners, suppliers, traders and various government institutions on the other. The representation of groups among the poor may be based on ethnic or community identity, a common pattern of exclusion with respect to rights or income sources, or other factors which do not directly identify a group of workers. And the subject of negotiation is not necessarily wages and other employment conditions, but may also be the provision of government services, training and credit, social protection or employment opportunities.

In this process, trade unions can be powerful allies for the poor. Convention No. 87, 1948, on Freedom of Association and Protection of the Right to Organize, is clearly relevant, but in practice the existing associations and trade unions do not necessarily directly represent the interests of all the groups concerned. Indeed, a widespread complaint is that national trade union bodies represent mainly those in relatively better-paid, stable jobs. While in some countries this is undeniable, unions may, of course, have a direct impact as the organizers of unskilled wage workers who are often members of poor households, and there are many cases where unions attempt to mobilize casual and irregular workers, or assist homeworkers to negotiate better terms and conditions of work. But unions are best at organizing in large enterprises and plantations, where many people are working within a limited amount of space and where working conditions are comparable. The role of trade unions as organizer is much more complicated in the rural, small-scale and informal sectors where wage workers are scattered among many different enterprises and areas, and where self-employment is widespread. This implies that a variety of forms of organization are likely to be needed. For instance, among the self-employed, organizations aimed at community solidarity and mutual help may be most effective. And it would appear to be important to aim for solidarity between trade union organization and other popular movements which may more effectively reach the poor.

As matter of fact, various unions have shown interest in working with the urban informal sector as well as with the rural poor and have developed contacts with the unorganized poor. This was mainly motivated by the need for new membership. For example, almost half of the members of the Ghana Agricultural Workers Union were at one time small-scale peasants receiving special services from the union, and the union still has a strong presence among the rural poor in Ghana. The Agricultural and Plantation Workers Union of Uganda is also active in the rural areas and is attempting to organize rural women. The National Union of Free Trade Unions of Côte D'Ivoire (Dignité) organized the market women and other self-employed workers in national associations, which are now linked with that organization. The Central Organization of Trade Unions of Brazil (CUT) played and continues to play an important awareness-creating role for the grass-roots communities in the rural and urban informal sectors. For instance, it provides civic and organizational courses for local leaders to enable them to resolve community problems.

The degree of organization at grass-roots level is the basis for any form of political power, i.e. the ability to influence decision-making of other groups or the government. In some cases organizations extend beyond the local level, and are able to operate at the national or regional level. This is usually the result of successful examples in one locality, which are then replicated in other parts of the country or even abroad. Examples of such processes are the *Sarilakas* ("own strength") projects in the Philippines, *Bhoomi Sena* ("land army") in India and the Organization of Rural Associations for Progress (ORAP) in Zimbabwe.

With the advent of greater democracy in many developing countries various groups among the poor have greater opportunities to organize themselves openly. National or international NGOs can play a powerful representative role, and so can political parties, even though they may wish to influence rather than to be influenced. Here also the new wave of democratization can be to the advantage of the poor. In a democratic state, active bargaining takes place between voters, the parties, the candidates for office and the elected representatives. The resulting politics are the manifestation of the increased influence poor people can wield by becoming organized in a society where politicians must be responsive to the voters.

But poverty persists in democratic states, and more is needed to tip the balance of power in favour of the poor. Thus, mobilizing support at the national and international level is a vital part of a comprehensive anti-poverty strategy. Eradicating poverty is an aim that concerns — and is to the benefit of — society as a whole. But anti-poverty policies may not always be in the direct, short-term, interest of all groups in society. Any government in a democratic society will therefore have to enlist support from a variety of socio-economic groups, and be prepared to stand up to conflicting interests, in order to implement an effective anti-poverty strategy.

7. Some tentative conclusions

The review of strategies and policies presented in this section and in Section II can be summarized around three main preoccupations. One set of issues relates to *development strategy and economic growth* and their impact in reducing poverty levels. A second relates to questions of *redistribution towards the poor*, principally through transfers in cash or in kind, but also through measures which alter the structure and regulation of the labour market in favour of the poor, through the provision of social services which enhance human capital, such as education and health care, or by administrative means which ensure the supply and price of basic commodities. A third group of issues relates to the *promotion of employment*, particularly employment which integrates the poor into the mainstream of earnings and activity. Underlying all three approaches are questions about what it is in the structure of economies that causes them to have significant, sometimes large, fractions of the population in poverty, relative as well as absolute. And this in turn throws up a number of non-economic questions relating to the structure of society, the nature of governance and the representation of different social groups.

With respect to the effects of development strategy and growth, a first tentative conclusion would be that the requirements for generating growth on a global scale are not well understood, especially growth which favours the poorer countries. The reversal in the dominant approaches to development strategy which has occurred in recent years, away from intervention and import substitution and towards liberalization, underlines this point. Growth has in fact occurred. But it has been unevenly spread over the developing world and the reasons for the success of some countries and the failure of others are contested. Secondly, and more importantly from the point of view of anti-poverty policies, it is clear that even if countries experience growth, a reduction in poverty is not an automatic consequence. Higher incomes in the modern sectors of developing countries do not necessarily trickle down to the poor, in either the rural or the urban sectors, and unmodified programmes of structural adjustment aimed at setting the preconditions for growth are likely to lead to greater poverty in the short term, perhaps also in the longer term. But growth certainly makes things easier for governments which are committed to tackling poverty.

What, then, of redistributive policies? Broadly defined, these subsume a wide range of measures including direct income support, the redistribution of land and other assets, nutrition and basic needs programmes, programmes aimed at improving human resources, food subsidies and price controls, programmes of social security and social protection, and legislation which protects the poor, especially women and children, from exploitation in the labour market. The review notes a number of successes from policies of this kind. And because these policies are more specific and more targeted than macro-economic policies, both successes and failures are more easily identified. But the review also notes a number of factors which limit the scope and magnitude of redistributive policies, at least when taken in isolation from other changes. Resources and the capacity to mobilize them are clearly the major constraint: national budgets are small, both because of the overall level of income and because of the span of the tax base, which frequently does not reach outside the modern sector. And structural adjustment programmes tighten the constraints further. Equally important, however, is the political feasibility of redistributive policies. The poor in developing countries tend to be disenfranchised, either de jure because of a lack of democracy or de facto because of their lack of economic power or inability to organize. The consensus for redistributive policies rests largely on the goodwill of the better-off, who cannot easily be coerced by the poor. Particularly where poverty is widespread and where large-scale transfers would be required to make any impact, the possibilities of achieving consensus are limited.

Finally, it is in the area of employment policies that the ILO has made the greatest contribution. There are two sides to the issue. On the one hand, increases in the demand for labour are the means by which overall growth can be distributed to the poor in a way which produces a lasting change in the primary distribution of income. On the other hand, improvements in the supply of labour, especially in terms of skills, and in the functioning of production systems and of labour markets are required in order to ensure that the demand be made effective in a way which increases access to incomes for the poor, and does not concentrate the gains on groups who are already better placed. Poverty reduction requires that growth be directed to the outsiders more than the insiders. Success in employment generation automatically improves the feasibility of redistributive policies, both because it brings the primary distribution of income closer to that required on social and humanitarian grounds, and also because it increases the tax and social security base from which resources can be drawn.

There are a large number of facets to policies for employment promotion, and many of them have been touched on above. In particular, they include measures aimed at improving labour market outcomes in terms of access to employment and remuneration, especially for the poor and vulnerable groups. Employment in this context means both wage and self-employment, and a wide range of approaches has been deployed to promote them. But in the end it is the simultaneity and coherence of policies which matter most. It is no use improving the employability of the poor if the jobs are not there. At the same time, people who are undernourished, in poor health, or without basic education are unlikely to be productive even if jobs are available. But conversely, the investment in human capital cannot be made without the resources which come from growth. Some form of structural adjustment may or may not be a necessary condition for growth: but it is an uncertain condition, since in the first instance it throws people out of work, the conditions for their reinsertion may take a long time to arrive, and it may harm the human and economic base for its achievement.

Thus, the chief conclusion of this report is that no single analytical approach, paradigm of policy stance can by itself produce the required results. Partial or piecemeal approaches do not seem to work, and what is needed is an approach which combines both socially sensitive macroeconomic policies with the more direct policies associated with the promotion of employment and with a redistribution of assets and income towards the poor.

IV. Strategic options for the future

1. The context

Despite the hopes and expectations of the past, poverty not only persists today but is intensifying in some ways and in some regions. Decades of sustained effort to promote development have had an effect on poverty that can at best be regarded as mixed. It is true that poverty has declined in rapidly-growing Asian economies — but the group of countries which has been able to maintain high rates of economic growth over long periods is small, and high growth is in any case not a sufficient condition for poverty reduction. Meanwhile, whole regions, notably most of sub-Saharan Africa, have suffered systematic impoverishment. At the same time, in wealthy countries the 1970s and 1980s have seen growing deprivation, as increasing numbers fail to gain access to the economic mainstream and are shunted off to the margins of society. At both national and international level, there seems to be a delinking of the fortunes of rich and poor. Poverty in Africa appears to have no adverse consequences for the growth of the global economic system; deprivation in advanced societies does not affect the enjoyment of their growing wealth by the affluent. The prevailing development path seems to have built into it a process which excludes some while including others, which restricts opportunities rather than broadening them, and which undermines solidarity and systems of social protection.

What changes in the global economic system provide the background to these trends? It is common to point to at least three: a growing internationalization or globalization; a decline in the capacity of production systems to create jobs; and a transformation of institutional frameworks towards market relationships.

While globalization surely affects poverty, the process is far from clear. Many poor countries are on the fringes of the global economy: globalization may increase poverty by exclusion. A new division of labour may emerge, in which poor countries are trapped in low-wage, low-skill production ghettoes; but here the relationships are uncertain. What is sure is that information and communications flows increase international awareness, generate new wants and new deprivations. The delinking between rich and poor within countries may accompany a linking of rich and rich between countries, as high-consumption life styles globalize. It is also true that the internationalization of economic systems implies that autonomous national action may not, by itself, be sufficient to reduce poverty; and in the absence of an international commitment to poverty reduction, this means that state policy against poverty is weakened on a global scale.

The changes in production systems are still more ambiguous. Growing unemployment in the majority of countries suggests that there is something new in the output growth path, that capital-intensive technology or inflexible institutions lead to a failure of growth to create jobs. In low-income settings this is accompanied by an informalization of labour relationships and production; this is also true in many high income settings as well. Increasing poverty seems an inevitable outcome, though whether the problem lies in the production system or in the design of macro-economic and macro-social policy is far from obvious.

The growing reliance on market relationships reflects a shift in the dominant ideology towards a liberal model of economic relationships. How this affects the poor depends on the nature of the non-market institutions which disappear. The steep decline in the benefits provided by state-sponsored systems of social protection and redistribution in ex-socialist countries, for instance, is clearly a direct cause of growing poverty. The discussion in Section II also suggests that at least part of the recent growth in poverty in countries in Africa and Latin America can be attributed to the liberalization implicit in structural adjustment, especially in so far as market forces undermine institutions which provide security, protection or income opportunities to low-income groups. The market may also under-mine the vested interests of the affluent — but on the whole, the rich are better placed to defend their interests than the poor. A particularly important issue, from the point of view of the ILO, is the growing individualization of economic relationships, so that the collective organizations of the ILO's constituency, in particular the State and the unions, suffer a decline in authority and influence.

The conclusion cannot be avoided that the universal reduction in poverty that was confidently foreseen a few decades ago has not been realized. The reasons can be contested — were the wrong policy instru-ments used, were the right policies not applied with sufficient vigour, was the problem macro-economic failures, lack of solidarity or the power of vested interests...? — but the persistence of poverty cannot. That poverty and prosperity co-exist suggests that we can no longer convincingly argue that they are mutually inconsistent. True, there are threats on the horizon to which persistent poverty may contribute: uncontrolled migration and refugee movements, the fragmentation of societies, or exclusion and re-gress of substantial parts of the world which put political stability in peril. But the most powerful argument against poverty is not self-interest, but moral. The case is therefore strong for a rethinking of the economic and political framework which has guided action against poverty in the past — and this applies to the policy community at large, and not only to the ILO.

2. The elements of a strategy

The importance of poverty to the ILO is attested by the foregoing sections. Both instrumental and final arguments can be deployed:

instrumental, in that the elimination of poverty is a precondition for much else — the elimination of child labour, the protection of working conditions, or the general provision of social insurance surely all depend heavily on the effectiveness of strategy against poverty. But the ILO also has a direct mandate to act against poverty as one of the primary objectives of social policy. As we have seen, much work has been done. But if there is one clear conclusion that the analysis in the sections above can offer, it is that action against poverty has been greatly weakened by its fragmented and partial nature. How can wage policy be divorced from employment policy? What sense does it make to treat social security as if it had no relationship to macro-economic policy or the informalization of economic relationships? Each action against poverty faces diminishing returns on its own — but there are substantial complementarities and mutual reinforcements which are possible if an integrated approach is adopted; there are also contradictions, but they should be identified and tackled.

The discussion above offers many elements which may contribute to the design of such an integrated strategy. In this, the complementarity of opposites is worth stressing the following.

International or national: national action against poverty is essential, but the financial capacity for action in many developing countries, even medium income ones, is tightly constrained. International solidarity is also needed, not only in terms of resource flows but also by changing the rules of the international economic system in favour of poor producers and consumers.

Macro or micro: much of the discussion of Section II focuses on macro-economic policies and strategic intervention; much of the discussion of Section III on the micro-level. Again, these are complements and not alternatives. Micro-interventions will be needed to raise labour capability and access, but these will be ineffective without a good macro-economic strategy that generates adequate labour demand. Similarly, programmes designed to directly reduce poverty in particular target groups can contribute to successful structural change in the distribution of assets and opportunities, but structural change may itself be necessary for targeted interventions to have more than marginal effects. For instance, interventions aimed at poor women are unlikely to offset the feminization of poverty unless combined with structural changes in the way economic systems provide opportunities for women in general.

Transfers or change in the primary distribution of income: programmes of transfers alone, as the analysis in Section III suggests, impose intolerable resource burdens on the State which imply that they cannot provide the sole answer to poverty. They need to be supplemented by policies to change the primary distribution of income, such as land reform. But no attainable primary distribution of income, however equitable, will eliminate the need for transfers.

The State or the people: the role of the State is vital for the redistribution of incomes and the reduction of poverty, yet alone is insufficient; grass-roots movements, community actions, the mobilization of poor groups and other actions from the base appear to be essential for successful poverty alleviation.

The conclusion is that a broad-based approach which can integrate and balance these different elements is necessary. But is this broad canvas something that the ILO can tackle? The ILO may have a mandate for action against poverty, but the problem goes far beyond the ILO's capabilities alone. What are the specificities of an ILO vision of the problem?

At the core of an ILO vision is a notion of society. Within society, solutions are achieved through social dialogue and consensus-building — or if consensus cannot be achieved, by building broad coalitions to overcome vested interests. This means that the labour market, for instance, is a locus of dialogue and consensus, and not just resource allocation. Since conflicting interests are involved, there is a need for rules which obtain respect from the parties involved, implying regulation. Because such regulation cannot be achieved by individuals, there is a stress on the importance of social groups and of collective action.

The ILO concern with social justice leads naturally to a stress on rights and standards: rights, as the basis for participation by labour in society; standards, as a means to express those rights. With respect to poverty, the prevailing philosophy can be expressed as a right to inclusion, in the sense of participation, protection, access to decent jobs and decent incomes. But the fulfilment of this right depends on economic preconditions — and to meet these preconditions it is necessary to build up the capacities of labour and of the corresponding systems of production. Thus, the achievement of rights involves the development of both economic and social capability.

There are corresponding priorities in macro-economic policy as well. Inclusion, integration and access to incomes all imply the centrality of employment creation as an economic priority. More generally, the need to build social objectives into macro-economic policy implies a stress on redistribution, equity and solidarity. This is not limited to national policy, but also has implications for the design of international economic systems which respond to poverty-reducing objectives, e.g. through internationally agreed systems of social protection, or through modifying the operation of international markets for goods and services in order to defend the ability of workers to obtain a decent remuneration for their work.

All this implies a priority to the creation of social institutions, as means of promoting both economic and social goals. Such institutions may include organizations or administrative systems, they may include legislation and the means for its enforcement, they may include values and patterns of behaviour in the workplace and the labour market which are accepted by all the parties concerned.

3.   The challenge for the ILO

The potential contribution of the ILO to action against poverty is considerable, and the argument so far is that the elements of a strategy are present in its work. But the history of its work in this domain, outlined in the foregoing sections, suggests that success has been patchy. There have been periods when the ILO made considerable contributions to quality research, but these periods have not been prolonged. The internal divisions of the organization, such as the divide between legislative and normative action on the one hand, and other forms of social and economic policy on the other, have yet to be overcome — and yet this would be a precondition for the integration of action against poverty in different domains. Many specific programmes have contributed to action against poverty; but they did not add up to more than the sum of their parts.

What are the key challenges that the ILO must now face if it is to contribute decisively to the development of new strategies against poverty?

First, there is an analytical challenge. The ILO needs to make a serious attempt to analyse afresh some of the key issues: how to prevent trade-offs between economic and social goals from dominating economic policy and sapping efforts to attain social objectives; how to tackle the political economy of redistribution; how to design integrated strategies in which macro and micro interventions are mutually reinforcing; how to mobilize the different social actors at both national and international levels and convince them that they have a common interest in poverty eradication.

Among these, perhaps the most crucial in the current climate of liberalization is the first. There is a global debate over how far it is possible to promote social goals without subverting them by undermining economic progress, and it is one in which the ILO should be more active. In its simplest terms, the conventional economic argument is that direct intervention in markets in favour of the poor is self-defeating, for it generates inefficiency and inequality. Thus, protective labour standards are said to reduce employment and create islands of protected workers in a sea of informality. Minimum wages, it is argued, protect the few at the expense of the many. The ILO cannot simply reject these arguments as contrary to its dogma, but needs to assess them objectively and see how they can be overcome. For it is quite likely that they can be overcome, if sufficient attention is paid to the design of institutions which bypass or redirect trade-offs, promote productivity gains or provide a basis for consensus-building. But this requires an intensive effort of quality research, which mobilizes both the ILO's constituency and the academic community. Similar considerations apply to other on-going debates, such as those over the social clause in international trade.

Second, there is a philosophical challenge. Much of the work of the ILO is built around the notions of rights and standards. The challenge here is to establish a moral baseline in which universal labour standards are seen as part of a package which also encompasses the right to social inclusion and freedom from poverty. Given the normative perspective of much of the ILO's work, it seems essential, if a concern with poverty is to permeate the work of the organization as a whole, that the relationships between these different objectives in different domains be clarified. Once this is done, an effort is required to build a strategy against poverty which responds to a range of diverse objectives; not all these objectives will necessarily be consistent, and a consensus on the ranking of goals will be hard to achieve, but if there are inconsistencies they need to be transparent: if the issue is fudged, its moral force will be undermined. A successful mapping out of rights and social objectives and their relationships with economic strategy can provide the basis for action against poverty to be presented to the international community as a global responsibility.

Third, there is a political challenge. For a strategy against poverty to be viable, it is essential to mobilize both intellectual and political support. The basic needs strategy of the 1970s may have had the intellectual support, but it was sadly short of political backing; this was surely a major reason for its rapid demise. A strategy against poverty through labour protection and employment promotion may have political support, at least in some quarters, but without sufficient intellectual backing it can make little headway. Both in-depth social analysis and close attention to the political economy are therefore required.

As far as the ILO is concerned, the bedrock of its political support is necessarily its tripartite constituency, who have to be convinced that a broad-based and effective strategy against poverty is in their long-run interests. But the ILO and its constituents need also to reach out towards the representatives of other interest groups and other organizations, especially with a view to the more effective mobilization of the poor, but also because a highly decentralized mode of operation seems likely to be both efficient and desirable in its own right.

The other important point is that the ILO cannot act alone. Its domain may be central to a strategy against poverty, but it shares this domain with many other organizations; what is more, there are additional, different aspects of poverty which intersect with the concerns of the ILO. Alliances and coalitions are required with other organizations in the national and international systems which treat these issues from different perspectives. But for the ILO to be an effective and leading member of such alliances, it must first reassess and renew its own approach and capabilities.

Bibliographical references

Adelman, I. 1978. *Income distribution policy in developing countries*. Oxford, OUP, 346p.

ARTEP. 1981. *Basic needs and minimum wages in Thailand*. Bangkok, International Labour Office.

—. 1987. *Structural adjustment: By whom, for whom: Employment and income aspects of industrial restructuring in Asia*. New Delhi, International Labour Office, 97p.

Berar, A. 1988. *Women and rural development: What have we learnt?* SAREC Seminar. Geneva, International Labour Office, 14p.

Collier, D.; Radwan, S. 1986. *Labour poverty in rural Tanzania*. Oxford, Clarendon Press, 143p.

Dasgupta, P. 1989. *Well-being: Foundations and the extent of its realization in poor countries*. London, London School of Economics, LSE-STICERD, Development Economics Research Programme Discussion Paper No. 19.

Galtung, J.; Wirak, W. 1977. "Human needs and human rights. A theoretical approach", in *Bulletin of peace proposals* (Oslo), 8(3).

Ghai, D. et al. 1977. *The basic needs approach to development*. Geneva, International Labour Office, 113p.

Ghai, D. 1987. *Successes and failures in growth in sub-Saharan Africa*. Geneva, International Labour Office. WEP Working Paper.

Ghai, D.; Smith, L. D. 1987. *Agricultural prices, policy and equity in sub-Saharan Africa*. Rienner, Boulder, Col., 174p.

Ghose, A. K. 1987a. *Agriculture-industry terms of trade and distributive shares in a developing country*. Geneva, International Labour Office, 63p. WEP Working Paper.

—. 1987b. *Trends and fluctuation in rural poverty in India: An explanatory framework and some conclusions*. Geneva, International Labour Office, 56p. WEP Working Paper.

Green, R. H.; Allison, C. 1986. "The World Bank's agenda for accelerated development: Dialectics, doubts and dialogues", in Ravenhill, J. (ed.): *Africa in economic crisis*. Basingstoke, Macmillan.

Griffin, K.; Khan, K. 1978. "Poverty in the Third World: Ugly facts and fancy models", in *World Development* (New York), 6(3), pp. 295-304.

Guhan, S. 1992. *Social security for the unorganised poor: A feasible blueprint for India*. Madras, Madras Institute of Development Studies.

Hoeven, R. van der. 1987. "External shocks and stabilization policies: Spreading the load." in *International Labour Review*, 126(2), pp. 133-150.

—. 1993. "Can safety-nets and compensatory programmes be used for poverty alleviation", in Hoeven, R. van der; Anker, R.: *Poverty monitoring: An international concern*. London, Macmillan.

Hopkins, M. J. D.; Norbye, O. D. K. 1978. *Meeting basic needs: Some global estimates*. Geneva, International Labour Office.

Hopkins, M. J. D.; van der Hoeven, R. 1982. *Basic needs in development planning*. Geneva, International Labour Office.

Infante, R. (ed.). 1993. *Deuda social. Desafío de la equidad*. Santiago, International Labour Office, PREALC.

ILO. International Labour Office. 1950. *Action against unemployment*. Geneva, 260p.

—. 1969. *The World Employment Programme*. Report of the Director-General. International Labour Conference, 53rd Session. Geneva.

—. 1970a. *Poverty and minimum living standards: The role of the ILO*. Report of the Director-General. International Labour Conference, 54th Session. Geneva.

—. 1970b. *Towards full employment: A programme for Colombia*. Geneva.

—. 1971a. *Concepts of labour force utilisation*. Geneva.

—. 1971b. *Matching employment opportunities and expectations; a programme of action for Ceylon*. Geneva.

—. 1972. *Employment, incomes and equality; a strategy for increasing productive employment in Kenya*. Geneva.

—. 1976. *Employment, growth and basic needs: A one-world problem; The 'international basic needs strategy' against chronic poverty, and the decisions of the 1976 World Employment Conference*. New York, Praeger. xi, p. 223.

—. 1977a. *Poverty and landlessness in rural Asia*. Geneva.

—. 1977b. *Meeting basic needs: Strategies for eradicating mass poverty and unemployment*. Geneva.

—. 1982. *Resolution concerning statistics of the economically active population, employment, unemployment and underemployment*. Thirteenth International Conference of Labour Statisticians, Geneva.

—. 1984. *Into the twenty-first century: The development of social security*. Geneva.

—. 1987. *Report of the High Level Meeting on Employment and Structural Adjustment.* Geneva.

—. 1988. *Rural employment promotion.* International Labour Conference, 75th Session. Geneva.

—. 1989. *Rapport au gouvernement de la République camerounaise sur l'extension de la protection sociale aux populations non salariées.* Geneva, OIT/TF/CAM/R.13.

—. 1990a. *Informal sector and urban employment – A review of activities on the urban informal sector.* Geneva, WEP Technology and Employment Branch.

—. 1990b. *The promotion of self-employment.* Report VII. International Labour Conference, 77th Session. Geneva.

—. 1991. *The dilemma of the informal sector.* Report of the Director-General. International Labour Conference, 78th Session. Geneva.

—. 1992. *Democratization and the ILO.* Report of the Director-General. International Labour Conference, 79th Session. Geneva.

—. 1993. *World Labour Report,* Geneva.

ILO. International Labour Organization, 1944. *Declaration concerning the aims and purposes of the ILO.* Philadelphia.

Jamal, V.; Weeks, J. 1987. "The vanishing rural-urban gap in sub-Saharan Africa", in *International Labour Review* (Geneva, ILO), 127(3).

Jamal, V. 1988. "The African crisis, food security and structural adjustment", in *International Labour Review* (Geneva, ILO), 127(6).

—. 1993. "Structural adjustment programmes and structural adjustment: Confronting the new parameters of African economies".

JASPA, 1982. *Rural-urban gap and income distribution in Africa.* Addis Ababa, International Labour Office, JASPA.

Keynes, J. N. 1936. *General theory of employment, interest and money.* New York, Harcourt Brace Jovanovich.

Levitsky, J. 1993. *Innovations in the financing of small and micro enterprises in developing countries.* Geneva, International Labour Office.

Lydall, H. 1975. *Trade and employment.* Geneva, International Labour Office.

Maldonado, C. 1993. "Building networks: An experiment in support to small urban producers", in *International Labour Review* (Geneva, ILO), 132(2), pp. 245-312.

Marshall, A. 1893. *Official Papers.*

Mukherjee, S. 1979. *Restructuring in industrialized countries due to an increased trade between developed and developing countries.* Geneva, International Labour Office.

Paukert, F. 1973. "Income distribution at different levels of development: A survey of evidence" in *International Labour Review*, 108(2-3), pp. 97-126.

PREALC. 1983. *Empleo y salarios.* Santiago, International Labour Office.

—. 1987. *Beyond the crisis*. Santiago, International Labour Office.

—. 1988. *Meeting the social debt*. Santiago, International Labour Office.

Radwan, S. 1977. *Agrarian reform and rural poverty*. Geneva, International Labour Office.

Radwan, S. (ed.). 1989. "Rural labour markets and poverty in developing countries", *International Labour Review* (Geneva, ILO), 125(6).

Rahman, A. 1983. *A pilot project for stimulating grass-roots participation in the Philippines*. Geneva, International Labour Office.

—. 1984. *Participatory organizations of the rural poor*, mimeo. Geneva, International Labour Office, Rural Employment Policies Branch.

Renshaw, G. 1980. *Employment, trade and North-South co-operation*. Geneva, International Labour Office.

Rodgers, G. B. 1984. *Population and poverty: Approaches and evidence*. Geneva, International Labour Office.

Rodgers, G. B. (ed.). 1989. *Urban poverty and the labour market: Access to jobs and incomes in Asian and Latin American cities*. Geneva, International Labour Office.

Rodgers, G. B.; Rodgers, J. M. (eds.). 1989. *Precarious jobs in labour market regulation: The growth of atypical environment in Western Europe*. Geneva, International Institute for Labour Studies.

Rowntree, B. S. 1909. *Poverty: A study of town life*. London, Macmillan.

Sen, A. 1975. *Employment, technology and development*. Oxford, Clarendon Press.

—. 1981. *Poverty and famines*. Oxford, Clarendon Press, 257p.

Siddiqui, A. M. A. H. (ed.). 1990. *Labour laws and the working poor*. Bangkok, International Labour Office-ARPLA.

Starr, G. 1981. *Minimum wage fixing*. Geneva, International Labour Office.

Tilakaratna, S. 1987. *The animator in participatory rural development: Concept and practice*. Geneva, International Labour Office.

Tokman, V.. 1992. *Beyond regulation: The informal economy in Latin America*. Boulder, Col. Rienner.

Tripartite World Conference on Employment, Income and Social Progress and the International Division of Labour. 1976. *Employment, growth and basic needs: A one world problem*. Geneva, International Labour Office, 177p.

UNDP. United Nations Development Programme. 1991. *Human development report*. New York, OUP.

World Bank. 1981. *Accelerated development in sub-Saharan Africa: An agenda for action*. Washington.

—. 1990. *World Development Report*. Washington.

—. 1992. *World Development Report*. Washington.

2   Comments on "The framework of ILO action against poverty"

Paul Streeten[1]

It has taken the more enlightened advanced societies three centuries to achieve the civil, political and social dimensions of human development. The eighteenth century established *civil* rights: from freedom of thought, speech and religion to the rule of law. In the course of the nineteenth century *political* freedom and participation in the exercise of political power made major strides, as the right to vote was extended to more people. In the twentieth century, the welfare state extended human development to the *social* and *economic* sphere, by recognizing that minimum standards of education, health, nutrition, well-being and security are basic to civilized life, as well as to the exercise of the civil and political attributes of citizenship. These battles had not been won easily or without resistance. Each progressive thrust has been followed by reactionary counter-thrusts and setbacks.

The struggle for *civil* liberty was opposed, after the French Revolution, by those fearful that it can lead only to tyranny; the fight for *political* participation on the grounds that it would bring about enslavement for the masses. We are now witnessing one of these counter-attacks on the *economic* liberties of the welfare state, and on some fronts there is evidence of partial retreat. The argument again is that the opposite of the intended results is achieved. Just as civil liberty was said to lead to tyranny, and political liberty to slavery, so compassionate concern for the poor, it is now said, can lead only to their pauperization.[2]

The ILO's report, "The framework of ILO action against poverty" (henceforth called the Report) refers to this debate on its ultimate page.

---

[1] Professor Emeritus of Boston University and a consultant to the United Nations Development Programme.

[2] See Albert O. Hirschman, *The rhetoric of reaction: Perversity, futility, jeopardy.* Cambridge, Massachusetts, Harvard University Press, 1991.

The ILO, and right-minded people generally, have set their face against this line of argument and believe that human progress is possible, though not inevitable, along all three fronts, and particularly in the fight against poverty. Only then can we at last falsify St. John's famous pronouncement, that "the poor always ye have with you".

When discussing the ILO and its concern with poverty in the developing countries, it is helpful to remember its origins. It was founded in 1919, after the First World War, in order to protect the standard of living of the industrial workers in rich countries against the cheap imports made by sweated labour in low-income countries. It has propagated trade unions on Western lines, collective bargaining, minimum wages and welfare legislation. It has set uniform standards for safety and health that have been criticized by some as excessive and inappropriate for low-income countries, such as restricting hours of work, and it has propagated anti-forced labour conventions.

Critics have said that these provisions, while they sound fine, have made it more difficult to raise employment, to increase equality, and to eradicate poverty in labour-surplus poor countries. The small and relatively well-off group of employed workers in the organized sector, whose incomes are among the top 5-10 per cent of the population, have acquired vested interests in sophisticated, capital-intensive products and processes that give them high incomes but leave the rest unemployed, under-employed, and poor. ILO policies have, in some cases, reinforced urban bias. (The Report says disarmingly "ILO research on employment and poverty has been rather reluctant to tackle the possible trade-offs between wages and employment" (see Section II.3.B). The role of trade unions in developing countries is *different* from that in advanced countries. They should act as a channel of communication between the Government and the wage-earners (as well as between employers and workers); they should organize training and productivity campaigns; they should reduce industrial tensions and unrest. They can also promote social services, organize cheap holidays and welfare facilities, etc. (Some of these functions are discussed in Section III.6 on "The organization of the poor").

We might want to concede that even forced labour may be justified in some conditions. A form of conscripted national service for rich and poor youths for public works can mobilize a grossly underutilized labour force, train people for productive jobs, and give meaning to their lives. Objections are raised on grounds of inefficiency and human rights. As to efficiency and motivation, more research is needed on different forms of labour mobilization, motivation, morale and incentives. Even in the least favourable circumstances, such as prisoner-of-war camps or penal institutions, useful work has been carried out, as the current United States protests against the imports of goods produced by Chinese prison labour show. As to human rights, it can be argued that labour conscription in poor countries with labour surpluses is the equivalent of taxation in advanced countries. When communal obligations cannot be discharged by money payments in the form of a compulsory income tax, conscription may be one way to avoid the perpetuation of injustice, privilege and poverty. As Joan Robinson said in a different context, the only thing that is worse than being exploited is not being exploited. (I do hope that saying such monstrous things to an ILO audience will not bar me from future meetings.)

Of course, the ILO has adapted to a changing world. As the Report says, wages in the urban organized sector have dropped enormously in sub-Saharan Africa in the 1980s, and defending them has become a legitimate anti-poverty activity. The ILO's technical assistance (about which the Report says little) has been extremely useful, and some of the standard-setting that has been criticized was addressed when it launched the World Employment Programme. An important and neglected point in favour of the ILO is that it is the only UN agency that transcends the inter-governmental level and can be regarded as a genuine form of international participation. It consists of representatives of trade unions, employers and governments. Those who are critical of the power of governments, who advocate participatory development, and wish to apply it to international organizations, should welcome this. At the same time, the tripartatite organization of the ILO is not particularly responsive to the needs of the poorest or even many of the poor.

Minimum wage legislation and trade union pressures for minimum wages do not normally contribute to poverty reduction if the wages are confined to an urban labour aristocracy employed in the formal sector and are at the expense of lower total employment levels.[3] The Report stresses that urban wages were substantially reduced in the 1980s (Section II.2), but, as has already been said, this is true mainly of Africa and not of many other parts of the Third World. There are, however, important exceptions

---

[3] However, David Card and Alan Krueger have recently found that for some fast food restaurants in New Jersey and neighbouring Pennsylvania (as a control group, where minimum wages did not go up) higher minimum wages have led to *higher* employment. The fast-food restaurant operates with a couple of vacancies it cannot fill because it does not pay enough. When the minimum wage is raised, new supply emerges. (Sylvia Nasar in *The New York Times*, Sunday, 22 August 1993 and David Card and Alan Krueger, "Minimum wages and employment: A case study of the fast-food industry in New Jersey", a paper presented at the NBER Summer Institute, Harvard University, July 1993).

to the rule that high minimum wages hurt the poor. For example, if the higher minimum wages, that apply only to the formal sector firms, induce them to subcontract labour-intensive activities previously carried out within these firms, to informal firms to which the law does not apply; or if the previous wages were so low that workers suffered from undernutrition and their productivity is improved. (This might be added in Section III.4.A to the conditions determining the contribution to poverty reduction of minimum wage legislation).

Poverty is sometimes used interchangeably with vulnerability in the Report. But poverty is different from vulnerability. Diversified subsistence farmers may be poor but are not vulnerable. When they enter the market by selling specialized cash crops, or raising their earnings by incurring debts, or investing in risky ventures, their incomes rise, but they become vulnerable. There are trade-offs between poverty and vulnerability (or between security and income). Vulnerability is a function of external risks, shocks and stress, and of internal defencelessness.

It is true that the World Bank has done much work on poverty in recent years (see Section I). But the emphasis has been on "poverty alleviation" (a somewhat anaemic term, or, changing the metaphor, a bit of band aid, which regrettably, the Report also uses) instead of poverty reduction, or poverty eradication, or uprooting poverty. In spite of all the talk of structural adjustment, the Bank avoids talking much about the necessary structural measures, and touches only gingerly on delicate topics such as radical land reform and asset redistribution. Being a bank, it rightly approaches poverty alleviation as contributing to higher productivity. While consumption goods like beer, television and Hondas are not further questioned and regarded as ultimate ends, education, health and nutrition have to be defended as "human investment" that contributes to production and productivity growth.

Has structural adjustment exacerbated poverty (Section I, passim)? The answer is controversial. It depends on the counter-factual, what would have happened in the absence of adjustment? The poor would probably have been worse off. Alternatively, what would have happened if adjustment had built in from the beginning a "social dimension"?

A switch to tradables, if these are labour-intensive agricultural products, is likely to benefit the poor, if not the poorest of the poor (see Section II.2). The theory is that developing countries have a comparative advantage in labour-intensive goods, and real wages will therefore rise. This assumes flexible prices and mobility between sectors. But if both the tradables and the non-tradables sectors consist of labour-intensive, small-scale and capital-intensive, large-scale sub-sectors, and if the formal sub-sectors benefit while the informal sub-sectors are harmed, the poor lose. And some non-tradables, like construction and government services, are labour-intensive, while other tradables, like mechanized plantations, are capital-intensive, so that the poor would suffer.

The elimination of food subsidies was neither universal, nor, where it occurred, did it necessarily hurt the poorest, who had not benefited from them. Other cuts in public expenditure have not always harmed the poor. Real wage reductions, if combined with a substantially greater volume of employment, can benefit the poor. There may be short-run pains and long-run gains to the poor. Sometimes it is the absence of adjustment that has exacerbated poverty, and, as Michael Lipton and the Report itself (see Section II.2) have said, sometimes it is the absence of the *structural* in the "structural" adjustment package that has done so. The precise meaning of "structure" and "structural" is, of course, open to a wide range of interpretations, as Fritz Machlup has pointed out.

There is frequent talk in the Report of the importance of "productive employment". In Section I the Employment Convention No. 122 is cited. It declares the need for "an active policy designed to promote full, productive and freely chosen employment". I suggest that two adjectives should be added: "remunerative" and "satisfying" or "fulfilling."

The poor's need is not just for more work and for more production. It is for more income. Employment can be highly productive, but all the gains in productivity can be passed on in the form of lower prices to the buyers, who may be quite rich, or to foreigners, or both. The self-employed in the informal sector, exploited plantation workers, and sweated labour in cottage industries can be very productive, but their work is often unremunerative.

The second suggested addition to employment is "satisfying". With modern technology and the electronics revolution we have the opportunity to substitute machines for drudgery and the most boring tasks. We can ask that work should be interesting and even fun. If it is not, thought should be given to how it can be more easily married to play. The Report rightly points out that man (and woman) cannot live by income alone; that recognition is also needed (see Section II.3.A). The underclass in Kurt Vonnegut's novel *Player piano* who get handed out goodies by the managerial rulers, but do not participate in active work, eventually rebel. But boring, unsatisfying, unfulfilling, alienating work can have the same effect. How can the problems posed by repetitive industrial work be solved, not, or not only, by more pay and fewer working hours, but by removing the tedium?

On the other hand, I have some hesitation about "freely chosen". Of course, advocating forced labour is, as we have seen, highly controversial, largely because of its well-known inefficiency, but also because of its conflict with human rights. But as particularly the ILO employment mission Report on Sri Lanka pointed out, aspirations can go beyond opportunities. If we all wanted to be Pope, and were not prepared to accept any other job, there would be a lot of unemployment. Attitudes to work, and to what kind of work is acceptable, are at least as important as skills and aptitudes. And it is a matter for policy, particularly educational policy, not only to make us do what we want, but also to make us want what we do or have to do. But because attitudes to work are more difficult to measure than school attendance, literacy and years of schooling, they tend to be neglected in analysis and policy.

I agree that the recommendations of the ILO missions were "truly comprehensive" (see Section II.2). On the other hand, to say that one "could find few countries which had fully adopted the comprehensive policy recommendations emerging from WEP research" is surely an understatement. In spite of increased understanding of unemployment, underemployment, disguised unemployment and poverty, these problems are in many parts of the world more serious than ever. Why? Three answers are possible. First, the world environment may have changed so drastically that the old models, theories and recommendations, though correct for their time, are no longer applicable. Second, the recommendations of the Employment Missions may have always been wrong, either because they recommended the wrong things or because they omitted to recommend the right things. Third, there is the possibility that though analysis and recommendations were correct, the advice was not taken.

There may be an element of truth in all three answers. The world environment has certainly changed radically. Stagnation has replaced rapid growth and unemployment has become world-wide. Poverty has been globalized. J.K. Galbraith's famous dictum about "private affluence amid public squalor" has, with the growing number of homeless, drug addicts, hungry, destitute, and criminals in the advanced countries now to be complemented by "private affluence amid private squalor." Global interdependence has grown, international migration has become important, trends in demography and labour markets have changed, and technological innovation has accelerated. In the ex-Soviet Union and Eastern Europe we have witnessed a transition from the zoo to the jungle.

Although mistakes were made, some of the new problems are the result of the successful solution of a set of previous problems. It is the rapid rise of industrial production that has led to migration to the towns and the growth of open, urban unemployment. It is also the rapid growth of industry that has shown up agriculture as the slow-coach and focused attention on rural development. It is the success in education that has led to the brain drain. It is successful import substitution that has led to the capacity for good export performance. It is the successful reduction of mortality rates, by itself surely a welcome development, that has led to the population explosion.

Perhaps the main reason why the recommendations of the missions have not been universally accepted is that they were politically naïve. The assumption was that if a policy is shown to be sensible in the light of the declared objectives of the government, it would be adopted. By postulating implicitly a false theory of government behaviour, the ILO approach was guilty (like most others at the time) of only a partial analysis.

Where the ILO mission reports were defective, therefore, was in the analysis of the political economy or the politics of reform: of why so many excellent recommendations remained unimplemented; of what the political constraints on reform are (positive political economy), and how a political constituency or coalition for progressive reforms can be built (normative political economy). And this defect is still to be found in the Report before us. Apart from organizing the poor in a democratic society[4] and some discussion of autonomy, participation and empowerment of the poor (see Section III.6), there is no discussion in the Report of how to create the political base for anti-poverty action. This may involve (1) recruiting the interests of the rich and powerful[5] (e.g. "the economy of high wages" or their interest in healthy, skilled workers, or in shorter working hours that lead to higher output); or (2) exploiting differences and clashes within the ruling groups) as in nineteenth-century England between Tory landlords and Liberal industrialists); or (3) organizing action groups, altruists, idealists, NGOs, "trustees for the poor" (G.M. Meier), "guardians of rationality" (J.M. Keynes), and others with a disinterested interest in removing poverty; (4) taking advantage of outside pressures from bilateral aid donors and international agencies for policies for poverty reduction.

---

[4] I like the passage that says "The poor are often so involved in their daily struggle for survival that they have neither the time nor energy left for organized contact with the outside world." Oscar Wilde said "the trouble with socialism is that it takes too many evenings". The same can be said for participation.

[5] Amartya Sen wrote "I sometimes wonder whether there is any way of making poverty terribly infectious. If this were to happen, its general elimination would be, I am certain, remarkably rapid". "The political economy of targeting", World Bank Conference on Public Expenditures and the Poor: Incidence and Targeting, 17, 18 and 19 June 1992, Washington, DC. It would, however, be possible for the poor to be put into quarantine.

Research into such political constituencies and interest coalitions should replace the present empty talk of "political will" (see Section II.5.B).

The Report says that "the basic needs strategy met with relatively little success" (see Section II.2). The opposition was confined mainly to international debates. At home, many of the plans and speeches endorsed basic needs fully. The Kenya development plan 1979-83, the Philippine plan 1978-82, the Indian plan 1978-83, the sixth plan of Nepal 1980-85 and others explicitly announced efforts to provide for basic needs. Admittedly, action lagged. In its JASPA missions, the ILO continued to promote basic needs, responding to country requests in Africa into the 1980s. But the reason for this lack of success was, as in the case of the employment strategies, lack of a political base. In the new bottle of Human Development, the old basic needs approach has found wide appeal. Since its first Human Development Report, the UNDP has been asked by many developing countries to sponsor Human Development missions. Defined as incomes + social services + participation it has also been advanced by the World Bank in its 1990 World Development Report on poverty.

The Report says "A programme of transfers sufficient to satisfy basic needs was simply beyond the resource capacities of the States where it was most needed", and again "Resources and the capacity to mobilize them are clearly the major constraint: national budgets are small..." (see Sections III.5 and III.7).

At first sight, this seems plausible. Poor countries have perhaps 1/50th of the income per head of rich countries. On the other hand, the proportion of the population aged 5 to 15 and to be educated (primary and secondary education) is perhaps twice as large as in rich countries (25-30 per cent compared with 15 per cent) and teachers' salaries, which are near or below the national average in rich countries, are four or five times (in Africa seven times) the average in poor countries. This means that a vastly greater share (typically eight to ten times as much) of a much smaller national cake would have to be devoted to education, with the inevitable result that less would be left over for the implementation of other objectives.

But on further reflection, I wonder how severe the resource constraint is compared with the lack of political commitment and of a political base. The very same countries that pleaded financial and fiscal shortages spent a multiple of the required sums on their military, on large prestige projects, on loss-making public enterprises, not to say anything about corrupt pocketing of funds and capital flight.

Between 1960 and 1988 military expenditures in constant dollars quintupled in the developing countries. This was twice the rate of growth of incomes per head and almost equal to total expenditure on health and education.[6]

Within the social sectors, tertiary education for the children of the middle classes and expensive, curative, urban hospitals absorbed a multiple of what was needed for primary education and preventive rural health services. In 1988, Iraq and Somalia spent five times as much on their military than on all education and health; Nicaragua, Oman, Ethiopia, Pakistan and Syria between two and three times as much, and even Tanzania spent more than 100 per cent. The ratio of soldiers to teachers is 6.25 in Iraq, 5.91 in Somalia, 4.16 in Ethiopia, 3.50 in Nicaragua, 3.02 in Syria, 3.00 in Mauritania, 2.91 in Cyprus. Only Costa Rica has a ratio of 0 and no poverty to speak of.

The Report talks of a "Basic Needs Strategy." I submit it is better regarded as an approach, a part of a more general strategy that has other objectives and policies as well. Otherwise there would be either an absolutism attached to meeting basic needs, which governments and, indeed, common sense, would find repugnant. Or, alternatively, it would become such a large holdall of received wisdom as to become all things to all men. As an approach, an adjunct, a complement or a supplement, it is entirely compatible with promoting advanced technology, environmental protection, private foreign investment, rapid economic growth, defence and security, and other non-basic needs objectives. By bringing out some distinct features, it is intellectually more satisfactory to treat it as an approach than as a strategy that either comprises all components of previous strategies or is narrowly focused on the attainment of all basic needs by everyone in the shortest time, to the exclusion of everything else.

I found the discussion of the distinction between structural change and direct improvements at the beginning of Section III excellent. The merits and defects of both are brought out well. I would go one step further and say that a series of direct interventions can undermine the whole structure of an iniquitous order and thus contribute to structural change. It is true, as the critics say, that each direct intervention may be twisted in favour of the ruling groups, if the income, asset and power distribution are initially unequal. What the late Raj Krishna called "first-round socialism" and I have called the "law of the racket" amounts to saying that even the best-intentioned schemes, implemented in an inegalitarian society, can be hijacked by the ruling groups. This applies to government interventions,

---

[6] This is, of course, also true for the industrial countries. It has been estimated that a 10 per cent cut in defence spending by the NATO countries could finance a doubling of aid.

to non-price measures, as well as to the market. And it could be argued against the piecemeal approach that sops to the poor may actually prevent the radical reforms required. In the jargon of economists, while the utility-possibility locus is shifted outwards in the neighbourhood of the old position, it intersects with the old utility-possibility curve, so that even more desirable positions are ruled out. But at the same time, a number of specific interventions, particularly if directed at crucial points, raising the confidence and empowering the poor, can, like a host of termites, eat into the woodwork of a rotten order and eventually bring it down. If such radical reform is the ultimate intention, I suggest that the words and the aim "poverty alleviation" should be replaced by "poverty eradication".

I entirely agree with the general conclusion (see Section IV) that it is a matter of "both... and" and not "either... or"; that what the Report calls the "complementarity of opposites" is often necessary, and that relying on only one approach can be either ineffective or even counterproductive. It applies to markets *and* states; to NGOs *and* governments; to the private sector *and* the public sector; to small-scale *and* large-scale enterprises; to domestic *and* foreign firms; to decentralization *and* central government action.

The main items that are missing from the Report's list of measures to be taken "if poverty is to be overcome" (Section II.2) are access to health services (including nutrition and family planning) and, as already said, the mobilization of political coalitions, apart from "the organization of the poor". The Report is altogether silent on the need for a *population policy and its links to poverty and the environment.* Yet the employment problem can be traced directly to the very high rates of growth of population and of the labour force, and poverty to large families and environmental degradation such as deforestation and soil erosion. Also the role of *services* and that of *international migration and refugees* deserve fuller treatment than the brief reference in Section III.4.B.

In Section III.7 on "Some tentative conclusions", the emphasis is placed on the generation of primary and secondary incomes: incomes through productive and remunerative employment (including self-employment), whether through macro-economic policies or more specific measures (meso- and micro-policies), and transfer incomes that create and improve human capital through better nutrition, health, education and training. What is missing may be called the creation of tertiary incomes: incomes for the *unemployables*, the lame ducks: the old, the infirm, the chronically handicapped, sick and disabled. The "centrality of employment creation" (see Section IV.2) does not look after them, particularly if accompanied by the breakdown of the extended family, and sometimes even of the nuclear family.

It could be argued that if society looks after the unemployables, although this will not add to productivity, it will tend to lower reproductivity. An important motive for large families, and particularly for having many sons, is to be looked after in old age or if an accident occurs. And this motive will be removed. (Here again the neglect of a discussion of population policy in the Report is evident.) But there are other good reasons to look after the unemployables in a civilized society.

The World Bank approves of government interventions only when they are market-friendly. I think I interpret the spirit of the Report correctly if I add that market-friendly interventions should be accepted only if they are people-friendly. For this to be so, several conditions have to be met, which the Report spells out well. Among them are a fairly equal distribution of productive assets, particularly land, the provision of certain public goods and of social services, participatory organizations and general access to power.

We often hear that the 1980s were "the lost decade." This is true only if we think in terms of countries rather than people. In the large countries of East, South, and South-East Asia poverty has been reduced. Average annual growth of income per head was higher between 1980 and 1989 than between 1965 and 1980 (3.2 per cent compared with 2.4 per cent). The percentage of the world population which enjoyed a growth rate of over 5 per cent grew from 10.6 per cent in the earlier period to 33.2 in the later. The trouble of the 1980s was that there was polarization: the proportion of those experiencing growth rates below 1 per cent also grew. But the majority of mankind saw their lot improved.

3   The ILO and poverty:
Reactions and debates

Following the presentation of *The framework of ILO action against poverty* and the critical review by Paul Streeten, there was a general debate, led by a panel representing different interests and perspectives among participants in the Symposium.[1] This debate identified many areas of agreement with the analysis presented in the framework paper, but also raised a number of additional issues crucial to the fight against poverty.

Employment, it was generally agreed, was at the core of successful action against poverty, but it was necessary to take into consideration the changing nature of employment resulting from recent economic trends and evolving social policy orientations. The discussion focused on issues such as resource constraints on policy against poverty, access to and discrimination in the labour market, and the growth of the informal sector, where the poor are concentrated and where conditions of work are often exploitative. The need for appropriate national and international policies and actions was stressed, with particular reference to the formulation and enforcement of international standards which could enhance access to the labour market while ensuring protection to all participants, and the need for investment in human capital development aimed at increasing the capacities, skills and productivity of the poor. The need for supportive institutions at national and international level was highlighted.

Resource constraints are frequently alluded to as one of the major obstacles to taking effective action against poverty. However, it was argued that the economic constraints on poverty eradication are frequently exaggerated, as the problem often stems mainly from the allocation of resources. For example, many countries spend much less on social sectors

---

[1] The members of the panel were Susil Siriwardana, Rodney Bickerstaffe, Nora Lustig, Jean-Jaques Oechslin, Jan Breman and Vremudia Diejomaoh. While many of their views are reflected in the summary presented here, this is a synthesis of differing perspectives, to which the panellists would not necessarily subscribe. It attempts to summarize the main points emerging from the discussion, rather than offer a "consensus".

than on defence or large prestige projects which have no direct impact on the poor. Other factors that have constrained national governments' ability to allocate scarce resources to poverty eradication programmes include debt servicing and capital flight. This points to the importance of the international financial system in ensuring that resources are available specifically for policies against poverty.

The fundamental requirement, it was repeatedly underlined, is for there to be the necessary political will and commitment at both national and international levels to seriously address the causes of poverty. Poverty eradication was clearly recognized as the prime objective of a multi-dimensional approach to development, of which labour market policies form an integral part.

In addressing these issues, the *conceptualization of poverty* takes on great importance. There are many faces of poverty, and understanding them is crucial prior to taking steps aimed at resolving the problem. "Alleviation" of poverty and "eradication" of poverty, often used inter-changeably, are in fact two different but potentially mutually reinforcing objectives. The alleviation of poverty involves minimizing the consequences of poverty: providing food and shelter to meet basic needs, ensuring the survival of victims. These measures tend to consist of transfers of income and are at best ineffective or very marginal in providing a long-term solution. The eradication of poverty, on the other hand, requires the generation of income through long-term productive employment. It must also be recognized that poverty itself is a relative and often imprecise concept — for example one might distinguish between the "poor" and the "poorest of the poor". The poor may become economically viable if their vulnerability is reduced, for example if they are able to move from subsistence farming to a cash crop, raising their income and consumption levels. The "poorest of the poor", on the other hand, include many who are totally without assets and have only their unskilled labour power to rely on, generating incomes insufficient to cover even the most basic food requirements and subject to debilitating working and living conditions.

I. Global changes

Poverty needs to be considered afresh in the light of the employment impact of current *global economic processes*. Globalization of production and markets, the widespread application of new technologies and rapid population growth, all of this occurring in the 1980s and early 1990s in a climate of prolonged recession and low economic growth, was associated with a spread of poverty and unemployment in many parts of the world. Structural adjustment and stabilization policies have, for the most part, failed to reverse this trend. In the industrialized countries, economic restructuring has resulted in growing unemployment and the re-emergence of poverty and exclusion. The transition to the market that is under way in the countries of eastern Europe and the former Soviet Republics is not reproducing the "economic miracle" of the South-East Asian countries. Instead, poverty and mass unemployment are becoming evident. In Africa, in particular in Sub-saharan Africa, and in Latin America, the 1980s have been dismissed as the "lost decade" as real incomes fell dramatically. In Asia, on the other hand, in some countries at least, high growth rates have permitted a decline in poverty despite growing inequality.

Participants in the debate placed this issue in a North-South perspective, and the question was raised as to whether the process of *globalization*, whose link with poverty has yet to be properly investigated, should be perceived as an opportunity or a danger for labour. The view was expressed that the opening up of developed countries' markets to the products of developing countries was more of an opportunity than a danger, due to its potential for employment creation. However, it was also argued that the gains and losses depended crucially on the terms and conditions established within both global and regional integration schemes. For example, in the case of the North American Free Trade Agreement (NAFTA), would wage levels in the United States fall as a result of competition with a lower-wage labour force? What would be the net effect on poverty in the United States and Mexico? The distributional impact of globalization both within and between countries needed to be better understood.

International economic policy thus needs to be linked to international social policy. The most prominent aspect of this linkage, which came up during the Uruguay Round of trade negotiations, is whether minimum labour standards should become an integral part of regional and global trading arrangements. A trade union view, for example, is that minimum social standards underpin the road to prosperity and to increased employment and therefore, in order that workers may benefit from a globalized market, it is necessary to include a social clause in regional and global trading agreements. This debate is of evident importance for understanding the impact of global change on the level and incidence of poverty.

Changes in the global structure of *technology* utilization have been influenced by the ease with which capital relocates under globalization. There is an additional threat here to levels of employment and wages, through the widespread use of new technologies that displace unskilled labour. At the same time, new and advanced technology has a potential for employment creation. In industrialized countries, where the adverse employment impact of technological innovation is larger, there were in the past other non-skilled employment opportunities, particularly in the public sector. But, with the cutbacks in public sector investment, this source of employment is in decline. Technological change needs to be supported by high levels of aggregate demand if it is not to lead to problems of structural unemployment. Consistency between macro-economic policy and technology policy is required, but this is difficult to achieve in a globalizing environment.

The impact of *population growth* on poverty was noted by many as a major determinant of poverty that had not been fully discussed in the ILO paper, in particular the link between population growth, the physical environment and poverty. There was specific concern about its impact on average earnings, on the bargaining power of the population, on the possibility of universalizing social services and on migration. It was argued that population growth is a symptom of poverty, not the cause, but there are important demographic aspects of issues such as social protection requirements, low levels of education, high levels of infant mortality or the position of women. So population issues need to be addressed, because they affect crucial relationships that underlie poverty.

Under the present global conditions, there is a real need to redesign *macro-economic policy* in order to provide the market with a role in poverty eradication. But in order for the market to effectively combat poverty, it is important that it should function in a "people-friendly" way, which in turn means that it is necessary for governments to make sensitive policy choices. Careful evaluation is required to assess the need for government interventions in markets, such as state control over the distribution of productive assets to reduce inequality; state provision of certain public goods — health, education, etc; or the creation of an enabling environment for the development of participatory organizations giving market power to the poor.

Global changes have strongly influenced the present character of poverty. It should not be seen as a problem confined to the South — there are more poor people all over the world today than ever before. The global character and international dimension of poverty means that it can no longer be resolved at the national level. And solutions should therefore be conceptualized, articulated and implemented at the global level, requiring new thinking and alternative, broader approaches that incorporate as wide a range of actors as possible.

II. Commitment

Despite decades of experience with anti-poverty measures, poverty has not disappeared. Why? It was argued that even the "right" policies and recommendations were bound to fail, because they were not supported by the necessary political environment for implementation. The fundamental requirement is *the commitment at all levels to poverty eradication*. The lack of a clear political will, weak political pressure groups and the absence of an appropriate political economy have undermined the fight against unemployment and poverty. Among the preconditions for effective policy implementation, the following are significant:

1. *The issue of poverty eradication must be on the agenda* on a continuous basis and at all levels — international, regional and national. In order to facilitate this, the analysis and recommendations of major international groups which have studied this problem should be borne in mind, including, for instance, the Brandt Commission Report and the Report of the Independent South Asian Commission on Poverty Alleviation.

2. *A wide community of interest has to be created around the issue of poverty eradication*, by building consensus among all those identified as having an interest in this objective. It is imperative to demonstrate to the different elite groups that poverty reduction is in their interest, and therefore that the issue is of relevance for them, too. In particular, the social conscience of the private sector needs to be strengthened. Trade unions also have an important role, extending beyond their membership.

3. Today, with most governments preoccupied with getting their macro-economic and budgetary situations right, the *role of the State in poverty eradication* has been weakened. To overcome this, it was argued that campaigns were needed to create effective political will for systematic action against poverty. It was necessary to create a conducive political environment, so that an appropriate development agenda built around the objective of poverty eradication could be promoted.

4. *Alliances must be built between the social actors and also across international organizations*, in order to further emphasize poverty reduction. As in the past, international organizations have an important role to play, not only by focusing on the international dimensions of poverty, but also by promoting development strategies aimed at poverty reduction at the national level. Collaboration

between international organizations becomes all the more vital as their efforts are increasingly constrained by the realities of the international economic and political order.

The inadequacy of past and present development strategies is evidenced by the unacceptable magnitudes of poverty in the world today. This further highlights the need for a political commitment to a multi-dimensional development strategy. Such a strategy might well involve an open economy, industrialization, liberalization and export-led growth; but it needs also to encompass policies for poverty alleviation which could yield results in the short term, including emphasis on policies for agricultural development and food security, productive and remunerative employment creation, and the provision of a basic level of social services. The latter also requires a supportive State and the organization of the poor. If the appropriate linkages could be established to harmonize and achieve complementarity between the different aspects of this type of strategy, poverty eradication could be feasible. However, it was also noted that political conflicts may render such broad strategies impossible to implement, as is so tragically evidenced by the prevailing situations in some African countries. In such cases — and there are too many visible today — conflict resolution has a vital role to play in poverty reduction.

III. Regulation

In the search for solutions to the present conditions of growing unemployment and restricted access to the labour market, two contrasting approaches were evident. One is the claim put forward by many governments and employers that jobs can be created if labour costs, in terms of wage levels and social protection levels, are reduced. The other is the argument put forward by the trade union movement against "social dumping", proposing instead an approach that attempts to combine social cohesiveness with competitiveness, and greater equality with new working practices. Underlying this is the belief that labour market access can be improved while maintaining minimum social standards.

Because of these contrasting views, the relationship between *labour market regulation* and poverty came under close scrutiny. From the workers' point of view it is accepted that this is a controversial issue, but stress is placed on the moral dimension — a minimum level of labour market regulation is essential in order to respect basic human rights and human dignity. Employers, on the other hand, express an equally strong argument on efficiency and cost grounds, which holds that excessive regulation adds to the cost of the production process, thus acting as an impediment to employment creation. However, it was also argued that the history of the developed countries suggests that labour standards have been instrumental in increasing productivity and facilitating the effective redistribution of the benefits of growth.

Labour market regulations play a very important role in that they exclude a number of exploitative practices from the competitive game — producers cannot undercut each other by hiring children, relaxing safety norms, evading contributions to social security, paying below the minimum wage, etc. Many such regulations contribute directly to reducing poverty. However the adoption, enforceability and coverage of these standards are not universal in all countries. In many countries, labour market regulation is effective only in modern sector wage employment, a relatively small part of the labour market in much of Africa and parts of Asia and Latin America. With growing unemployment and the cutback in the number of new jobs created, it was argued by some speakers that there is a need to investigate and review the effects of particular types of regulation with respect to the possible trade-off between the implementation of minimum standards and the level of employment, within the broader question of the contribution of labour market regulation to strategies against poverty.

The complexities and the difficulties encountered when looking at the enforceability of standards, and at the potential benefits from their implementation, raised a number of important research issues. Among the questions that were suggested as priorities for further investigation and analysis were those relating to the sequencing and manner in which standards may be introduced; the identification of target groups so as to ensure the maximum degree of beneficial coverage; the merits and demerits of different types of regulations; and the role of the ILO in different aspects of this process.

IV. Job access and discrimination

Unequal access to jobs and discriminatory practices are only just starting to be recognized as significant in the relationship between employment and poverty. While the causal relationship between discrimination and poverty is increasingly evident, systematic data to comprehend the magnitude of the problem are as yet unavailable. Statistical methodologies traditionally used in labour market analysis do not usually take discrimination according to gender, ethnicity or race into account. However, such factors have an important bearing on what happens to people at the lower end of the income spectrum. With respect to women, for instance, there has been a widespread increase in the numbers of female-headed households that are forced to survive below the poverty line, with labour market vulnerability an important cause.

Labour market access would be facilitated if the conditions that perpetuate labour market discrimination were identified and transformed. The "culture of poverty" concept, which is sometimes advanced as an explanation of the inadequate labour market situations of the poor, was refuted on the grounds that it misrepresented the position of poor who, rather than being content with their lot, were seen to be constantly fighting against the legitimization of inequality. This was particularly evident at the micro-level, for example in some Asian villages. The issue is also significant in industrialized countries, where increasing violence and social unrest are closely associated with growing unemployment and poverty. A crucial issue here was seen as permanent exclusion from the labour market, a major cause of poverty.

The increasing integration of rural and urban labour markets was noted as an important development. The conventional assumption is that the labour market in developing countries is segmented into clearly defined rural and urban labour components. This was challenged; the market for unskilled labour was integrated, and integration was also promoted by the dismantling of formal sector employment and growing informalization of work in terms of both forms and patterns of work and payment structures. The character of the labour market itself has changed. Poor unskilled workers in rural areas no longer constitute a purely agricultural labour force and increasingly they seek access to employment outside agriculture and outside the village. They are not in fact excluded from the labour market, they are very much part of it. But it is the conditions under which they are engaged that reinforces their poverty.

One mechanism by which poverty is reinforced within the labour market was identified as labour circulation. Continuous migration creates a labour force which is not only insecure but also vulnerable. Labour mobility may be a means of overcoming poverty, but it may also be a cause of poverty. This emerges also at the international level. International migration from developing countries is a drain on human resources — in terms of skilled and semi-skilled labour — and in a resource-scarce country this can have a significant poverty impact. However, it was noted that the inward remittances of migrants play an important part in improving the living standards of their family members who are left behind. In the destination countries, however, migrant workers may displace local labour and adversely affect incomes at the lower end of the labour market. Migrant workers are often vulnerable to exploitative practices which reinforce their poverty and social exclusion. Given these contradictory and conflicting effects, internationally acceptable rules are needed to govern migration and protect migrant workers, which recognize the importance of labour market access in reducing poverty.

V. Some specific priorities

The importance of *capacity building* and *human capital development* in poverty eradication was widely acknowledged. This is particularly the case for investment in *basic education, training and skill diversification*. For example, it was noted that those developing countries that had made a major investment in education had also demonstrated relative success in eradicating poverty, as in the case of several East Asian countries. Education and information, particularly with respect to the new technologies being introduced in manufacturing and services, can equip a population to be better prepared to take up the employment opportunities that become available. This issue is not confined to developing countries; it is also of crucial importance to developed countries.

The appropriate and rational expansion of the public sector is another means by which governments can address the poverty problem. The public sector may need to be restructured, but it remains a central mechanism to provide basic welfare to all citizens through health care, education, housing and other social services, thereby redistributing income and creating new sources of employment. However, basic social services and social safety nets must be integrated within broader economic policy, and not merely be considered as a soft policy option.

The growing informalization of work and its link with poverty were discussed in the light of the importance of the *informal sector*. This sector appears to have a vast capacity to generate employment, particularly in developing countries but also in developed countries; but many of the jobs which are created remain outside regulatory frameworks and provide only poverty-level incomes. Much more attention needs to be paid to how this dualization can be overcome, by establishing rules which apply equally to all sectors of society.

VI. Institutions and mobilization

The importance of *supportive institutions* was strongly emphasized, both in relation to the participation and organization of the poor, and in terms of the role and power of non-governmental organizations (NGOs) and other pressure groups. It was recognized that often the obstacles to poverty eradication are political and not economic, technical or financial. It was agreed that empowerment and organization of the poor and their participation in the design, execution, implementation and monitoring of anti-poverty projects is of fundamental importance. However, organization at the grass-roots level alone is not sufficient to ensure the eradication of poverty, and these efforts must be supported by easy access to economic and financial resources and sensitive State mechanisms. In this regard, lessons learned from actual situations where the poor have demonstrated the ability to organize and, through their own actions, have transformed their income-generating capabilities, were recognized as a valuable contribution to any poverty eradication strategy. Women are often in the vanguard of such movements. More theory, conceptualization and analysis of experience is required.

With regard to effective representation for the poor, it was noted that this issue cuts both ways, as both trade unions and employers' organizations need to capture this potential constituency in order to ensure their own legitimacy. Many of the poor fall outside the formal labour market, are therefore excluded from traditional trade union activity and, as a result, may even view trade unions with hostility. This is particularly evident in some parts of the informal sector where barriers exist to organizing labour, articulating solidarity and expressing mutual support. It was suggested that it might be easier for employers' organizations to be active in the informal sector, as they may be well placed to represent the interests of small scale entrepreneurs. However, there is much wage labour in the informal sector as well. The representation of this constituency will be important in an anti-poverty strategy.

Emphasis was placed on how the international and global institutions could be made more participatory and, thus, more responsive to the needs of the poor. At the national level, issues of participation and decentralization were addressed not only in relation to the possible decentralization of government activities, but also in terms of how trade unions, NGOs and other institutions of civil society (including the private sector) could be brought into the development process and also how these institutions could themselves be made more participatory. It was felt that the ILO had an advocacy role to play here, as it is unique among international institutions in its tripartite structure. By building upon the participation of governments, employers and workers it could aim to mediate between all the social and institutional actors committed to poverty eradication.

4   Growing points in poverty research: Labour issues

Michael Lipton[1]

J O D

I.   Meaning and measurement: Effects of a focus on labour

1.   Receipts: Low or inadequate for conversion into well-being?

We all concur — as Jan Breman pointed out in the discussion of this paper — that poverty is "about" much more than income and consumption; that, just as Sen [1975] stressed the "recognition aspect" of employment, so we need to be aware that being recognized (and recognizing oneself) as poor is part of the misery of *being* poor. Yet it is a small part, compared to (say) a much increased risk of seeing one's children die. In any event, because of the career structure and limitations of most economists, poverty is almost always measured by asking whether a person's *level of receipts* falls below some norm. "Receipts" are usually proxied by the flow of consumable commodities per person per year, because that flow is deemed less unstable and less hard to measure than income (but see Section I.2 below). Let us ignore, for a moment, the issue of what to include in "receipts" (rights, security, etc.). An important question is: in defining what level of "receipts" constitutes poverty, is the norm the same for different people, times or conditions?

The "norm" has to refer to a level of receipts sufficient to provide well-being. But well-being does not depend on *receipts* alone — even in the broadest sense, going well beyond consumption and even income. Well-

[1] Institute of Development Studies, Sussex University. The author wishes to acknowledge extensive research assistance, discussion, and bibliographical help from Suma S. Athreye, Science Policy Research Unit, Sussex University. The commentators I found especially helpful included Eddy Lee, Jan Breman, Nora Lustig, Vremudia Diejemoah and Myra Buvinić.

being also depends on *requirements* and on *conversion capacity* from receipts into requirements. People who are smaller, or do less work, have lower total energy *requirements*, and can therefore thrive on fewer calories — and therefore less consumption expenditure — than others. Even if two people have identical height, weight, work and leisure, one of them may be more "efficient" in calorie *conversion* (for example, with a lower resting metabolic rate), and will thus reach a given level of well-being at a lower level of calorie intake. That person may well be adequately fed even at an income level below the "food-poverty line" (see below), while the less efficient calorie convertor is inadequately fed although above that income level.

These issues are much discussed in the nutrition/poverty literature [Dasgupta, 1993; Payne & Lipton, 1994]. In practice, a line of "food poverty" or "ultra-poverty" is often defined as at the level of receipts at which an "average person", i.e. with average requirements and conversion efficiency, just gets enough energy to meet requirements. But, in practice, many people below that line will tend to select low levels of effort and earnings because they *require* less food energy, and/or are better at *converting* it into bodily and working needs. Such people may be desperately deprived and poor in many ways, but more calories are not their top priority, and often they are not food-poor. (Recent work by Behrman, Bouis/Haddad and others suggests calorie-income elasticities as low as 0.1-0.4 even in the poorest quintiles in some developing countries: see [Lipton, 1989], and Section II.4 below.) In other cases, the most cost-effective way to end under-nutrition is not to raise food intake but to reduce unwanted energy requirements, especially for fighting disease or walking long distances to work, water or fuel.

There is a widespread fear that, by pointing these things out, we "blame victims" for their poverty. Far from it; the aim is to see what can be done to reduce its ill-effects. Sometimes, this depends partly on the victims, as in the case of possible learning from "positive deviants" in infant feeding practice [Zeitlin et al., 1987]. Sometimes the issue is proper location of interventions: in some regions, poor people's top priority may be more food; elsewhere, for example during civil wars, reduced (unwanted) requirements; elsewhere again, measures to improve conversion. In many cases extra food is provided to people whose main needs are different. In general, most people would much prefer "reduced disease, and hence reduced requirements to fight it" to "extra income to buy food, medicines and health care to fight disease". To allocate public expenditure in response to such preferences is not to be dismissed as palliation, rather than eradication, of poverty.

What relevance has this to labour research and policy? Economic (market or home-farm) labour typically uses 300-800 calories per working day for poor employed labourers in developing countries. There is enormous variation, some of it policy-determined (see discussions below). Fieldwork also confirms significant variations (i) in the relative efficiency of different persons in using energy to do the same pair of jobs, (ii) in the energy required by different, physically very similar, persons to do the same task in (apparently) the same way, (iii) in the energy requirement, and other aspects of strain, involved in doing the same task in different ways. Great emphasis is correctly placed in poverty-directed policy-making upon bidding up the demand for labour via labour-intensive growth paths [World Bank, 1990]. If "labour-intensive" means "effort-intensive", this path may harm some people if they are forced to compete by greatly raising their energy requirements, and if this is not readily compensable by selection of higher intakes, or better conversion. The interfaces among nutrition, ergonomics and economics are an important, largely unexplored aspect of anti-poverty policy — and an aspect highlighted by thinking about definitions. Similarly, diseases *of work* — including industrial accidents, and scorpion-bites on the farm — cause poverty by reducing income *and* increasing requirements, yet are seldom touched by "poverty research".

2. Inadequate receipts: quality of life, consumption, income, food?

This is familiar territory [Sen, 1981, 1985; Dasgupta, 1993]. *Consumption*-per-year is usually preferred to *income*-per-year, as a welfare measure, on grounds of greater stability, better reflection of commodities enjoyed, and more reliable measurement; but these arguments are in fact quite dubious. For standard economics, income includes a normally privately "optimal" proportion of savings. Indeed, savings (including grain storage) are chosen by some very poor people as their only means of consumption smoothing, in view of their lack of access to credit markets at any price [Stiglitz & Weiss, 1981]. Most poor people "dissave" most of the time, but this is exaggerated by measurements that fail to record savings in non-monetized forms, or as outlays on human capital formation.

Food typically comprises about 80 per cent of consumption (and income) among people at risk of being undernourished because they lack resources. Energy (calories), rather than protein or micro-nutrients, are overwhelmingly their main food deficiency that is clearly related to income or other resources [Lipton, 1983].[2] Hence estimates of extreme poverty tend to spotlight levels of consumption at which *average* food energy requirements are not met by typical persons; but (see above) there is good reason to expect most (not all) low-income individuals to be untypical in that they have *below-average* energy requirements, despite their (usual) need to do unskilled work.

Most efforts to expand poverty indicators beyond food-consumption-income measures are not satisfactory. As Dasgupta [1993] remarks, the 1990-93 "human development index" is not a significant improvement on the "physical quality of life index" developed by Morris [1979]: in each case the items excluded (e.g. rights), the items included, and the weighting among included items are all arbitrary. That is inevitable; when we estimate income, the price system allows us to add the values of different commodities (albeit with many serious problems), but no logic exists to add the value of one year's higher life expectancy and of one year's extra education.

Listing values of desirable variables (literacy rates, calories per head) helps policy advisers to allocate *specific* resources. If they know that Region A has few hungry adults but many illiterate ones, Region B the reverse, they can use limited resources to provide more schools in A, and more command over food in B, rather than vice-versa. But this does not help policy advisers to allocate or prioritize *overall* resources (finance) or opportunity, or to "measure poverty". In short, scalars of poverty stop at (inadequate levels of) income or consumption; vectors of well-being should certainly include literacy, life expectancy, safety, rights; but the logic and use of scalars and vectors should not be confused.

What is the relevance for labour research? In many parts of the world, the working poor are not ultra-poor or food-poor, but lack claims on health care or on children's schooling, or rights of organization, assembly and industrial action. Which lacks are most felt? Jodha [1988] showed that many Indian rural people — shown to have got no less poor in income or nutrition terms — felt themselves to be much less poor because they no longer relied on caste "superiors" for security. The preferences of adult working people show where *they* feel the shoe pinches, yet are not often sought by researchers. Alas, there is little *disaggregated* empirical work on how the components of deprivation interact. We know, of course, that primary education has a high private economic return to the poor in

---

[2] However, very recent work seems to imply that some nutrients, especially Vitamin A, iron and zinc may catalyze higher levels of efficiency in converting food energy into requirements [Beaton et al., 1993; Payne & Lipton, 1994].

general; we do not know to what extent, and how, the process works in particular cases — its impact must surely depend on the structure and rate of growth of national income, and hence of demand for various sorts of educated workers. More narrowly, we know that (private) consumption expenditure on food and (public) outlay on child health care are synergistic in reducing poor children's death-rates, i.e. a fixed sum of money achieves most impact on those rates if it is divided between the two sorts of use [Taylor et al., 1978]; but such relationships and synergisms in anti-poverty policy are generally very little explored, especially for adults and workers.

3. Private, public and total receipts

The great majority of estimates of poverty relate to receipts from private sources — employment, self-employment, and private assets. Nordhaus and Tobin [1972] developed an approach (later incorporated into the "new household economics") in which estimates of "full (private) income" are made, which add, to private receipts, the value of leisure — and more recently, home production (e.g. cooking). That process has not been applied yet to the setting of a level of receipts that constitutes a "poverty line"; but, even when this is done, it will leave the issue of non-private receipts unaddressed.

There are two sorts of non-private receipts: from common property resources (CPRs) and from State-provided commodities. (Neither category should be confused with "public goods".) Like self-consumed peasant produce, CPRs and state-provided commodities are not market-priced, but unlike it they do not usually correspond to very similar products with "farm gate" or "market" prices which can be used to permit commensurability with private income. Therefore, though CPRs [Jodha, 1986] and State-provided commodities [Datta & Meerman, 1980] loom larger in the receipts of poorer than of richer people *per head* — not necessarily per household [ibid.] — they are seldom calculated in poverty estimates.

This need not matter if *rankings* of groups (e.g. regions) of policy-targeted people in order of poverty — and hence of "qualification" for anti-poverty policies or resources — are similar. But this need not be so. Group A may have a smaller proportion of members with private receipts signalling poverty than has Group B — and hence may have a higher measured poverty incidence; yet Group A may have much more access by lower-income persons to CPRs or State support, and hence lower true poverty incidence.

This might be relevant to labour-related poverty research. Various forms of formal or informal workers' protection, workers' health services, sanitation and water supply, or unemployment insurance, may well now be provided by State action or as CPRs in a non-uniform way, e.g. in cities but not villages, or for contract labourers but not casual workers.[3] This could cause the true and apparent rankings of groups, by poverty, to diverge. Also, the historical evolution of labour-related CPRs and State services is very unlikely to produce the outcome most cost-effective in reducing poverty now. Why should almost all public-works schemes be rural, and almost all slum upgrading schemes urban?

4. Receivers: person, adult-equivalent, household

Very many so-called "poverty surveys" — and some practical schemes, like India's IRDP — have used a household's total income to measure whether receipts are below the poverty line. Even if there were no information or incentive problems, this would be quite useless. Larger households tend to contain more earners. So households with low total income (consumption, receipts, welfare) are a meaningless amalgam of households with few members and households with low income (consumption, receipts, welfare) per person. Datta and Meerman [1980] are among many who have shown that even the ranked quintile by income, etc. per household is an extremely bad predictor of the ranked quintile by income, etc. per person.

Does income or consumption *per person* suffice to indicate poverty? Children need less food than adults (and the poor typically spend as much as 80 per cent of income on food). Poor households have much higher child/adult ratios than do other households. It would seem to follow that various forms of adult-equivalencing [Deaton & Muellbauer, 1980] are needed before we compare poverty incidence or severity. In reality, however, the poverty ranking of groups, regions or places is surprisingly little affected by the choice between receipts-per-person and receipts-per-adult-equivalent. However, since the poor do have fewer adult-equivalents per person than the non-poor, measurements of "food poverty" that ignored these differences would overstate it.

---

[3] Dr. E. Lee comments that some forms of labour regulation and other social intervention may well have increased the beneficiaries' security and hence *subjective* freedom from poverty. This is confirmed by Jodha [1988], who — in the spirit of Hagenaars and van Praag [1985] — shows that perceived poverty in selected Indian villages has declined much more than measured (income- or consumption-based) poverty, and that the beneficiaries state that they feel less poor because dependency on local "big men" has been replaced by some sense of independent security. These *gains* to some poor people are consistent with *losses* to other poor people to the extent that enforced, or feared, labour regulation reduces demand for labour.

In practice the household is almost always the *location* where income, consumption, receipts, and (rarely) requirements or conversion efficiency, are measured, for all household members. Since an individual is poor if, and only if, his or her receipts fall below some (perhaps nutrition-related) norm, we need either information or assumptions about intra-household distribution. Poverty measurements usually assume that this distribution is proportional to need, and to that extent cannot over-estimate (and normally must under-estimate) the severity, but not necessarily incidence, of poverty. However, food distribution — except in North India, Bangladesh and Pakistan — is surprisingly close to that assumption [Harriss, 1993], and shelter distribution at household level presumably is very close.

One area of relevance for labour research is at the intersection with requirements (see Section I.2). Labour tasks, and *possibly* labour energy requirements, appear to be more unequally distributed within households, especially by gender, than income or consumption. Indeed, the "double day" appears to bite hardest for the poorest women (Section II.2), especially in rural areas.

5. Adequacy per receiver: absolute or relative?

Almost all serious discussions of poverty in developing countries now concentrate on *absolute* poverty. This is not because inequality is uninteresting, or irrelevant either to poverty or to efficiency and growth. The point is simply that "relative poverty" is a misleading and muddled concept. (1) If the poorest X per cent of people are in relative poverty, it can never increase, decrease, or vary among countries. (2) If all those in a nation with below Y per cent of its average GNP are in relative poverty, there is more of it in Brazil than in Bangladesh; that was even the case when the World Bank used to define "poverty" as *either* absolute poverty *or* income-per-person below 30 per cent of average GNP. (3) Relative *deprivation* is a rigorously definable condition (corresponding to Adam Smith's celebrated remarks concerning the then popular expectation of linen sheets as a sign of decent living levels); but its indicators, and therefore levels — measured and analysed mainly by sociologists [e.g. Runciman, 1966] — depend on people's expectations, past experience, and role models, as well as on their "objective" poverty and on interpersonal inequality; indeed, the relationship between absolute and perceived poverty is an important topic [Jodha, 1988; Hagenaars & Van Praag, 1985] but distinct from the issues discussed here.

Various components of the "relative poverty" muddle can be unravelled, and their relevance to absolute poverty measured and explained. The incidence, intensity, and severity of poverty can each be expressed as functions of *(a)* average consumption (or income) per person (or adult equivalent); *(b)* an appropriate measure of its distribution between rich and poor — only on strong assumptions the overall Gini coefficient, more frequently an Atkinson index, or even, simplistically, the ratio between average consumption (or income) of the poor and that of the non-poor; and *(c)* an index, usually the Gini, of distribution *among* the poor [see e.g. Lipton & Ravallion, 1994].

There remains the question of the relative role of *(a)* and *(b)* above, as — together with *(c)* — they jointly determine poverty. First, are they independent? It is widely believed (e.g. by Dasgupta [1993]) that Anand and Kanbur [1989] have disproved the Kuznets hypothesis that inequality first rises, then falls, with average GNP. However, earlier ILO research [Lecaillon et al., 1984] proved that the relationship did work, but only as regards inequality between the top 5 per cent and everyone else. For purposes of the impact on *poverty*, then, rich-poor inequality and income-per-person can probably be measured independently.

Second, what is the independent impact of growth and rich-poor inequality on poverty? Most recent evidence shows that — because of the evidence that growth commonly doubles real average income in 20-40 years, whereas rich-poor distribution is normally slow to alter — growth plays a much greater part in poverty reduction than does changing distribution.

However, several caveats are needed. First, this evidence does not prove trickle-down. (i) There are striking, proven examples of rapid growth without poverty reduction (e.g. Brazil in the 1950s and early 1960s).[4] Conversely, (ii) there are important instances of specific redistributions, usually of land, that reduced poverty substantially in the short term, even in the absence of growth in real income per person (Kerala) or (iii) — because they set the stage for, and were part of, an accelerated growth process — even more in the long term (China, the Republic of Korea). Second, there are some countries such as Bangladesh with such very low average income that only substantial redistribution *and* growth can substantially reduce poverty within, say, 25-50 years. That is also true of some middle-income countries, such as South Africa, for a very different reason: that their initial rich-poor distribution is so

---

[4] Malthus's [1798] celebrated — and justified — criticism of Adam Smith was that Smith, having rightly argued that technical progress together with free trade could *increase real income per person* through specialization, wrongly inferred that this would, of itself, *reduce poverty*.

exceptionally unequal that even very rapid, but distribution-neutral, growth would reduce poverty only very slowly.

The above discussion avoids the question of intra-poor distribution (see Section I.10). Yet this will affect the impact, on incidence (as well as, more obviously, on severity and intensity) of absolute poverty, of any given 1 per cent rise in average income of the initially poor — whether due to distribution—neutral growth, to rich-poor redistribution, or to any mixture of the two.

Are there any implications for labour research or policy? While the *research* activities of IILS-WEP-ILO have paid great attention to unorganized, informal and rural workers, the tripartite structure of ILO may lead their *Conventions and action* in directions that raise the relative incomes of the moderately poor, rather than that of the poorest; or even towards labour regulations, and influence on wage or contract arrangements, that damage some of the poorest. I do not know enough to assert this firmly, but the danger is obvious. Labour research should therefore concern itself with establishing, in specific case studies and in cross-sections, (1) the statistical patterns of growth, distribution and therefore change in well-being among various groups of formal-sector, informal-sector, and non-working poor *vis-à-vis* poorest, and (2) the impact, on such changes, of wage régimes, labour régimes in general, and of adherence to (or avoidance or erosion of) ILO Conventions and actions in particular. We return to this issue at the close of Section II.3.D.

6.   Transient, chronic, or instantaneous?

Most surveys record *instantaneous* responses to questions about consumption in a given *reference period*. Such surveys cannot estimate whether a person's consumption in that reference period is "typical". Therefore, they cannot decompose poverty into chronic and transient, let alone ascribe transient poverty as between its origins — e.g. in the life-cycle (such as the times when there are several small children and only one working household member) or in external events (e.g. illness or drought). A very few panel studies do allow some inferences, however. In India, about a third of poor people appear to be in more or less transient poverty — poor for less than one year in three — and only about half appear to be poor almost every year [World Bank, 1990; Ryan & Walker, 1990]. I concur with Jan Breman's reactions, in discussion: (i) this is a counter-intuitively large incidence of transient poverty in the total; (ii) the relevant studies are few, rural and Indian only; (iii) transience of poverty, even if important, does not allow any inferences against the "inheritance" of exposure to poverty risk, e.g. via landlessness, ill-health, or the need of frequently poor parents for income from children's labour even at the cost of education.

Interestingly, Gaiha's sample shows that the transient poor seem likelier to be in the very poorest groups, than do the chronic poor. This confirms that our natural intuition — that poverty is less harmful if "shared around" via transience — is mistaken. Famine, after all, is an extreme case of event-specific transient poverty. And life-cycle poverty — probably the main cause of transient poverty — concentrates on young couples with several small children [Lipton, 1983a] and on widows [Drèze, 1990]: very vulnerable groups. But the extent and type of transience is very important, because policies suitable against transient poverty are *different* from those relevant to chronic poverty. Transient poverty, but not chronic poverty, can be dealt with by consumption smoothing. The capacity of credit agencies to offer sustainable "consumption smoothing" via peer monitoring is a public good, justifying state subsidy to appropriate credit *admini-stration* (rather than to borrowers via capital or interest), often mediated via NGOs or ad hoc borrowers' organizations such as rotating savings and credit organization (ROSCAs) [Besley, 1994; Hoff et al. (eds.), 1992].

Transient/permanent poverty measurement has some labour-specific research and policy implications. Common sense suggests that labour income, especially if casual, is much more subject to downward fluctua-tions — and to risk that a *given* fluctuation may lead to transient poverty — than asset income. However, two studies suggest that this is false *in semi-arid rural areas* [Ryan & Walker, 1990; Sambrani & Pichholiya, 1975]. To what extent will decasualization, either as a market trend (e.g. with the switch from ox-drawn to tractor cultivation) or as a rule or convention, affect transient and chronic poverty? Will the effects of income stabilization, in reducing transient poverty for households of workers who shift from casual to contract status, outweigh the effects of lost employment in increasing both transient and chronic poverty, especially for casuals who are rationed out of the market? The response depends on the evidence regarding the extent to which involuntary unemployment — as against impeded workforce participation — is implicated in transient and chronic poverty (Section II.3). If this is a large and growing problem, then the extent to which some form of basic unemployment insurance, probably via employment guarantee schemes rather than via social security, can offer improvement needs to be explored [Hanson & Lieberman, 1989].

7. Poverty: primary, secondary or observed?

Just as instantaneous survey estimates of poverty in a single reference period seldom address the transient/chronic distinction, so also do they neglect the distinction between primary poverty, i.e. absence or deprivation of resources to meet requirements such as those for food and shelter, and secondary poverty, or household management that prevents inherently sufficient resources from meeting those requirements. This distinction, due to Rowntree [1901], now sounds unfashionably paternalist and victim-blaming. Yet there is no doubt that — usually through circumstances that they cannot readily alter, and that policymakers can — many households suffer poverty despite having, in principle, adequate resources. Reasons vary from addictions (cigarettes, bidis, alcohol, and other soft and hard drugs), through intra-household maldistribution (on women's superiority as resource-allocators towards children's food needs see Kennedy and Peters [1992]), to energy dispersion via long walks to, from, and among workplaces.

The overarching principle is that poverty can be caused by inadequate *resources*, i.e. levels of consumption or income, per person or per adult equivalent, below the poverty line; by excessive *requirements* that are reducible without harm or even with benefit, e.g. to fight preventable disease or to walk miles to work; or by low *conversion efficiencies* from resources into requirements. Only the first of these three leads clearly to primary poverty. The last two often lead to secondary poverty. They are often due to policy errors or to constraints at community level, rather than to private mistakes. And they are much neglected by policymakers. Are there any specially labour-related areas of enquiry?

Presumably one should concentrate on (potentially) poor people's conversion of energy from food intake into income [Payne & Lipton, 1994]. This conversion depends on *(a)* food energy needed for basic bodily functions and discretionary activities (Section II.4); *(b)* "chemical efficiency" with which remaining food energy is converted into usable working energy; *(c)* "mechanical efficiency" of converting that working energy into movement [Dasgupta, 1993]; *(d)* "ergonomic efficiency" of converting movements into tasks; *(e)* "economic efficiency", price and technical, in selecting low-cost tasks and converting them into high-value output; *(f)* distributional factors affecting the proportion of output value that reaches the (potentially) poor. Economists have concentrated overwhelmingly on *(e)* and *(f)*.

One could easily drown in a research agenda stretching from *(a)* to *(f)*, involving WHO and FAO alongside ILO, and going deep into fundamental research linking nutrition, food, health, working performance and labour economics. I suggest the ILO/IILS/WEP brief, given its own resource constraints and comparative advantage, should probably home in on labour *policy* issues related to the reduction of poverty via improved conversion efficiency. A useful area of work would home in on policies to ensure that improved linkages — especially in *(b)*, *(c)* or *(d)* above — were converted into reduced poverty, rather than merely into a higher supply of labour at a reduced rate of reward (along a fixed, and perhaps not very wage-elastic, demand curve for *employed* labour).

However, comparative advantage is not the only criterion of research specialization for agencies such as ILO/IILS/WEP. The need to remedy research neglect is another. This suggests researching the extent to which poverty could be reduced by policies to facilitate (1) substantial cuts in addictive consumption, both by switching income from *bidis* or *ganjam/dagga* to food and by increasing earning power, (2) less costly substitutes for snacks at the workplace, (3) reduced work-related illness and incapacity.

8. Inadequacy for what? Poverty and ultra-poverty lines

Suppose we are measuring instantaneously-observed absolute poverty, reported for a reference period. Where does one draw the line? The issues are discussed in Lipton and Ravallion [1994], Lipton [1983b], and sources there cited. A household is normally deemed to be above the line of food poverty, or ultra-poverty, if and only if it receives consumption or income per adult equivalent or per person, sufficient — with compositions of outlays among foods, and between food and non-foods typical for a household of the size, structure, and income level — to meet dietary energy needs (defined, for dietary energy and for most other nutrients, as 80 per cent of WHO/UNU/FAO (1985) levels, partly to allow for below-reference body weight of poor adults). A more generous poverty line could reasonably reflect, on similar assumptions, the consumption or income level above which net savings in the broad sense, i.e. including private outlays on education and durable consumer goods, is observed in the typical household.

There are no direct implications for labour-related research and policy. Indirectly, it may be useful to identify labour conditions (including activity, occupation, timing and location) associated with higher incidence, intensity and severity of poverty — and to assess causal linkages. It should be noted that the same level of poverty is normally associated with significantly different levels of income and/or consumption expenditure, in regions with different main food staples [Foster et al., 1984]. In the spirit of the previous section, it should also be noted that requirements of work (including travel costs) or domestic life, and conversion efficiencies, can also affect the moderate poverty and ultra-poverty lines appropriate for an individual or a group.

9.   Do lines mark thresholds?

There are several distinct senses in which a poverty line might mark a threshold, such that being above it was qualitatively different — for an individual's well-being or conduct, and/or for appropriate policies towards that individual — from being below it. It is an empirical issue whether variability, in relevant respects, is significantly greater between poor and non-poor than it is among the poor and/or among the non-poor. There is considerable evidence of threshold levels of nutritional (especially energy) adequacy in the sense that only below such levels is there significant risk of impaired survival chances, immune response, and mental and physical performance (see reviews in Lipton [1983b] and Payne and Lipton [1994]); hence an ultra-poverty line does seem to mark a threshold. As for the moderate poverty line, the existence of positive expected net savings capacity is in a sense a Micawber threshold [Dickens, 1849-50, Ch. 14], separating accumulation from decumulation of the present value of a person's human and physical capital stock.

The policy significance is twofold. If well-being, and/or capacity to pull oneself up by one's own efforts, increases sharply *above* the threshold of a poverty or ultra-poverty line, there is a stronger efficiency case for concentrating efforts on helping those below, rather than above, that line. Much less consonant with our moral intuition is another implication: that the cost of achieving a given welfare gain is reduced by concentrating resources on people (regions, groups) just below a poverty line, rather than further below it. The notoriously misdirecting criterion of a policy, that it should reduce poverty incidence without concern for severity, may not be so stupid after all. Yet "triage" [Paddock & Paddock, 1967] is inescapably repugnant. Hence the implication of particular thresholds *and* generally increasing marginal disutility of deeper poverty, taken together, may be as follows: relieve the *poorest* (or get as many as possible above a basic food-poverty line) first, but thereafter concentrate on support to push the *marginally*-poor above the moderate-poverty line, into sharply higher prospects of subsequent well-being or capacities for (unsupported) accumulation. Whether rough-and-ready, acceptable, implementable policy sets could conduce to this apparently complex pattern is, of course, an open question.

Two discussants (Dr. Adesima and Dr. Lee) rightly emphasized (i) the need for policy to avoid "setting the poor against the poorest" and (ii) the absolute priority for attacking extreme, life-threatening poverty. Over and above those goals, however, and despite our intuitions about smoothly diminishing marginal utility of income — and despite political correctness too — there is something to be said for getting the only-just-poor into self sufficiency (and into a position to pay taxes for subsequent poverty reduction), even at some cost in terms of foregone reductions in poverty somewhat further down the income scale.

10. Adding up below the line: FGT and all that

Counting the poor, without asking how poor they are, provides a very weak basis for discovering how much a group or region requires — through its own efforts, subsidies, or a mixture — in the context of a resource-constrained policy for poverty reduction. Alternative ways to aggregate poverty "below the line" are summarized in Kakwani [1993] and Lipton and Ravallion [1994]. These poverty indices all share some desirable characteristics of the 1976 Sen index [Sen, 1981] — but avoid its two counter-intuitive characteristics: that poverty is not additive among groups [Kakwani, 1993], and that some second derivatives of poverty, with respect to components of the Sen index, are non-positive [Lipton, 1985a].

All the modern poverty indices increase with (a) poverty *incidence*, or the proportion of a population below a poverty line, (b) poverty *intensity*, or the gap between income (or consumption) at the poverty line and that of the average poor person, as a proportion of the poverty line; (c) income (or consumption) *inequality below the line*, usually expressed by the Gini among the poor. Much the most used index now is the Foster-Greer-Thorbecke index P_2. P_2 — usually expressed per head of population — is the sum of the *squares* of differences between consumption (or income) at the poverty lines and that of each poor person. If a population of four people (A, B, C and D) have consumption levels of 1, 2, 3 and 4 units, and the poverty line is at 3, then

$$P_2 = [(\frac{3-1}{3})^2 + (\frac{3-2}{3})^2] \div 4$$

so that $P_2 = 0.14$. (Only the consumption of A(1) and B(2), not of C or D, affects the value of the poverty indicator, because C and D are not in poverty.)

There is much debate about appropriate poverty indicators, much of it not in my view very relevant to labour research or policy. Two points need attention. First, it is never right to continue using incidence on the grounds of data availability. If (and only if) a survey generates data usable to calculate incidence, then it also generates data usable to calculate P_2. It is not even true in general that small-sample properties are less favourable for P_2 than for incidence; and the policy consequences of measurement errors are in general smaller for P_2 [Kakwani, 1993]. Second, the considerations rendering P_2 an attractive poverty index — satisfaction of certain plausible axioms; sensitivity to, and credible weighting of, incidence, average intensity, and inter-poor distribution; and data parsimony — also make analogous indices attractive for other characteristics with increasing marginal disutility, such as land hunger [Sanyal, 1988] and undernutrition.

II. Correlates, causes and consequences

1. Bivariate characteristics and multivariate models of poverty

Enquiries into "characteristics of poverty" abjure counterfactual models of causal sequences. Policy analysts therefore cannot slice into the correlations and conclude (for example) that poverty may be effectively attacked by first reducing hunger or *vice versa*. The characteristics approach may, however, be a first step to causal modelling. For example, Klitgaard [1991, Chs.10-12] rightly confronts economists for ignoring links between poverty and ethnicity (and possibly discrimination); yet in fact there is a three-stage sequence of enquiry. First, we need to establish the bivariate relationship: for example, in Malaysia [Anand, 1984], ethnic origin is associated with much less poverty than is intra-Chinese or intra-Malay inequality, but in Côte d'Ivoire [Glewwe, 1990; Kakwani, 1993] Voltaic nationality does seem strongly correlated with poverty risk. Second, we need to embed these relationships into a multivariate model: is ethnicity in Côte d'Ivoire associated with poverty independently, or as a proxy for certain sorts of low-wage casual work? Third, we need to order the model causally. The last two steps can be combined, e.g. by testing a simultaneous-equation system. However, sorting out the bivariate relationships between poverty and its characteristics, and comparing bivariate and multivariate results, are essential *prerequisites* to formal modelling of causal sequences involving poverty.

Moreover, even if no causal statements can be made simply by establishing bivariate attributes of poverty groups, these attributes may provide useful indirect indicators of which persons are likely to be poor. This, in turn, can permit successful "indicator targeting" of programmes to help poor people. If such indicators — e.g. shortness, slum residence — are not readily altered or simulated, they avoid the incentive and information problems associated with targeting on persons claiming to have low income or wealth [Besley & Kanbur, 1993; Glewwe, 1992]. At the cost of a few high-profile errors, the overall incidence of both Type A and Type B errors — alongside targeting costs, and stigma — may all be reduced.

If there is a large and significant zero-order correlation between poverty and another characteristic, we usually investigate higher-order partials and/or perform multiple regressions. However, conclusions about poverty can be misleading. Suppose that, on large samples in Country X, rural areas show a significantly higher P_2. Noting that a larger proportion of rural than of urban people are elderly, in big families, or female — also (let us assume) characteristics linked to high P_2 — we then regress P_2 on these characteristics as well as on a rural/urban dummy. If the beta on this dummy becomes non-significant, we should not be misled into concluding that rurality, as such, cannot be a cause of poverty. Features of rural (urban) life, created by nature or by policy, may harm (improve) the prospects for women, the old, or those in big families to reduce their poverty.

Sorting out such causal sequences is the business of both anthropology and econometrics. Only a handful of countries has big enough household samples for robust multivariate work, let alone for causal modelling and testing. To lay the basis for such work, we need *bivariate* results. Some are presented below as "characteristics of the poor". Pending multivariate modelling and testing, analysts can explore causal alternatives, but policymakers should not depend too heavily on the answers.

2. Demographic characteristics

A. Malthus

His challenge is often analysed (and, nowadays, rejected) at the *macro*-level, in *real* space, and relevant to *GNP per person* (via a population-resource "race"). Malthus himself saw demographic change — more interestingly — as a *micro*-economic problem. Except in the very long run, he normally interprets the problems in *price* space. And he sees it is a problem, not for "growth" or the limits to it, but for the prospects of improving the welfare of the *poor*.

We thus examine the "characteristics of the poor" as the centre of gravity of a rectangle — population, labour, food, assets — created by Malthus's challenge and the responses to it. *Population* growth, for Malthus, increased *labour* supply relative to demand, and (because of diminishing returns to labour) increased *food* demand relative to output. These increases tended, respectively, to push down the money wage-rate (and/or employment-per-person) and to raise food prices. These tendencies damaged poor people's nutrition. Therefore, "The object of those who really wish to better the condition of the lower classes of society must be to raise the relative proportion between the price of labour and the price of provisions" [Malthus, 1803/1960, p. 499]. Partly for ethical reasons and partly because of incentive effects, Malthus rules out artificial contraception, and most forms of income and asset redistribution (he advocated the very gradual phasing out of poor relief). We do not share these constraints. However, to a greater or lesser extent, many poor states "act as if" they do so. This should link poverty to those households with most members, especially children, and least land or other assets. This leads, in the demographic arena, to the question: to what extent is poverty associated with large or fast-growing households, high fertility, and (in some sense) consequential high mortality?

There are two other relevant sets of demographic characteristics of poverty groups: structural and cyclical. Does the structure of the poor population place it disproportionately, or increasingly, in female-headed households, or among women, children, or the old? Does the life-cycle move people, in large numbers, in or out of high risk of poverty?

B.   Household size, poverty, assets, status

Typically, larger household size is strongly associated with much greater risk of poverty [Birdsall, 1979; Meesook, 1979; Musgrove, 1980; Visaria, 1980; Lipton, 1983a, Lanjouw & Ravallion, 1994]. For example, in the poorest quintile of households in rural Thailand in 1975-76, 42.2 per cent had 9 or more members, as against 12.2 per cent in the richest quintile [Meesook, 1979, p. 65]. In urban Colombia in the 1970s, 78 per cent of households in the poorest decile contained 8 or more persons, as against 12 per cent overall [Birdsall, 1979].[5] There is now growing evidence that

---

[5] "Poor" means "having household income or consumption, per adult-equivalent, normally associated with inadequate nutrient (or energy) intake". No account is taken of

even the alleged exceptions (in West Africa and elsewhere) to the rule that "big households *tend to be* poor households" in fact conform to that rule [e.g. Glewwe, 1990; Kakwani, 1993].

There is a "family size paradox" [Krishnaji, 1984], or "demographic paradox of poverty" [Lipton, 1983a]. (1) Small households are less likely to be poor than large households. (2) Households with little status or few assets (especially land) are less likely to be poor than others. Yet (3) higher-status — higher-caste, non-immigrant, "better" job-holding, male-headed, etc. — and/or more abundantly asset-holding households tend to be *larger* than others [ibid.; Krishnaji, 1984, 1989; Shapiro, 1990]. For example, in 1961-62, rural households in India operating no, or below 0.2 ha., of farmland averaged 2.7 persons; 4-5 ha., 6.5 persons; and above 20 ha., 8.7 persons [Krishnaji, 1987, p. 893]. Since all these effects are probabilistic, there is of course only an oddity, not a contradiction, among them.

Historically, no oddity or paradox existed, because (1) above was false: poor households in most countries tended to be *smaller* than others. Children from non-poor households married younger; and, if poor households became large, adolescents were often put in service with non-poor households, "transferring" large size to them [Hajnal, 1982]. However, in today's LDCs, adolescents from non-poor households are likelier to delay marriage through education, and subsequently to have lower marital fertility, than those in poor households. These, in turn, have become less likely to be put out to full-time servant membership in non-poor households [Lipton, 1983a]. Hence today's demographic paradox of poverty: *poor* households tend to be bigger; households with land, status or assets tend to be less poor; yet *landed*, etc., households tend to be bigger, not smaller.

It is land or assets per person or per adult-equivalent (AE), not per household, that one would expect to be associated with low risk of poverty. In most cases in the above sources, however, even farmland-*per-person* increased with household size, though less sharply than land-per-household.

Exceptionally, Shapiro [1990] shows that, in the land-abundant conditions of Southern Zaire, an extra household *worker* was associated with a small (0.055 ha.) but significant *fall* in land farmed per worker, and attributes this to increasing marginal costs of supervising even family

---

possible economies or diseconomies of scale in consumption. For the USA [Lazear & Michael, 1980], substantial economies of scale have been demonstrated even for the lowest income quintile. However, this is very unlikely to apply to low-income countries, because 70-80 per cent of poor people's income (consumption) is used for food purchases.

labour in extensive agriculture, as portrayed by Binswanger and McIntire [1987]. However, this sequence fails in more intensive agricultures. There, how can poverty be strongly related to *larger* family and household size, and to low status and asset-holding (even per person), when the latter characteristics are strongly related to *smaller* family and household size? The three tendencies imply that, as a rule, each asset-holding or status-receiving group, e.g. the landless or the high-caste, must show a very strong positive linkage of large family size to poverty. The above evidence supports this, but does not dispose of the oddity.

C. Mortality

Evidence cited in Lipton and Ravallion [1994] and Lipton [1983a] shows that inter-group mortality differences are *(a)* heavily concentrated in the first five years of life, *(b)* increasing quite steeply with poverty, but also with asset deprivation, *(c)* sometimes apparently discontinuous, or at least strongly non-linear, around a very low level of nutritional status, income, and asset-holding. On their own — i.e. without allowing for actions by poor couples to (over)compensate for high child mortality, viz. early marriage and high marital fertility — these facts render large size of *poor* families more surprising, but of *assetless* families less so.

Cross-regional and cross-cultural mortality differences, however, are also big, even with similar severities of poverty. Much of this relates to disease and food environments. However, an unknown part of the difference is due to working requirements and circumstances, in particular those of pregnant women. Joint research between medical and social scientists might find promising routes to "uncouple" poverty from over-work, poor child care and high death risk; and hence to help poor people to escape from poverty.

D. Fertility

Higher mortality *on its own* would render large size among poor families *more* surprising. However, it is more than offset by their higher marital fertility. That is partly to replace, and insure against risks of, infant and child deaths; and partly because lack of access to affordable education, plus the need for income from child labour, often render it difficult for poor couples to "substitute (child) quality for quantity" [Becker & Lewis, 1974]. This helps to explain the "paradox of family size". It is further illuminated by the fact that — although income per person is negatively associated to fertility over most of the range — operated (but not owned) landholding per person is positively associated to fertility (Mueller & Short

[1982] for Botswana; Stoeckel & Chowdhury [1980]; Schutjer & Stokes [1984] for Thailand and Egypt; Mitra [1978, pp. 209-210] for India). This may be because family, rather than hired, labour per hectare economizes transactions-costs in own-account farming; or because [Chayanov, 1966; Nakamura, 1986] extra hands and mouths in a family raise the marginal disutility to it of incomeless leisure, relative to that of drudgery divided over the total family.

ILO/IILS/WEP has done much important population-related research [e.g. Rodgers., 1989]. Probably, its comparative advantage lies in exploring the links between changed — especially, improved — prospects for wages and employment, and subsequent fertility declines. There is reason to believe that the favourable links are strong, but delayed and perhaps non-monotonic. Can policy speed up or otherwise support the linkages?

E.   Age of marriage

Poorer households tend to have more births per marriage partly because (contrary to historical experience [Hajnal, 1982]), they marry earlier than other households in today's developing countries. However, the effects on *household* size are ambiguous. Couples start to have children sooner, increasing it; but children marry sooner, reducing it [Lipton, 1983a, pp. 24-27]. High-prestige occupations, joint or extended family structures, education, and income-per-person are independent correlates of later marriage of offspring [ibid.; Singh & Richard, 1989; Reddy, 1991]; it is more likely to pay them to stay at home, working part-time for their parents, to the extent that they have expectations of inheritance.

F.   Nuclear or extended?

Most of the above discussion assumes nuclear, not extended, families. For the great majority of the world's poor, this is valid. Nuclear households are proving to be the norm in more and more cases — developing as well as developed — where the debate switches from literary to empirical. Nuclear families are especially dominant among the poor, where parents have few assets to "will-shake" over — or to benefit from the complementary labour of — married children who seek to leave home [Krishnaji, 1984; Lipton, 1983a, pp. 27-32, and sources therein]. Hence complexity, i.e. jointness or extendedness, of households cannot explain poor people's larger household size, because complexity is linked to *high* (landed, chiefly, Brahman, etc.) status [ibid., pp. 30-31], perhaps as large landholders diversify income sources.

Labour participation, employment, and wage-rate, as they might differ between nuclear and extended families, are little researched. This is an interesting topic, but probably not a priority for *policy* research.

G. Is poverty feminizing?

Our conclusion, then, is that poorer couples' greater (need for) replacement and other fertility exceeds their greater (exposure to) mortality and hence raises their family size. More physical assets for the poor reduce it *only* if they substantially cut poverty. Education, of course, cuts both poverty and fertility (in normal circumstances: these are caveats). Since high fertility among the poor also *causes* high mortality via sib crowding — and impedes women, in particular, from advances out of poverty through productive work — the importance of appropriate intervention in this sequence is obvious.

This issue apart, until the Latin American evidence presented to this symposium by Buvinić [1993] was collected, the evidence was very strong that women are *not* in general over-represented in poorer households; nor among heads of households that are likelier to be poor (Visaria [1977, 1985] on Asia; Drèze [1990] on Karnataka, Maharashra and Gujarat in India; H. Standing [1985] on Calcutta; Haddad [1991] and Lloyd & Brandon [1991] on Ghana; and earlier sources cited in Lipton [1983b, pp. 48-53]). Further — except for some subsets of girls under five in North India [Levinson, 1974; Bardhan, 1982; Das Gupta, 1987] and Bangladesh [Chen et al., 1981; Muhuvi & Preston, 1991] — females are *not* normally exposed to excess poverty-induced nutritional risk *within* households, as Harriss [1986] shows for South Asia. As for Africa, among 12 African countries, only in Nigeria do pre-school boys have better anthropometric status than girls; in eight of nine country samples with significant gender differences in infant or child nutrition it is the girls who do better; and adult women generally show a better body mass index than men [Svedberg, 1990].

Nevertheless, women *are* especially severe victims of poverty, in three respects. First, they work for longer hours (household plus "economic") than men to achieve the same level of living. For example, in Peru, the excess female burden was worst for single-earner households, where female heads had to work 39 per cent more "market" hours than male heads; but even in multiple-earner households, market plus domestic work occupied female heads for 76 hours per month more than male heads [Rosenhouse, 1989]. Such burdens are heaviest for the poorest. The relative demands of child-rearing can be assessed by observing that the ratio of under-fourteens — and of under-fives — to adult women, doubles between the best-off and the poorest household quintiles in most samples (Visaria [1977, 1980] on Asia; Lipton [1983a, pp. 43-44]).[6] As women participate more in market work under pressure of poverty, their domestic labour contribution is *not* substantially reassigned to men [Bardhan, 1985; G. Standing, 1985].

Second — in part because women's culturally assigned, large share of domestic commitments prevents them from seizing new and profitable work opportunities as readily as men (Haddad [1991] for Ghana) — women's chances of *independent* escape from poverty are much worse than men's. Many LDC job markets appear to be largely segregated — into "progressive", poverty-escaping, and usually male; and "static", poverty-confirming and usually female (G. Standing [1985]; Anker & Hein [1985]; Guhan & Bharathan [1984] on silk-weaving in South India; von Braun et al. [1989] on irrigated rice-farming in the Gambia). Even more important than the domestic burden, in explaining this poverty trap, may be cultural discrimination against females in both education and — given education — in job assignments. (On Taiwan, see Greenhalgh [1985]; on Ghana, see Haddad [1991]; on Bangladesh, see Safilios-Rothschild [1991]). In rural India in 1981, men's probability of being literate exceeded women's by a larger proportion among the far poorer scheduled castes (22 per cent-6 per cent) and scheduled tribes (28 per cent-8 per cent) than among the population as a whole (40 per cent-18 per cent) [Bennett, 1991].

Third, in many cultures, widows face barriers against employment or remarriage, leading to especially high risks of poverty [Drèze, 1990].

Though the severity of income-based poverty is usually no more among women than among men, male-dominated societies make it harder for women (widows being an extreme case) than for men to escape from poverty [Alam & Martin, 1984; Schiegel, 1976]. These two facts imply that poverty is more likely to be chronic for women, and transitory for men. The "feminization of poverty" happens, not so much via higher incidence, but in the sense that turnover is lower among poor women than among poor men, so that expected lifetime disutility is higher.

The policy relevance for research in the UN system, above all ILO and UNESCO, is strong. What labour market conditions, and what material and cultural constraints, are associated with the trapping of poor women into *either* low participation rates — urbanization reduces the rates

---

[6] The increase, with deepening poverty, vanishes among the very poorest 5-10 per cent of households in most samples [Lipton, 1983a, pp. 43-45].

in *the poorest quintile* by 20-35 per cent [Lipton, 1983] — *or* into higher unemployment (see section 2.4), or, above all, into types of work offering few prospects for self-advancement? How can the organization of work, homestead micro-horticulture, and other occupations compatible with both skilling and domestic work, be arranged so that women can better escape poverty, yet employers are not faced with disincentives to labour-intensive activities?

H. "Juvenization" of poverty

This is a huge, and in Africa at least a proportionately worsening, problem. Yet the concentration seldom arises because their nutritional requirements are more neglected than that for adults in a *given* household [Schofield, 1979]. It arises because child/adult ratios are much larger in poor households. This is both because higher infant and child mortality (leading to even higher replacement fertility) is *caused by* undernutrition, and because higher child/adult ratios *cause* severer income-based poverty. In the early 1970s, the poorest quintile of households contained 25 per cent of children in rural India, and about 30 per cent in Colombia, Malaysia and Brazil [Birdsall, 1980, p. 39]. In five Andean countries, the probability that an urban household would be in poverty in the late 1970s was more elastic to child/adult ratios than to the proportion of adults working [Musgrove, 1980]. In rural India in 1972-73 child/adult ratios were above 0.45 among the poor, and around 0.35 among the non-poor [Lipton, 1983a, p. 71, pp. 102-103].

Heavy female burdens from the "double day" and child poverty often go hand in hand; hence, where children most need intensive parenting to grow up healthy [Zeitlin et al., 1987], they are least likely to get it. Typically, in poor Indian households in 1972-73, each adult was associated with 1.8 children; in non-poor households, with 1.1 [ibid., pp. 104-105]. In one Indian village, widow-headed households with no adult male derived 56 per cent of earnings from child labour [Drèze, 1990]! In a Bombay slum in the mid-1980s, a large majority of working children came from widow-headed households [Bharat, 1988].

The linked questions of the "double day" and child labour are *(a)* important causes *and* effects (not just correlates) of poverty, *(b)* areas where research has been distorted by rhetoric and "political correctness". There is serious empirical and analytical work to be done. Much of it relates to the interfaces between labour, health, education, and survival chances.

I.　Greying of poverty

In LDCs, the old have until recently comprised a much smaller proportion of the poor than of the non-poor [Lipton, 1983a], but this may be changing. Overall the over-65s comprised 3.8 per cent of South Asians in 1980, but are projected at 4.8 per cent in 2000 and 8.2 per cent in 2025; in other developing regions the expansion is faster, except in Africa where even by 2025 the proportion is projected at only 3.9 per cent [Deaton & Paxson, 1991, p. 2]. The old in the Côte d'Ivoire and Thailand have below-average income — but only because they are more rurally concentrated [ibid.]; and this does not prove that *proportions in poverty* are higher for the old. In Nigeria and India in the 1970s, the evidence was against this [Gaiha & Kazmi, 1982, p. 56; Hill, 1982, pp. 187-188].

However, more poor people survive into old age nowadays. Also, because of the income-dispersing effects of assetless widowhood (creating poverty) and spousal inheritance (creating wealth), inequality among the old may well be greater than among those of prime age. If so, similar average income per person in these two groups — as in the Deaton-Paxson evidence — would mean higher, perhaps much higher, poverty among the elderly. With the impending "greying of poverty" in most LDCs — though not in Africa — these issues merit further research. Their interaction with labour markets depends heavily on the extent to which *(a)* the poor *can* and *do* continue work into old age, *(b)* family, group, or state social security mechanisms exist through which the working population support the elderly poor. European experience suggests that such mechanisms should be financed by general progressive taxes (including profits taxes), not by charges to employers based on — and hence discouraging — large payroll size. Analogous effects in family and community old-age protection are largely unresearched.

3.　Labour and poverty

Population growth is supposed to worsen poverty through two routes in the Malthusian macro-model. First, it drives food prices up (Section II.4). Second, it raises labour supply, driving down wage-rates and/or employment. The counter-arguments, in the spirit of "new institutional economics", are that both fertility [Schultz, 1981; Simon, 1981] and technical progress [Boserup, 1965; Hayami & Ruttan, 1985, Simon, 1986] are adjusted, by rational individuals, to these harmful effects — thereby preventing them.

Only recently has it become possible to assess what *happens* to poor people as workers in LDCs. Tautologically, income per person is the product of (see A. below) the proportion of people who are of working age, (see B. below) the proportion of their time spent in workforce participation, (see C. below) the proportion of their participating time during which they are self-employed or employed, and (see D below) their income per unit of time worked. Poverty depends on the average levels of these four variables, on their distribution between poor and non-poor, and (except for the widest poverty incidence measure) on their distribution among the poor.

A. Proportions of working age

As we saw in Section II.2.H, the age-structure of poor households is unfavourable to workforce participation. In three large rural and urban state samples in India, the proportion of under-14s in 1972-73 decreased sharply as household expenditure per person fell, while the proportion of over-60s rose only gently. For example, in urban Maharashtra the proportions in poorest and richest household quintiles, respectively, were 49.6 per cent and 20.5 per cent for under-15s, and 5.2 per cent and 6.4 per cent for over-60s. *Thus the ratio of dependants to prime-age workers, the dependency ratio, among the ultra-poor was 54.8 per cent/45.2 or 1.21 for the poorest quintile — well over three times the ratio, 26.9/73.1 or 0.37, for the best-off quintile* [Visaria, 1977; Lipton, 1983a, p. 43, pp. 101-105]. Similar relationships prevail in numerous Asian data sets, rural and urban [ibid.; Visaria, 1980, Table 4]. Of course, the age at which economic work starts and ends is a behavioural variable, cultural and individual; and poverty compels some of the young and the old to work for reward, even when the norm is education or rest.

Yet a high ratio of young and old people to prime-age workers is a great drag on poor people's participation. This drag increases, at least relatively, with early development and urbanization. The rich-poor gap in the dependency ratio is proportionately greater in cities than in villages, and in more than in less developed countries and regions [ibid., Table 4 and p. 65; Lipton, 1983, p. 45]. These demographic dynamics of urbanization, and their impact on poverty, appear to be an important field for research, perhaps jointly by UNFPA with IILS/ILO/WEP.

B. Age- and sex-specific participation rates (ASPRs)

Three things drive the poor to seek higher ASPRs than others. Poverty itself increases the marginal rate of substitution of income for leisure [Robbins, 1930]. Second, as poverty deepens, so does the proportion of income derived from labour. Third, dramatically high dependency ratios increase the marginal utility of income-per-worker [Chayanov, 1966]; thus the Malthus effect, that high fertility raises labour supply (and thus depresses the wage-rate), operates long *before* the children reach working age.

In all income-groups, 90-95 per cent of prime-age men are in the workforce; it is, therefore, only for women, children and the old that ASPRs can vary *greatly* in response to poverty. Women's ASPRs increase, but only modestly, as household poverty deepens, but with limited benefits for the poor. *(a)* The effect fades out among the ultra-poor; the poorest 5-15 per cent of households show female ASPRs usually no more than the moderately poor, probably in part due to bad health and nutrition. *(b)* At a given income per person, the household's female ASPRs decline with rising ratios of under-fives to women and older children [Lipton, 1983, pp. 16-17; Dasgupta, 1977, p. 153]. *(c)* High female ASPRs may harm pregnant women (and unborn children) in extreme situations. *(d)* Women's participation and employment are in worse-rewarded tasks — and subject to more fluctuation — than men's (Section II.10). *(e)* Above all, female urban ASPRs — given the poverty level — are quite dramatically lower in urban than in rural areas; so their tendency to be higher among the poor is less useful to poor women as they urbanize [Lipton, 1983, pp. 23-25].[7]

In urban Gujarat, India, only 1 in 4 women *in the poorest decile* participated in market work in 1972-73 [Visaria, 1981, p. 13]. By 1983, among rural Indian women (over 15), 32 per cent were workforce participants, as against 35 per cent in the lowest four deciles; the urban proportions were 18 per cent and 23 per cent, respectively [Hanson & Lieberman, 1989].[8] This seems puzzling: urban women are usually better qualified educationally than rural women, and less often pregnant or lactating; and their children are more likely to be at school. Explanations may include greater underenumeration of women's urban work [ibid.], lower propensity of urban women to be household heads, factory scale-economies (and zoning laws) that militate against "economic" work at home [Lipton, 1983, p. 24], and greater urban risks of violence against women at work and travelling.

---

[7] At the symposium, Buvinić pointed out that Latin American rural-urban migrations — unlike those of most other developing countries — featured a high female/male ratio. This point *(e)*, therefore, may not apply in Latin America; more research is needed.

[8] Only to a very small extent can this be explained by the fact that the poorest urban deciles have somewhat higher real income and consumption per person than the corresponding rural deciles.

Urban proportions of populations (including poor populations) are rising. So are urban female/male ratios (once very low), especially for poorer adults [Lipton, 1983a, p. 51]. Therefore, *the reasons — and, if appropriate, cures — for urban women's low ASPRs should be high on the poverty research agenda.*

Child labour is demonstrably understated by large offical surveys, and much more prevalent in poorer households [Lipton, 1983, pp. 17-18]. More evidence is needed on causes and cures. Weiner [1991] develops a powerful case for enforcing India's paper protections for children. However, legislation cannot (should not?) prevent child labour, if it offers poor parents the only safe route to survival, unless alternative routes are offered — and financed.

C. Employment and unemployment

For Arthur Lewis [1954], mass rural unemployment prevailed in LDCs, creating the chance for "economic development with unlimited supplies of labour". For Hansen [1969], Myrdal [1968] and others, unemployment in areas of owner-farming was meaningless, empirically small, or a "bourgeois luxury" irrelevant to poverty. Since about 1980, with the emergence *(a)* of *hired work* as the main economic activity of the urban *and rural* poor, *(b)* of the economics of search costs, information and risk, and *(c)* of major new evidence from household surveys, a more measured view of unemployment's role in poverty has emerged. It is less important than low incomes at work, but, selectively by time and place, important still; and increasing.

Unemployment as a *usual status* over a long period, in countries without social security, truly is a bourgeois luxury [see e.g. Udall & Sinclair, 1982]. However, the *time-rate* of unemployment (TRU) — i.e. the proportion of days or half-days in a reference period, typically the week before survey, spent workless and seeking work — is substantially higher among poor workers and sharply so among the poorest, especially in towns, among casual workers and women, and for places, groups, and periods when most people are assetless and landless, unable to fall back on asset-based self-employment [Sundaram & Tendulkar, 1988]. In view of the extremely strong impact of farm and firm size upon labour/land ratios [Lipton, 1993a] *the linkage of "unemployment as a cause of poverty" to the case for land reform — and for urban and rural micro-enterprise — is blatant.* Unemployment itself is concentrated among the assetless and in areas, age-groups, etc. that are likely to over-represent the poor.

Relevant data for many countries are reviewed in [Lipton, 1983, pp. 42-54]; important new sources are Visaria and Minhas [1991] and Krishnamurthy [1988, p. 302, p. 306, pp. 309-312]. He analyses a huge and careful household sample for India in 1977-78. Only 3 per cent of the rural workforce were unemployed as a *"main activity"* during the previous month, and the incidence was very slightly higher for the non-poor. However, *time-rates* of male unemployment "for rural areas... steadily decline from about 15 per cent for very poor households to about 8 per cent... just below the poverty line, and continue to decline" above it. In towns the respective rates are about 20 per cent and 11 per cent — corresponding to the greater urban prevalence of hired (including casual) labour. Female TRUs were 1.3 (rural) to 1.5 (urban) times male, but among the urban poorest female TRUs were well below male rates (probably reflecting lower female urban ASPRs among "discouraged workers"). In rural areas, the mainly self-employed suffered a TRU of only 3 per cent, as against 15 per cent for those deriving income mainly from hired work; the respective urban figures were 6 per cent and 13 per cent. Much higher TRUs were suffered by workers in "unskilled" households, i.e. earning most income from rural or urban construction (15-19 per cent), transport (10-12 per cent), or mining (11-12 per cent), or *urban* agriculture (10-11 per cent). There are striking regional differences; the TRU was over 25 per cent in urban and rural Kerala, 14-15 per cent in Tamil Nadu, but 4-7 per cent in the Northern States. More research is needed — not only in India — into why "time unemployed", clearly a correlate of poverty, varies so greatly among places without *obviously* different relative factor prices or labour information régimes.

A huge research agenda, in which largely neglected issues of workforce participation should be considered *alongside* much more widely discussed unemployment data, awaits those concerned to improve the information base on labour and poverty. Liaison with information from agricultural production functions, and on the relations between size of firm, self-employment, and labour demand *and supply*, is part of this agenda. Of course the primary data base is much more in need of strengthening, prior to such research, in Africa than Asia. The JASPA work in Africa [JASPA, 1990] appears to confirm the strong impression from Asia, Latin America, and Europe that unemployment is a growing problem, and a growing explanation of poverty; but African TRUs are hardly ever estimated, and in several African countries (including South Africa) the distinction between unemployment and informal-sector activity is not made clear in the data available.

D. Wage rates

We have seen that workforce participation rates, especially those reflecting *supply* of unskilled casual hired labour, increase with poverty; and that time rates of unemployment, reflecting slackness of labour *demand*, also tend to do so. The prospect for wage-rates of poor people's (unskilled) labour is therefore bleak. This is especially the case in a Malthusian world of growing overall labour supply, unless offset (1) by rises in labour's marginal value-product due to intersectoral shifts or to sector-specific (and not too labour-saving) technical progress, and/or (2) if falling relative prices of food staples offset falling relative wage-rates.

In a world where growing proportions of rural people depend on wage incomes, the imperfect linkage of poverty to farm wage-rates in many countries is interesting, and suggests growing alternatives — urban, non-farm, or state-mediated — for the rural poor. Thus rural poverty fell in Indonesia, Egypt, Kenya, and (to a smaller extent) India around 1950-75; yet real *farm* wage-rates showed no clear uptrend [Lipton, 1983, pp. 86-87]. In India, "the marked increase in [agricultural growth after Independence] to 2.4 per cent p.a., over its long-term trend rate of just under 1 per cent p.a., [had by 1978 not accelerated] rural real wages [beyond] the long-term trend rate of less than 0.5 per cent p.a." [Lal, 1988, p. 283], probably due mainly to rising rural labour supply. In 1976-88 agricultural wage-rates appear to have risen by 2.5 per cent in India, 1.1 per cent in Sri Lanka and 11.5 per cent in Pakistan — though by 0 per cent in Bangladesh and -1.1 per cent p.a. in the Philippines [Gaiha & Spinedi, 1992]. The real wage rises were probably due mainly to world food price trends, not to labour-using technical change; elasticity of employment to cereals yield has fallen sharply since the early 1980s [Lipton with Longhurst 1989, pp. 84-85]. A model that reportedly "tracked agricultural wages closely" suggests normal (negative) and substantial effects of Asian agricultural labour supply on farm wage-rates, except in Pakistan, where a strong *positive* effect was found [Gaiha & Spinedi, 1992, p. 468].

It looks as if it is not rising real farm unskilled wage-rates — but rather skilling, sectoral shifts, increased cereals yields even on handkerchief-sized farms, remittances, or (seldom) rising employment — that accounts for falling rural poverty in most of Asia. Skilling, and associated human capital formation, raise productivity "even" in basic farm tasks [Jamison & Lau, 1982], and help people to escape from low real wage-rates in unskilled agriculture by shifting or diversifying sector, or place, of work. In Malaysia, Thailand and Korea, it was arguably this skilling process that eventually led to the "Lewis-Fei-Ranis" outcome:

absolute decline in farm labour supply. Post-primary education also helps this process by inducing lower fertility.

The emphasis of the World Bank [1990] on *technology and incentives via domestic institutions and policies* that absorb labour is justified. It *appears* obvious that minimum wage laws, restrictions against redundancy, etc., harm the poorest by discouraging employers from using labour. But ILO and other research suggests a more complex reality. In some circumstances, the poorest can be net gainers, even if a minimum wage law for those in work does (inevitably) reduce employment. It depends on, for example, whether those in (or at risk of) unemployment tend to be secondary workers, in households with a securely employed or self-employed primary worker — and, of course, on the wage-elasticities of demand for labour. However, very careful enquiry is needed into the employment and wage structures of poor (and potentially poor) households, from an adequate sample survey, before adopting policies that set a minimum wage significantly above the level justified as a market signal. Experience from Zimbabwe to Kerala (India) does suggest a serious impact on the job prospects of the poor.

Perhaps even more important, what happens to poor people's wage-rates (and welfare) if world-scale technical progress, and the relative factor and product prices with which it interacts causally, tend to displace labour (and the output-mixes that are made labour-intensively)? *Technology and incentive outcomes* are ultimately determined globally for all but the biggest LDCs; and the global trends (as Western unemployment suggests) are extruding labour. The bad news is that unskilled farm wage-rates therefore seldom rise much (at least so long as farm labour supply grows). The good news is that, as shown, poverty can nevertheless fall sharply.

E. Structure of work

Total work done can be classified by type of contract, worker, work, or employer. Related to *type of contract* are: casual/long-term, factory/out-work, piece rate/time rate, informal/formal, and employee/self-employed/family. Related to *characteristics of worker* are: migrancy, nationality, age, gender, and educational level. Related to *type of work* are: location (e.g. urban-rural), economic activity (e.g. by SITC classification), skill level, and part-time/full-time. Related to *type of employer* are size of unit and (again) location and nationality.

Some of these characteristics show systematic links to poverty incidence or severity. In particular, casual work is strongly linked to high poverty incidence, apparently in large part because casual workers face a relatively high unemployment risk [Visaria, 1980; Lipton, 1983 and citations therein]. Clear inverse-U-shaped age-wage rate relationships, and positive education-wage rate relationships, have also been established, matching poverty risks. So has the fact that apparently strong gender-wage rate relationships break down when task and day-length are held constant [ibid.]. More will be said about the crucial economic-activity/poverty linkage below, but first a word of caution is needed.

Unlike analyses of participation and unemployment, even as correlates of poverty, the analyses of "structure of work" do not, even implicitly, distinguish between supply and demand factors. Nor do these analyses usually separate the poverty linkages of cross-sectional differences among individuals (or households) in a variable such as education, from those of its increase over time in an economy. Taken together, these two omissions create a serious danger of drawing wrong policy conclusions from a "fallacy of composition". For example, from the almost universal finding that *individuals* with more education[9] enjoy lower poverty risk, it does not follow that educating more people in a *nation* will lower poverty. The first, partial-equilibrium, question is: will a minority of poor persons, if it becomes able to *supply* a higher level of education, increase expected earnings, income from self-employment, or ability to achieve welfare from a given income? Suppose the answer is yes. Then the second, general-equilibrium question is: does *demand* for educated services grow commensurately with supply? If not, the extra efficiency-units of labour-supply due to a more educated workforce may — even if enriching the persons whose level of education rises — crowd out from the labour market, and hence impoverish, other workers. This is especially likely to affect poorer, less-skilled workers, in a process of "qualification escalation". Conversely, suppose that demand for educated work rises faster than supply. This will normally accompany (1) rising GNP but also (2) a rising share, in GNP, for educated and usually non-poor workers; if (2) is faster than (1) then the incidence of poverty — and probably higher-order indicators such as P_2 — must worsen.

Obviously, these remarks are not made in order to denigrate education as a remedy for poverty. Both cross-section and time-series studies reveal

---

[9] Secondary-school completers (and above) in cross-section studies show a persistently higher rate of "usual status" or "long-term" *unemployment* than others (Dev et al. [1991] for India; Vandemoortele [1991] for Africa); but this proxies, not poverty, but ability to live off family income while searching for secure or well-paid work. In cross-sections of workers below secondary completion level, time-rates of unemployment (and wage-rates and poverty) decrease with increased education.

its power, at least given rising demand for the commodities produced by the educated (Section II.7). The point is to warn against over-simple policy readings of the growing, and in some respects exciting, evidence on work structure and poverty. To give another important example: it is becoming clear that in towns informal-sector employment is *not* strongly associated with poverty; and that in rural areas non-farm activity (RNFS), partly because less strongly associated with casual labour than is farm activity, *is* strongly associated with reduced poverty risk. In most countries, such findings do greatly help in locating "markers" of what sorts of areas, groups, etc. are more likely to be severely affected by poverty. But the findings do not, as a rule, allow us to conclude that — for example — a growing share of urban labour supply to the informal sector will not increase urban poverty, or that State acts of stimulus should be transferred from agriculture to other rural activities in order to reduce rural poverty. First, there are interaction effects — e.g. RNFS growth appears to be fastest in areas where farm growth has been fastest [Hazell & Ramaswamy, 1992; Dev, 1991]; and in urban areas informal-sector growth may depend on formal-sector growth. Second, we do not know if it is extra *supply* of informal (relative to formal) urban labour — or of non-farm (relative to farm) rural labour — that is associated with lower poverty, or extra *demand*.

The usual assumption behind many "new" policies is that supply management is required. Yet it is at least probable that growing demand (and not at all supply) for urban informal or rural non-farm activity is growth-linked, and in turn responsible for poverty reduction. Absent growing demand, attempts to reduce poverty by encouraging the supply of urban informal-sector [de Soto, 1989] or RNFS activity may be like pushing on a piece of string. Moreover, both RNFS and the urban informal sector are *(a)* heterogeneous and *(b)* infrastructure-dependent. *(a)* In Egypt, Indonesia and India, it is rural commerce, transport and construction — not crafts and manufactures — that have proved dynamic, labour-absorptive, and "linked" to farm growth [Dev, 1991; Unni, 1991]. *(b)* Across Indian Districts, RNFS growth — much more than farm growth — has been highly responsive to the density of local rural bank branches [Binswanger & Khandker, 1992].

No data set, by relating work structure (e.g. by activity, status, "outsidership", formality, etc.), to the incidence and severity of poverty, so far enables us to disentangle the supply-demand and cause-effect conundrums. In presenting a few possible implications of recent findings, we suggest a tentative interpretation only, in the hope of stimulating proper modelling and testing.

There is quite widespread evidence that rural households which earn a high share of income from the non-farm sector have relatively low risk of poverty. But that statement skates over the (very rudimentary) *causal* evidence. Three things seem to be clear. First, agricultural labour is especially poverty-prone — either as such (on India see Dev et al. [1991]) or because it is especially likely to be casual labour and therefore liable to unemployment [Visaria, 1980]. In this case, those engaged mainly in the RNFS are helped to escape poverty because RNFS work is more likely than agricultural work to be self-employed (entrepreneurial), or else long-term employed (craft, apprentice, family) — in some cases because of the greater *permanence* of RNFS enterprises (for Mauritania see Coulombe & McKay [1991]). Second, diversity of income sources, and hence multiple family bases (locations), are associated with both membership of the RNFS and reduced risk of poverty due to downward income fluctuation, as in Zimbabwe [Jackson & Collier, 1988]; this is especially likely to link the RNFS to the escape from poverty where the agriculturally self-employed are *worse* off than labourers, as in Mauritania [Coulombe & McKay, 1991], and/or where, as in Burkina Faso, "larger" landholding signifies concentration on agriculture, lack of access to RNFS, and hence *greater* poverty risk [Delgado et al., 1991]. Third, much RNFS activity (52 per cent in a study of 288 households in Zimbabwe [Helmsing, 1991]) is highly seasonal, thereby offsetting seasonal poverty for rural people with impaired capacity to save, borrow or store.[10] The linkage of RNFS activity and poverty escape is therefore associated with *either* overall *farm* poverty, as in parts of Africa, *or* seasonal and annual fluctuations associated with casual (and principally agricultural) *employee* status.

Apart from the general finding that RNFS activity at household level reduces poverty risk — via diversification, outsidership, reduced risk of casual work and unemployment, or simple avoidance of low-returns farming — there is some evidence on poverty correlates in respect of the structure of work *within* agriculture:

1. *Involvement in cash cropping* is in numerous studies associated with reduced risk and severity of poverty. Often, this reduction clearly occurs *after* cash-crop involvement, and is not found in control groups not similarly involved [Maxwell & Fernando, 1989; von Braun &

---

[10] This widespread observation (e.g. Hopper [1955]), that rural people increase RNFS work and income in agriculturally slack times, is quite consistent with the evidence against "distress diversification" (e.g. Dev [1991]; Unni [1991]), i.e. that localized fast RNFS growth follows fast, not slow, growth of local farm output.

Kennedy, 1986]. However, the impact of higher real income, based on cash-cropping, upon poor people's nutrition is small and slow, and sometimes absent or not significant [ibid.]. This may reflect the fact that work on cash crops increases the energy requirement, or [Kumar, 1977] reduces mother's capacity for child care, at least seasonally. An early compilation of village studies suggests that the incidence of undernutrition — and perhaps of poverty as a cause of it? — is significantly (at 5 per cent) less in villages with a mixture of cash crops and self-consumed food crops, than in villages with a great preponderance of either [Schofield, 1979].

2. *Reliance on landless labour*, as opposed to farm self-employment, is a major poverty correlate in Bangladesh [Ravallion, 1990]. A very small sample of elderly people in the same country [Cain, 1991] suggests that wage work is much more closely related to landlessness among the elderly than among younger landless people, who more often engage in trade. In India *as a whole*, poverty incidence is much higher among landless workers than among small farmers [Dev et al., 1991, part 2.14]. However, this does not apply in semi-arid areas of India for farmers with below 3 ha. [Lipton, 1985], nor in similarly dry African countries such as Mauritania [Coulombe & McKay, 1991, parts 3.4, 3.12] and Burkina Faso [Delgado et al., 1991], where farming often proxies *lack* of access to poverty-reducing opportunities for rural trade or artisanship.

3. Greater reliance on (i.e. income or employment share from) *common property resources* is associated with higher poverty incidence in rural Tanzania [Collier et al., 1986], as in rural India [Jodha, 1986]. This is despite the substantially smaller inequality in CPRs than in private resources, but probably due in part to the major reduction in CPRs [ibid.]. Communal land tenure is associated with *lower* poverty risk in Mauritania [Coulombe & McKay, 1991, part 3.21], probably because both are associated with cattle ownership.

4. *Formal-sector work* (indifferently whether public-sector or private-sector) is associated with lower poverty risk, but almost certainly only because such work proxies educated labour [Coulombe & McKay, 1991]. In Tanzania, education militates against low wage rates even for unskilled farm labour [Collier et al., 1986]; this carries over to effects on total farm household income, and poverty risk, in the Indian Punjab [Chaudhri, 1979] and more generally [Jamison & Lau, 1982].

We have much to learn about the impact of work structures on poverty risk. For example, it is clear that almost everywhere the proportion of poor people dependent mainly on rural or urban employment is rising, relative to the proportion dependent mainly on income from farming. Yet a little own-farm activity may provide a "reservation wage" that increases immunity from poverty both directly and via improved bargaining capacity with the employer.

ILO will presumably want to concentrate on answering questions that could be relevant to policy *and* where the poverty impact of policy improvements is, or can be made, unambiguous. On the last issue, the recently contentious question of child labour [Weiner, 1991] illustrates the problems. If the horrendous abuses (millions of children denied schooling; probably hundreds of thousands with jobs impairing life expectancy, health, or eyesight) are remedied by a legal crackdown alone, family (including child) nutrition may well suffer. Yet some countries did successfully stamp out child labour —Sri Lanka, China? One needs to ask how a damaging short-run poverty impact was avoided in such cases. More generally, if a particular labour structure — such as a small RNFS — is associated with poverty, we need to know why, and in particular whether societies with that structure differ mainly in respect of labour supply or of labour demand.

4. Food, nutrition and poverty

Part 1 reviewed the case for using an "expected food energy adequacy" level of expenditure income or (per adult equivalent) as an ultra-poverty cut-off. The overall relationships between food, work, energy, income and welfare are shown in Diagram 1. Much recent research has been concerned with thresholds, turning-points and non-linearities in these relationships. If such thresholds, etc., tend to occur, it is at very low levels of (for example) body mass index, energy intake, or income; above such levels, affecting some 15-25 per cent of non-famine populations in low-income countries, adaptations — e.g. in the speed with which a task is performed — are possible (though often costly) in the event of energy stress. In brief, the ultra-poor need "food first"; the moderately poor can more quickly get less poor if they obtain assets and opportunities (for summaries of evidence see Lipton [1983b]; Payne & Lipton, 1994]).

Diagram 1: Conversion efficiencies

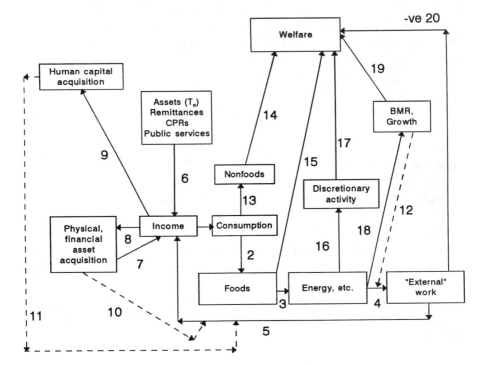

Paths: 1-5 Central path
          6-9 Other income-related paths
          10-12 Work-enhancer paths
          13-20 Welfare paths

All this relates to labour research in three main ways. First, those at risk of extreme poverty adapt in many ways — some more costly, or more likely to reduce prospects of escaping poverty, than others; these alternative modes of adaptation may suggest forms of work structure, options, or organization likely to help or harm the poor. Second, relatedly, the income-elasticity of demand for calories (CIE) has in several recent studies proved "surprisingly" low [Behrman & Deolalikar, 1988; Bouis & Haddad, 1992]; one of many plausible explanations relates to the fact that leisure will normally be substituted for income as *income* rises, thereby reducing energy requirements, but with an offsetting "substitution effect" of work for leisure if the *wage-rate* is rising. Third, the timing and intra-household allocation of energy stress *among* the poor may have major, researchable implications, differing among types of labour, and of policy to affect the balance among those types; the food-related issues are treated here in Section II.4.C; issues of timing of work and labour income are deferred to Section II.10.

1. Adaptation and labour research

In an important, challenging contribution to the economics and moral philosophy of poverty, Dasgupta [1993, p. 474] makes the surprising suggestion that — because unable to adapt to undernutrition without severe damage by other means — the very poor (landless) are driven to price themselves out of the (rural unskilled) labour market, where the landed deficit farmer "can undercut" them. This is supposed to happen because the landless: "must" earn sufficient to meet their *total* energy requirements; have no land of their own to help in this task; and are too weak to do so from agricultural labour (and to meet its *extra* energy costs) unless they receive a quite high piece rate.[11] At a lower rate — which it pays a deficit (part-time) farmer to accept, because he *does* have land of his own to help feed him — the very poor (on Dasgupta's account) find that farm labour is a less efficient way to use energy than is CPR activity, scavenging and begging. These latter activities, however, earn too little energy to enable the very poor to escape poverty. Rationed out of farm labour by the only means of adaptation available to them — viz. by rejection of (farm) work with relatively low work-to-food conversion efficiency — the very poor are rationed into residual activity that earns so little as to lock them into their poverty.

The Dasgupta argument (1) is one of a big set of positive-feedback, vicious-circle explanations of the "too poor and hungry to work hard" type, (2) thus belongs to a set of explanations with much to commend it, and of high relevance for labour research, but (3) in my judgement, is not a very convincing example of these explanations, because it is hard to reconcile with some widely observed facts, and in particular with the nature and scope for *adaptation* [Dubos, 1965; Payne & Lipton, 1994].[12]

---

[11] The argument is complicated by Dasgupta's assumption that, for the big farm-employer to maximize profit, he has to pay an efficiency wage rate — maximizing his net return from the worker, allowing for the impact of the wage-payment on her nutrition and hence work — to each work-seeker (landless and deficit-farm landed alike).

[12] Dasgupta (pers. comm.) stresses that the one-period sketch of his model, reported above, does not do justice to the full, two-period formulation. On day one, initially "equal" landless workers present themselves for day-labour. At the efficiency-wage, some are rationed out of work. On day two and subsequently, these increasingly undernourished workers become progressively less prepared to accept (harder) day-labour in preference to

Dasgupta (Chs. 14-15) may well be right to cast grave doubt on the argument [Sukhatme & Margen, 1982] that the undernourished can significantly respond to energy stress by biologically raising either metabolic efficiency (e.g. lowering BMR) or working efficiency. However, these *intrapersonal*, *short-term intertemporal* and *biological* adaptations to energy stress are much less important as "weapons of the weak" than three others [Payne & Lipton, 1994]. These are *(a)* short- and medium-term *behavioural* adaptations (to physiology and other sources of energy balance) especially at work; *(b)* *long-term* intertemporal (including inter-generational) biological adaptations of physiology to the nature and timing of energy stress; *(c)* cross-sectional (i.e. *interpersonal*), static (atemporal) specializations — by households, in response to the fact that they comprise different sets of persons, of given physiology — that involve selecting many things, including types of work, along the lines of least comparative disadvantage. *A crucial area for food/labour research is to identify sets of policies, behaviours, and labour-market environments that, without disastrously disrupting the above coping strategies, create options for people, now locked into them, to find poverty-escaping alternatives.*

(a)   Lean, short, or hungry people do a given job in different ways from heavy, tall, or well-fed people. The former group, unless "severely undernourished" according to conventional anthropometry, need not be less energy-efficient (i.e. need not use up more food calories per unit of work done), and certainly need not be less task-efficient (i.e. need not use up more food calories per "piece" of output produced). Jobs done slowly *may* be done better, per calorie of food used up, than jobs done energetically.

(b)   Families, if poor and hungry for generations, select against genes (and children) that carry high dietary energy requirements. Mild to moderate stunting in youth is in effect selected for — so as to avoid the much graver risk of wasting in adulthood. Stunting, even if mild, is indeed "no more healthy than scar tissue is healthy" [Martorell, 1985], but until the risk of burning (undernourishment) is abolished, scar tissue (shortness, leanness, and low BMI) may be the least bad option. Its consequence is that:

(c)   The "hereditarily" landless/poor/small will specialize in work where they have least comparative disadvantage. Need this trap them into poverty? No, because fortunately some such types of work actually

---

(less well-rewarded) residual work on begging, CPRs, etc.

often show *absolute* advantage for the small. Dasgupta rightly emphasizes that big people have high VO_2max — prolonged maximum oxygen processing capacity. This indeed provides big people with absolute productivity advantage over small people in work mostly involving heavy lifting, such as lumbering or cane-cutting. However, small people have as high, or even higher, VO_2 max *per kg of body weight* than large people. Also, being small, they need to spend lower proportions of working effort in moving their bodies around, alongside the hoe or the ploughshare. This provides small people with absolute, not just comparative, advantage over large people, in terms of calories of food required per piece of work performed, if that "piece" requires mainly movement of the body, not heavy lifting, pulling or pushing. Most agricultural tasks in fact fall into the former category. This is consistent with the nearly universal observation that the very poor and landless spend a *larger* share of work time in hired farm labour than do the moderately poor or non-poor small farmers, and receive a *smaller* income per hour, though not usually per piece. Dasgupta's argument that the poor and undernourished are driven biologically to be on offer to the farm employer only at an efficiency-wage that — in competition with the deficit farmer — prices them out of unskilled labour markets (because CPR, etc., work is more energy-efficient for the poor) runs against these facts — and against the steady decline of CPRs and of poor people's income and work from them [Jodha, 1986].

I *hypothesize* that the conflict between theory and fact arises because Dasgupta's outcome, with the very poor rationed out of farm labour and into CPR work or begging, is in fact a knife-edge, or at best a middle régime. In "bad" cases, people who cannot afford the calories for farm work are liable to starve. In "good" cases, such people engage in adaptation — short-term behavioural, and long-term biological (though probably rather little short-term biological adaptation *à la* Sukhatme-Margen) and hence we see a set of chosen specializations by very poor (small) people in unskilled labour markets. The *test* of my hypothesis is the forms taken by such specializations; if it is correct, its *labour policy implication* is the need selectively to train, empower, or "enasset" precisely workers in those specializations. If technology is flexible enough — and if derived demand for trained, etc., labour is reasonably price-elastic! — this is quite a promising way forward. Skill and education are complementary with higher wage-rates even in "unskilled" farm labour [Jamison & Lau, 1982]. Neither the acquisition nor the exercise of such skills usually requires a high or rising VO_2 max, though exceptions do exist.

B. Income-elasticity of demand for energy

Recently, a major challenge to the view that undernutrition is due mainly to poverty has arisen from Behrman's work, and more generally from a number of observations that, properly measured, *energy intake* at the mean rises by only 1 to 3 per cent in poor populations when income (or expenditure) rises by 10 per cent [Bouis & Haddad, 1992; Behrman & Deolalikar, 1988]. This finding — together with the fact that expenditure-elasticity of *food outlay* among the very poor is increasingly found to disobey Engel's Law, i.e. to be not significantly below unity [Bhanoji Rao, 1981; Lipton, 1983b; Poleman & Edirisinghe, 1983; Hassan & Babu, 1991] — strongly suggests that the poor as a whole do not perceive extra calories (as opposed to pleasanter, more varied diets) as an over-riding unmet need. However, more carefully considered, these findings redirect our attention to three critical distinctions: between *(a)* the undernourished ultra-poor and the "under-opportunitied" moderately poor; between *(b)* the effects on calorie requirements of extra income due to extra work, to higher wage-rates, or to non-labour sources; and between *(c)* use by poor people of extra resources to increase calorie intake and use to increase calorie adequacy relative to requirements. All these distinctions, in the light of Behrman's work, are of crucial importance for labour research.

A large majority of studies, investigating elasticities of (i) health and work performance with respect to energy intakes, (ii) calorie intakes with respect to income or expenditure (CIEs), find sharp increases — perhaps simple thresholds [Lipton, 1983b], but probably more complex non-linearities [Pelletier, 1991] — around low energy intake levels, usually below those typical of "poverty line" levels of income per consumer unit. CIEs estimated at the mean, therefore, considerably understate CIEs for, say, the lower quartile. This is true even if the "mean" is for total populations around, or even somewhat below, the poverty line. Further-more, even if the lower quartile's CIE is also as low as 0.25 or thereabouts, the response of health and work performance to even a modest increase in energy intake — and hence in income, even with a fairly low CIE — could be substantial, either because of thresholds in (say) immune response functioning around some level of energy adequacy, or because energy intake is closely clustered around the apparent requirements level, as appears to be the case for the rural poor in an excellent Indonesian data set [Ravallion, 1990].

The above helps to explain the importance of income and expenditure to energy and health/work-performance, even with a low observed CIE at the mean — i.e. a *low beta* in (log-linear) regressions of properly-measured energy intake on properly-instrumented[13] total income (or expenditure), together with other explanatory variables. However, there is also reason for concern about the *low r^2* in such regressions (typically, "poverty" plus other variables "explain" only 5-15 per cent of interpersonal variation in energy intakes), and about the often *low or marginal t-statistics*.

I conjecture [1989] that this is largely explained by the aggregation of such equations across three types of source of extra income-and-expenditure. These three sources modify the effect of extra income (and total expenditure) on the *choice* of amount of energy, i.e. calories, purchased, because the sources have quite different likely impact on energy *requirements*. Income can increase (or be more for some people than for others):

(a) because more effort is put into work at the same rate of reward, so that energy requirements rise;

(b) because the wage-rate rises, so that energy requirements may rise or fall, according to whether substitution-effect (of income for leisure) outweighs or is outweighed by income-effect [Robbins, 1930]; or

(c) because non-labour income, e.g. remittance income, rises, normally with the result that the duration and/or intensity of work effort are reduced, so that energy requirements fall — in which case some of the extra welfare is taken by replacing labour-income by leisure.

These three cases respectively amplify, complicate, and diminish the direct effect of extra income, via extra demand, upon extra energy intake. Since measured CIEs are estimated in equations that seldom include dummies (or other methods) to separate the cases, we may conjecture that low r^2's and t-statistics are likely. Field research is needed to quantify (or refute) this conjecture.

Such research will help to show *what* sort of work situations do — and do not — help *which* poor people to escape undernutrition. Other

---

[13] See Behrman [1991], who proves that lower (and more accurate) estimates of CIEs are normally obtained by *(a)* proper measurement, involving, among other things, allowing for meals eaten at work (largely by the poor) or served to workers (largely by the non-poor), *(b)* proper instrumenting of total expenditures — necessary because food expenditure is so large a part of them that their residuals and its own (and therefore, to some extent, those of energy intake) usually show strong positive correlation.

relevant variables involved may include intra-household energy allocations (and hence perhaps worker/dependent ratios); manner of working (piece, duration, etc.); non-energy nutritional content of foods (iron, vitamin A or zinc may "potentiate" the capacity of energy intake to enhance health or work performance); and timing or frequency of energy intake. However, before testing for the impact of many complicating variables, the first step is to estimate CIEs — in various poor urban and rural situations — allowing for changes, or differences, in rates of wages (or self-employment earnings), in worked time, and in non-wage income. This is, in my view, a high priority for research by, or supported by, ILO and/or FAO.

C. Timing, location and allocation of energy stress

A major recent trend in applied development research has been the emphasis on food security — in the extreme case, from famine — and on the reduction of vulnerability, achieved mainly by stabilizing and increasing "food entitlements" of groups at risk [Sen, 1981], as the main way to attack poverty. Accompanying this has been emphasis on localized, and intra-household, variation in the adequacy of food to meet energy requirements. Most of this literature, though not Sen himself, tends to run together two separate issues:

1. To what extent is undernutrition[14] caused by — or (not the same thing) cost-effectively treated by improving — levels of nearby food availability, food production, energy requirements of work or illness, or "simply" real income (usually the main determinant of "entitlements" to available food) for groups at risk? Note that membership of such groups varies over the life-cycle; and that the "best" way to raise real income (and hence market-based food entitlements) of the poor may be to improve incentives[15] or technologies for food production, which is usually more unskilled-labour-intensive (and with a higher employment multiplier) than are most alternative rural or urban production activities.

---

[14] Despite a modest amount of recent protein revisionism, it remains the consensus that the overwhelming majority of sufferers from PEM (protein-energy malnutrition) would get sufficient protein, if only their current food intake were boosted by raising energy levels. Micronutrient deficiencies are of widespread importance, but the most cost-effective and sustainable treatment is seldom (as it often is for PEM) to increase poor people's incomes.

[15] Most research, however, indicates that dearer food harms the poor on balance in the short-to-medium term; even among the *rural* poor (even in most of Africa), a substantial majority comprises net food buyers.

2. To what extent are undernutrition and poverty caused by fluctuations, local differences, or intrahousehold misallocations, either in access to work and income (Section II.10) or in food availability or need (see this section)? Note that, even if a village, household, or person has adequate average command over food to meet requirements — i.e. even if nutritional inadequacies happen only when there are fluctuations, highly localized differences, or intra-household misallocations of foods, tasks, or both — it does not follow that the most cost-effective remedy for inadequate nutrition is to reduce intra-household misallocations, localized variations, and/or fluctuations. Raising the typical poor household's average income may be a much cheaper, or even the only feasible, remedy — whether for the household itself or for policy-makers.

This said, timing, spacing and intra-household allocation — both of food and of the sources of energy needs, notably work and illness — are associated with a lot of energy stress. "Only" 3-7 per cent of under-fives in LDCs are severely undernourished, and the proportion has been falling [Bengoa & Donosa, 1974; Keller & Fillmore, 1983; Garcia & Mason, 1992]; yet some 15-25 per cent of populations in low-income countries have incomes carrying serious *risk* of severe undernourishment [Lipton, 1983b]. Who gets "caught" varies over seasons [Chambers et al. (eds.), 1981], localized harvest failures, life-cycles, and with price-induced fluctuations in entitlements [Sen, 1981]; across space; and according to allocation rules and decisions.

On timing, Edmundson and Sukhatme [1990] conclude that the *main* problem of low energy intakes is that normal reserves may not suffice to cope with extra stress. In rural India, the very poor at any time — i.e. those whose energy adequacy is likeliest to be threatened — are less likely to be in chronic poverty (throughout the period of the panel), and much more likely to be in transient poverty, than are the moderately poor [Gaiha, 1989]. Bhattacharya et al. [1991], for six villages in West Bengal, confirm that the poorest suffer much more fluctuating — but not less — daily intake of staple food than the moderately-poor. In Bangladesh, where girls aged 2-5 are clearly likelier to die than boys, it is in times of acute need that this differential is clearest [D'Souza & Chen, 1980]. Sen [1981] points out that the largest death-rate gaps between labourers and farmers usually appear during, or just after, periods of acute failures in entitlements to food.

The fact that energy stresses, or its consequences, fluctuate does not, of course, prove that it is more cost-effective to treat (or to help people treat) energy-balance *declines*, rather than low *average* adequacy. The lag structures need more research: in Côte d'Ivoire higher food prices (i.e. lower real incomes) do more damage — especially for the poorest households — to shorter-run indicators of nutrition status such as children's weight-for-height and adult BMI, but amount and quality of localized, precisely defined health infrastructure does more to affect long-run child nutrition indicators such as height-for-age [Thomas et al., 1992, p. 5].

Compared to the mass of work on *timing* of energy stress (see the reports in Sahn (ed.) [1989]; Payne & Lipton [1994, Ch. 2]) — and although casual empiricism suggests *locational* differences in stress are almost as important for the poor — very little work exists on such differences. Yet there is:

(a)   a known geography of diseases (e.g. malaria) and of deficiencies of micronutrients (e.g. iodine);

(b)   some evidence that diseases interact, to produce bad health outcomes, with energy stress (see Stephenson et al. [1986] on schistosomiasis);

(c)   reason to believe that micronutrient deficiencies, e.g. of zinc, iron or vitamin A, do so also.

On food allocation by households, Harriss [1986] surveys evidence demonstrating bias against girls aged 0-5 for Bangladesh, parts of Northern India, but not elsewhere in Asia; Svedberg [1990] demonstrates the absence of nutritional gender bias in Africa. Girls' inferior access to health care, rather than to food itself, is often the main cause of their worse nutritional status and performance where it exists for dysentery treatment in Bangladesh). This illustrates *both* that nutritional status depends on illness as well as food intake and work, *and* (as per Drèze & Sen (eds.) [1991]) that poverty can often be uncoupled from undernutrition by appropriate public action.

How food security is allocated depends on who allocates, not just on who earns. What can be called the liquidity theory of marginal income — that men's becomes alcohol, but women's becomes breastmilk — is naïve about fungibility, income pooling, and household decision structures. Female-headed households do seem to show a significantly higher calorie-income elasticity than the typical male-headed household (Garcia [1991, Table 5] for the Philippines] and the effect is stronger in poor households, in both Kenya and Malawi [Kennedy & Peters, 1992]. However, this may well be because female-headed households are smaller, especially among the poor (Greer & Thorbecke [1986, p. 86] for Kenya).

Year-to-year variations in a family's access to income and other claims, and hence to food adequacy — being dependent on weather and prices as well as on life-cycle events — are not individually (or collectively) predictable, but may be directly or indirectly insurable. Seasonal variations are individually (and collectively) predictable, but not insurable. A large number of studies [Sahn (ed.), 1989; Chambers et al. (eds.), 1981] show that poor people experience substantial variations in seasonal and annual food adequacy. This is partly because variations in labour requirements for energy often aggravate (rather than offsetting):

(a)   variations in food intake, and in its determinants such as employment income, food prices, and home stores; and

(b)   variations in non-labour requirements for energy, e.g. to fight infections.

These "perverse" correlations do not indicate failure either of individual adaptation or of market functioning. In Bangladesh, individual adaptation to seasonal energy stress is — as it must be — so finely tuned that births, and therefore conceptions, are so timed as to reduce risk of overlap of the most critical times for energy adequacy (second half of wet season) and for child immunity (during the switch from passive to active immunity, i.e. age 6-12 months) [Schofield, 1974].

There is growing evidence that seasonal fluctuations in body weight are much too small to "capture" the required responses to varying energy stress [Ferro-Luzzi, 1992]. It probably has to be discretionary activity, work *methods*, or (to a small extent only) BMR that is "adapted". Over the longer span, plasticity of response - the ability of an organism to adjust growth-rates to stress, and then catch up — declines rapidly in the early years of life [Eveleth & Tanner, 1976].

Policy-makers are often rightly advised to seek labour-intensive options, so as to pull up demand (and thus wage-rates, in some cases, as well as employment) for the labour of the poor. A familiar caveat is the need to avoid doing so just when seasonal peaks of employment already create "islands" of labour scarcity, even in oceans of labour surplus. Less widely recognized is the need to check that the timing *and allocation* of extra labour requirements does not damage poor people at periods of energy stress. For example, Kumar [1977] has shown pronounced seasonal variation — from positive to negative — in the effect on the nutritional status of children of extra work and income for their mothers.

5. Land ownership and poverty

The modest aim of most of the research reported here is to track the bivariate links between poverty — its incidence, severity, location, timing — and other variables, ideally at individual or household level, but otherwise through cross-sections of places, or time-series of a particular area. Where causal inferences seem possible, they are suggested. This partial-equilibrium approach is at best risky and doubtful, but it is all we have; general-equilibrium models are interesting, but have many problems and anyway exclude many key "political economy" variables. However, in the case of land, it is especially dangerous to equate modest, partial-equilibrium statements such as "Landless X is much likelier to be poor than landed Y" to interesting, general-equilibrium statements like "Areas of nations are likelier to contain many poor people — other things being the same — if they have unequal land rights and much landlessness".

Land distribution affects the demand for consumer loans, and hence the market for savings and investment. Land distribution also affects the transaction-costs of labour use by farmers, and hence not only the demand and supply of labour, but also the direction of indeed technical progress. Finally and less quantifiably, land distribution affects the gains and losses to rural élites from most sorts of State action. So the direct effect of land-rights on poverty cannot be even approximately reduced to the "crude question" of whether the landless are poorer than the landed — especially since a growing majority of the rural poor, and almost all the urban poor, derive more income from work than from operating farms, and are net buyers of farm products. The land-poverty relationship — and the argument for (or against) land reform as a remedy for poverty — must be evaluated increasingly by its effects on those who remain poor workers and net food buyers, rather than on potential land-reform beneficiaries.

Nevertheless, the "crude question" is important in itself. In 1983, of Indian rural households living mainly from farm employment income, 45 per cent were poor — as against 24 per cent of households living mainly from farming. In 1987-88, of the 35 per cent of Indian households mainly engaged in agriculture, but owning or renting in no (or below 1/10 ha.) of land, some 43 per cent were poor; of those cultivating 0.1-0.4 ha., some 26 per cent were poor; and the proportions fall steadily to 10 per cent for 8 ha. and above [Dev et al., 1991, pp. 58, 88]. Landholding size is a quite good correlate of reduced poverty risk in Bangladesh, though poverty reduction by land-contingent targeting has limited scope [Ravallion & Sen, 1992]. Smaller holdings tend to comprise better land [Bhalla & Roy, 1988], so that this cross-section relationship would be even stronger if land were measured in efficiency-units. The landlessness-poverty link is so strong, in part, because those earning income mostly as farm employees do not, in many cases, have more access to non-farm income if they are landless than if they also operate a small farm (see Shankar [1993] for a study of three villages].

The landlessness-poverty link is generally confirmed by single-village studies [Lanjouw & Stern, 1991]. However, in arid and semi-arid areas, it breaks down. In Rajasthan and Maharashtra in 1977-78 even 3 hectares of owned land — normally cropland — did not confer a lower incidence of poverty than did landlessness. In Northern Nigeria and Burkina Faso, landlessness may be a proxy for ability to work (at better returns) in the non-farm sector, and is not well correlated with poverty [Delgado et al., 1991].

The rural poor are (a) increasingly earning income from farm work rather than from land operation, (b) increasingly net food buyers, (c) much more often than was once believed in *transient* poverty, especially as drought reduces demand for hired farm labour. The impact of landlessness and smallholding on poverty, therefore, needs to be judged by its effects on the poor through these three channels.

Easiest is (a). Smallness and equality of operated landholdings almost always raise per-hectare labour input by a larger proportion than they raised the ratio of family to hired labour [Booth & Sundrum, 1984]. Thus even the demand for *hired labour* per hectare is greater on smaller farms, or after a redistributive land reform. Moreover, *supply of hired labour* from farmers themselves is less if land operation is more equal — because there are fewer farm families with farms so small that they have a lot of "spare" working time to hire out. For both reasons, the landless poor gain farm employment, if farms are more equally distributed among the landed.

As for (b), smaller farmers generally produce a higher ratio of food to non-food, but also retain a larger proportion of product for home consumption. If the former effect is stronger — and I hypothesize that it is — then the poor gain as net food buyers if land is more equal among the landed.

Least is known about (c). A priori reasoning suggests a mixed outcome, for the landless poor, from equal/smaller-scale farming. It is likely to be somewhat lower-risk farming. However, in bad years, small farmers are likelier than big farmers to find it feasible and profitable to displace a substantial proportion of their hired workforce with family labour. Yet, even in a bad year, the *total* workforce per hectare will be larger with small-farm systems.

All this assumes no change in "relations of production" between landowner, operator (manager), and worker. Tenancy almost always comprises a *net* transfer of land from big to small farms [Singh, 1990] thus reducing poverty both among the latter and — via *(a)* above — among landless farmworkers. Little is known about employment-per-hectare with various types of tenancy contract, holding land size constant. Systematic changes in labour contracts have been associated with changing landholding conditions during the "green revolution" in Indonesia [Hart, 1986] and the Philippines [Hayami et al., 1990], but the net impact on poverty is not clear.

In brief, the history of East Asia, Latin America, and even West Bengal does tell us that more equal smallholdings benefit the poor. But this involves much more than the direct gain of land, even together with benefits from the inverse size-yield relationship, evidence for which is strong [Binswanger et al., 1994; Lipton, 1993]. General-equilibrium effects, not just from flows of incomes and inputs but from (partly interlinked) non-land factor markets and from redistribution of power, also affect the small-farm poor. And it is on the poorest of all — the landless net food buyer — that analysis of the effects of land distribution should increasingly concentrate.

6. Other tangible assets

Even more than that other negative, the RNFS, "tangible non-land assets" (TNLAs) are very heterogeneous. Can anything useful be said about their impact on the poor? We should bear in mind two distinctions: between TNLAs (or rights to them) that multiply income from work (e.g. land farmed by a worker-owner) and those that add to it (e.g. interest-bearing bonds) [Lipton, 1985]; and between TNLAs (or rights to them) that, actually or potentially, tend to be owned or controlled by the poor and those (such as infrastructure) that may benefit the poor though seldom owned by them.

As regards TNLAs (including rights to them) tending to be owned or controlled by the poor, there are three issues. What types of TNLAs are "desirable" by and for the poor? What types of TNLAs are in fact likelier to be owned or controlled by the poor? What can research tell us about the likely fate of schemes to get TNLAs to the poor — and, in particular, are there implications for new labour research?

Presumably, the poor — as compared with other people — would select, and benefit from, TNLAs that:

(a) multiply, rather than merely adding to, unskilled work income, because workforce participation increases with poverty down to the ultra-poverty threshold (Section II.3.B);

(b) stabilize income flows, since the poor are most exposed to variability in income and nutrition, and most harmed by a given downward fluctuation (Section II.4.C, II.10);

(c) reduce risk (not the same thing), since the poor are more risk-averse, and less able to bear or diffuse a given risk, than the non-poor;

(d) are divisible into small units, preferably with diseconomies of scale at large holding sizes;

(e) are labour-intensive in maintenance, enhancement and use;

(f) tend to raise the returns to *other* assets, including land, over which the poor have claims.

There is astonishingly little evidence on the distribution of claims on total assets, let alone on specific TNLAs. Obviously, overall, the poor have a much smaller share of such claims than of income; of income, than of expenditure; of expenditure, than of food expenditure; and of food expenditure, than of dietary energy intake or adequacy. One of the very few studies, in 1971-72 in India, showed that total tangible assets — financial, land, other physical assets — were 294 times larger per household in the richest decile than in the poorest, i.e. at least 700 times larger per person [Pathak et al., 1977, p. 507]. Yet calories-per-person can hardly vary by more than, say, 3 to 1.

Contrary to widespread belief, the poor are *not* likelier, relative to the rich, to own cattle than to own land in India [Lalwani, 1991], and are much less likely to own cattle than to have significant (claims on common) land in Botswana [Watanabe & Mueller, 1982, Table 3].

Smallstock, however, are more "divisible" blocks of value (and therefore embody less risk) than cattle, and are much more likely to be owned by the poorer rural groups. Yet India's main programme for subsidized asset distribution to the rural poor (IRDP) has concentrated heavily on livestock. Seabright [1991] shows that landless households were usually unable to manage the two cows allocated profitably, because of the cost of acquisition even after subsidy; yet, although this was too *large* a cash commitment for the poor, per-animal labour costs were inflated by the *small* number of cattle per household. Owned oxen may well be more useful, as sources of income, to the landed poor than to the landless poor, both because of lower feeding costs and because ox ownership (without a perfect draught-hire market) may be required to enable a mini-farmer to cultivate on own account, rather than renting out.

With growing pessimism about land reform, poor people's acquisition of RNFS assets, usually supported by credit, has become a major thrust of rural anti-poverty policy in South Asia. Attempts to replicate Bangladesh's Grameen Bank are under way in several African and Latin American countries. There is a need for prior review of the existing ownership structure, labour-intensity, and potential "manageability" by the poor of the particular assets, which schemes such as IRDP and Grameen are to encourage the poor to acquire.

Just as ownership of RNFS assets, notably livestock, has been widely identified as the road to far rural poverty reduction, so ownership of one form of TNLA — housing — has been identified as an urban priority for helping the poor. Indeed, urban anti-poverty policy has until very recently been very substantially focused on site-and-service and slum upgrading. A better house is a relatively low-risk asset for the poor, but only because it does very little to enhance their capacity to earn income from (inevitably somewhat risky) production. Until recently, indeed, most housing-focused programmes did little to build in physical support facilities for informal urban production.

There remains the question of whether TNLA helps the poor most cost-effectively if they own or control it (i.e. if it is heavily concentrated on items suitable for the poor to manage) or if it is present in other forms, even if owned by the non-poor or the public sector. Work in progress at IFPRI indicates that, in Bangladesh, Zambia and elsewhere, the incidence of rural poverty is strongly and inversely correlated with both the per-person value of total infrastructure, and the presence of key specific items of infrastructure. There is a chicken-and-egg problem about such findings — maybe widespread enrichment justifies the provision of infrastructure, rather than being induced by it — but they are suggestive. Harriss [1993], analysing the causes of poverty reduction across three surveys (1958-66, 1982, 1991) in a village in West Bengal, gives first place (above even land reform) to extra employment for the landless due to groundwater infrastructures. Given wage behaviour in India, irrigation infrastructure appears to be a much more "pro-poor" (and pro-growth) recipient of public-sector subsidies than either fertilizers or even food [Ratha & Sharma, 1992]. A simple model of the rice and labour markets in Bangladesh produces a similarly encouraging result for infrastructures of "irrigation-induced technical change" [Ahmed & Sampath, 1992].

This is not meant to denigrate TNLA asset ownership or control as a cure for poverty. (Indeed micro-irrigation capital — land or pedal pumps

— has proved in Bangladesh to be much more likely to remain owned and controlled by the very poor, selling water to larger farmers, than is land [Howes, 1982; Shankar, 1992].) However, the "cure" has been advocated — and supported with large amounts of scarce credit — with astonishingly little analysis of which TNLA assets the urban and rural poor now own and can manage productively. Nor has there been enough concern for secondary employment effects of "TNLA reform": effects known to be highly favourable for land redistribution.

7. Education and skills

There is a mass of evidence about the impact of a person's education on private earnings, employment (and thus income), and productivity. There is also much evidence of the response of a person's output to education. Further, East Asian countries achieving rapid and relatively egalitarian growth are well known for high and widespread initial literacy before, and for persistent outlay on education during, growth accelerations.

Surprisingly little analysis exists, however, of the household-level or national-level causal sequences that are supposed to lead from education outlays, via educational "assets", to reduced poverty risk (as opposed to higher expected income for the educated). It is familiar that even literacy declines as poverty increases, and that the higher the indicator of education the faster is such a decline. One's first thought is that the rich buy a fair amount of education for their children, so that publicly provided or heavily subsidized education is likely to benefit mainly the non-poor. However, this assumes that public-sector spending on education in developing countries is initially mainly on primary education (see, to the contrary, Schultz [1988, pp. 606-607]); and that such education provides clear gains to the poor.

There is little doubt that farm productivity [Jamison & Lau, 1982] and even the incomes of farm labourers [Chaudhri, 1979], are increased by education. However, many of the gains, especially from female education, may be indirect. It has been shown to increase expected age of marriage and to reduce marital fertility, and reduce infant and child mortality (Rosenzweig & Schultz [1982] for Colombia; Behrman & Deolalikar [1988]; Bourne & Walker [1991]). *Completed* primary education seems to be required to produce some of these effects [World Bank, 1984]. Kerala's much better performance on indicators of "social development", despite very low average incomes, seems to be explained, in a careful cross-section of Indian States, by higher public expenditure on social sectors, mainly education [Raut, 1993].

There is much evidence that it is opportunity-cost relative to perceived benefits, not direct cost, that often constrains poor parents from having their children educated. For example, Botswana is one of the few countries where boys are more likely than girls to drop out of primary school, because it is the boys who are expected to mind the cattle. However, educational planning can itself reduce those opportunity-costs, e.g. by timing school into the agricultural slack seasons. And the laws could be implemented — e.g. on child labour in India [Weiner, 1991] — if the State so decided. Too little is known about the trade-off between short-run losses and long-run gains, to poor parents and their children alike; and labour-market pressures interact strongly with those losses and gains.

8.   Health

There are big differences in life expectancy, infant mortality, and risk of illness between rich and poor countries in terms of average income per person [Behrman & Deolalikar, 1988, pp. 633-634]. "Outliers" can often be explained in terms of either income distribution or the degree of public-sector health and nutrition-linked activity [Sen, 1980]; indeed, recent research by Ravallion (personal communication) shows that it is poverty incidence, not average GNP, that explains the bulk of many of these differences. Further, there are some clear indicators *within* countries that groups exposed to poverty suffer higher death rates than other groups: Mitra [1978] cites striking micro-evidence for landless labourers vis-à-vis farmers in India, and Lipton and de Kadt [1988, pp. 51-53] summarize evidence that death and disease are linked to rurality, low access to land, and shortage of non-farm assets in several countries.

Yet we are, frustratingly, unable to identify — let alone to interrupt — causal chains from poverty to ill-health, except via undernutrition. Partly, this is because *demand* for health-inducing services is variable, by choice, among people, even poor people, with different trade-offs between (say) longevity and enjoyment while alive. Partly, it is because *supply* of such services varies within countries in ways very imperfectly linked to poverty: urban-rural differences in age- and sex-specific mortality rates are substantial [Lipton & Ravallion, 1994] and strongly related to access to services [Lipton, 1977]. Further, there exist "equal-opportunity diseases" from which income, and all it can buy, provide no protection. Finally, a study from Colombia [Rosenzweig & Schultz, 1982, p. 58] indicates that urban (though not rural) "public health institutions are substitutes" for the health knowledge and child-care associated with education (and non-poverty).

An excellent survey [Behrman & Deolalikar, 1988] teases out the links connecting supply and demand for health to the main outcomes. Yet they find that variation in incomes, prices, and household characteristics such as mother's schooling are seldom associated with more than 10 per cent of interpersonal variation in health status [ibid., p. 660]. In practice, poverty is linked as cause or effect to numerous variables — large households with sib crowding, residence in unhealthy or remote places, highly seasonal work, periods of energy stress — known themselves to be causes of illness or risk of death. Incompletely specified simultaneous models may understate the direct and indirect health damage from poverty, just as crude bivariate correlations overstate them. Infection and disability are also *causes* of poverty via lost labour-time (for data see Lipton [1983, pp. 11-15]), and the official data measure the extent to which sufferers report a condition in the hope of cure, at least as much as the incidence of that condition. Where, as in Kerala, primary health care is relatively good, the proportion of casual working time "lost" to *reported* sickness goes up to 10-15 per cent, from the otherwise typical Indian figures of 4-6 per cent [ibid., p. 13].

The emphasis in health policy on *(a)* pesticides, water quality, and other environmental hazards [Lipton & de Kadt, 1988, pp. 33-40]; *(b)* nutrition; and *(c)* AIDS have left almost neglected some areas of central interest for labour research in the area of poverty. *(d)* Until recently, almost no attention has been paid to the health (and financing) effects of the ageing of populations — even among the very poor — in Asia and Latin America. The upper boundary of "working age", especially in casual and informal work, is bound to rise. What can be done to mitigate the health effects on the poor? *(e)* A big and neglected problem in "poor people's health" comprises industrial, and even more agricultural, injuries, especially during wet weather and in peak seasons; added to this is the revival of tuberculosis and malaria. What innovations in the workplace (from scorpion boots via DEET to simple retiming of operations) could reduce the damage?

Lanjouw and Stern [1991] provide one of several careful micro-studies to show that poverty risks — and risk of *decline* into poverty — are strongly associated with illness. In their Indian village, households with land and a fit adult male were at much smaller risk of poverty than were other households. Of course the causation is mutual. But labour-related policy, and research against poverty, need to attend more to health issues.

9. Variation in space: Rural-urban and other issues

It is useful to structure the analysis of poverty in LDCs into "rural" and "urban", to the extent that we can answer "Yes" to four questions.

First, do LDCs usually comprise urban and rural places that are clearly distinct, and in which most people reside and work? On the whole, the answer seems to be Yes [Lipton & Ravallion, 1994]. Second, do levels of poverty differ systematically and substantially between rural and urban places? The answer is clearly Yes. For 13 developing countries with reliable data for the 1980s, rural/urban poverty incidence ratios range from 1.3 to 2.5 in nine Asian and Latin American cases, plus Indonesia 3.7, Ghana 4.2, Côte d'Ivoire 4.6 and Kenya 6.0. These data understate rural-urban poverty differences [ibid., pp. 40-41], mainly because state-provided goods are more unequally distributed between city and village than are the goods normally included in assessing rural and urban poverty.[16] They also ignore the much more serious rural impacts of *fluctuations* in poverty. Third, do rural and urban poverty differ in structure or type, relatedly to a specifically rural and/or urban physical or socio-economic environment? Clearly, this is so. The rural poor are more dependent on agriculture — central to rurality — than the rural non-poor in South and East Asia and in West Africa [Quibria & Srinivasan, 1991, p. 49; Hill, 1982; Delgado et al., 1991]. Finally, is poverty importantly related to interactions, equilibria, or imbalances between *rural* and *urban* (i) people or groups, e.g. consumers or producers; (ii) impacts of decisions by governments; or (iii) land, water, or other physical factors? This is still controversial, but the balance of evidence seems to me strongly favourable, especially in Africa (Lipton [1977]; and see papers in Moore & Harriss (eds.) [1984] and Varshney (ed.) [1993]).

Within rural areas, the poor are heavily concentrated in remote and unreliably watered places. In 1972-73, of the 56 rural regions — each treated as (more or less) homogeneous in India's National Sample Survey — all nine with poverty incidence above 60 per cent averaged below 1,540 mm/year of rainfall *and* had below 17 per cent of farmland irrigated. Not

---

[16] At this symposium, Dr. Jamal drew attention to his work with Dr. Weeks, illustrating big falls in urban formal sector wage rates — and hence, it was suggested, in the urban-rural disparity — in Africa in the 1980s. However: *(a)* there is no evidence that urban-rural disparity in mortality or in levels of living has fallen; *(b)* apart from trends in the informal sector (and in rural incomes), public-sector outlays on rural and agricultural objectives have fallen, offsetting the undoubted decline in officially-sponsored distortions of prices and exchange rates against rural people [Lipton 1990, p. 75]; *(c)* continuing (slow) rural-urban migration in Africa, despite negative or slow growth in real income per person, casts serious doubts on claims that urban bias has been substantially corrected overall.

one of the six regions with poverty incidence below 15 per cent (and only four of the 15 below 30 per cent) had rainfall below 1700 mm *and* irrigation below 19 per cent of farmland [Lipton, 1992, p. 3]. By the early 1980s, across 58 rural regions, "a strong correlation between agricultural output per worker and daily wage rate is found" [Quibria & Srinivasan, 1991, p. 72], and this also applies to all-India time-series [Gaiha & Spinedi, 1992]. Economists should expect capital and labour mobility, and therefore should find all this surprising. Presumably the transactions costs of migration for the poor, and of capital mobility towards low-wage areas, have proved prohibitive. Certainly these findings underscore the evidence that (location in areas of) transient, specifically drought-induced, poverty is a major component of poverty overall.

Within towns, there is much quantitative geographical work (not discussed here) on the location of poverty, transport costs, etc. So far as I know, little has been done on the distribution of poverty incidence or severity *among* towns of different size or types. In Mauritania in 1989-90 only 10 per cent of households in "main economic centres" were poor, as against 40 per cent in "other urban areas", 49 per cent in "rural centres" and 61-65 per cent in "other rural" [Coulombe & McKay, 1991].

Nor is a lot known about urban poverty by occupational structures. This may be a serious omission. For example, census and survey data for developing countries show that 8-15 per cent of *urban* populations, even in large cities, live mainly off income from (urban) agriculture. Is this — as casual empiricism suggests — strongly associated with poverty, female workers or gardeners, and casual labour?

10. Fluctuations, variations and compensations

We saw in Section II.4.C that much poverty is due to *fluctuations* in income and hence command over food. Because declines are from a barely adequate average, they push the victims into poverty. In labour markets, the poor are normally characterized by greater short-run, seasonal and year-to-year variability — in real wage-rates, time-rates of unemployment, and age- and sex-specific participation rates — than the non-poor. Especially for the poor, such fluctuations are not mutually compensating. In slack times (and places), reduced participation (downward shift of labour supply curve) tends to raise the real wage-rate, but this is outweighed by reduced employment (downward shift of labour demand curve). Thus employment, participation and the real wage-rate *for the poor* tend to rise together and to fall together [Lipton, 1983].

Similarly, variations in location or treatment (e.g. between city and village; progressive and "backward" regions; women and men; or persons of different caste or ethnic group) tend to saddle the poorer area or group with low wage rates, employment prospects, and participation rates, i.e. to worsen the spatial distribution of income among the poor. Once again, most economists would predict that such spreads would "normally" be reduced by factor-market adjustment. Their persistence is due partly to informational issues; only to a minor extent to segregation or *wage*-discrimination against groups that over-represent poor people; and substantially to *access* discrimination, in which outsiders, low-caste persons, and women are associated with low-income tasks. In short, the summary of evidence in Lipton [1983, pp. 23-38, pp. 54-60, pp. 69-84] still applies, though an up-to-date treatment would place more emphasis on search costs and other informational issues [Stiglitz, 1988], on adjustment of labour disequilibria through non-labour markets [Binswanger & Rosenzweig, 1981], and on general equilibrium [de Janvry & Sadoulet, 1987].

The surveys, revealing the importance of fluctuations and transient poverty, seldom tell us *why* income fluctuates downwards among the poor or near-poor. There are three broad causes: life-cycle variation; decline in labour income due to bad harvests (so smaller farm employers neither need nor can afford to hire workers), falling relative prices of labour-intensive products, or recession and adjustment; and random events, especially illness. Quite remarkably little research has been done on the sorts of rural work that are more — or less — vulnerable to these three sources of downward income fluctuation. What sorts of urban, farm, and RNFS activity are more readily "kept up" by (for example) a near-poor household comprising a pregnant mother, a young husband, and two small children? What if such a family is in a moderately drought-affected village, or a town affected by retrenchment? There is huge scope, here and elsewhere, for the sort of research in which ILO/WEP/IILS has shown absolute (not just comparative) advantage in the past two decades. Such research has much to contribute to our understanding of the causes, correlates and cures of poverty.

Acronyms

AE	adult equivalent
ASPR	age- and sex-specific participation ratio
CIE	calorie-income elasticity (i.e. elasticity to income-per-AE of the intake of dietary energy per AE)
CPR	common property resource(s)
IFPRI	International Food Policy Research Institute, Washington, D.C.
IRDP	Integrated Rural Development Programme, India (publicity subsidized programme of loans for poor people to acquire non-farm assets)
LDC	less developed country
NGO	non-governmental organization
PEM	protein-energy malnutrition (undernutrition)
RNFS	rural non-farm sector
ROSCA	rotating savings and credit association
SITC	Standard Industrial Trade Classification
TNLA	tangible non-land assets
TRU	time-rate of unemployment
WEP	World Employment Programme (ILO)

Bibliographical references

Ahmed, A. U. et al. 1992. "Effects of irrigation-induced technological change in Bangladesh rice production", in *American Journal of Agricultural Economics* (Ames), 74, 1.

Alam, S.; Martin, N. 1984. "Limiting the women's issue in Bangladesh", in *South Asian Bulletin*, 4, 2.

Anand, S. 1984. *Inequality-development and poverty in Malaysia.* New York, Oxford University Press, for World Bank.

Anand, S.; Kanbur, R. 1989. "The Kuznets process and the inequality-development relationship", in *Journal of Development Economics*, 16.

Anker, R.; Hein, C. 1985. "Why third world urban employers usually prefer men", in *International Labour Review*, 124, 1: 73-90.

Bardhan, P.K. 1985. "Women's work, welfare and status", in *Economic and Political Weekly* (Bombay), 20, 51-52.

—. 1982. *Land, labour and rural poverty.* Berkeley, University of California.

Beaton, G.H. et al. 1993. *Effectiveness of Vitamin A supplementation in the control of young child morbidity and mortality in developing countries.* ACC/SCN(UN) and International Nutrition Program. Toronto, Toronto University Faculty of Medicine.

Becker, G.; Lewis, H.G. 1974. "On the interaction between the quantity and quality of children", in *Journal of Political Economy* (Chicago), 81: 2, pt.2.

Behrman, J. 1991. "Nutrient intake-demand relations: incomes, prices, schooling", mimeo, Department of Economics, University of Pennsylvania.

Behrman, J.; Deolalikar, A. 1988. "Health and nutrition", in Chenery and Srinivasan (eds.), 1988.

Behrman, J.; Srinivasan, T.N. (eds.) 1994. *Handbook of development economics*, Vol. III. Amsterdam, North Holland.

Bengoa, J.; Donosa, G. 1974. "Prevalence of protein-calorie malnutrition, 1963 to 1973", in *Protein Advisory Group Bulletin*, 4, 1.

Bennett, L. 1991. *Gender and poverty in India.* Country study. Washington, DC, World Bank.

Besley, T. 1994. "Saving, credit and insurance", in Behrman and Srinivasan (eds.), 1994.

Besley, T.; Kanbur, R. 1993. "Principles of targeting", in Lipton and van der Gaag (eds.), 1993.

Bhalla, S.; Roy, P. 1988. "Mis-specification in farm productivity analysis: the role of land quality", in *Oxford Economic Papers*, 40, 1.

Bhanoji Rao, V. 1981. "Measurement of deprivation and poverty based on proportion of income spent on food", in *World Development*, 9, 4.

Bharat, S. 1988. "Children of single parents in a slum community", in *Indian Journal of Social Work*, 49, 4.

Bhattacharya, N. et al. 1991. "How do the poor survive?", in *Economic and Political Weekly*, 26, 7.

Binswanger, H.; Rosenzweig, M. 1981. *Contractual arrangements, employment and wages in rural labour markets*. New York, Agricultural Development Council.

Binswanger, H. et al. 1994. "Power, distortions, revolt and reform in agricultural land relations", in Behrman and Srinivasan (eds.), 1994.

Binswanger, H.; Khandker, S. 1992. *The impact of formal finance on the rural economy of India*. Policy Research Writing Papers, No. 949. Washington, DC, World Bank.

Binswanger, H.; McIntire, J. 1987. "Behavioural and material determinants of productive relations in land-abundant tropical agriculture", in *Economic Development and Cultural Change*, 36, 1.

Birdsall, N. 1979. *Siblings and schooling in urban Colombia*. D.Phil. (unpublished). New Haven, Yale University.

—. 1980. *Population and poverty in the developing world*. Staff Working Paper No. 404, Washington, DC, World Bank.

Booth, A.; Sundrum, R.M. 1984. *Labour absorption in agriculture*. Delhi, Oxford University Press.

Boserup, E. 1965. *Conditions of agricultural progress*. Bombay.

Bouis, H.E; Haddad, L. 1992. "Are estimates of CIEs too high? A re-calibration of the plausible range", in *Journal of Development Economics* (Amsterdam), 39, 2: 333-64.

Bourne, K.; Walker, G. 1991. "The differential effect of mother's education on mortality of boys and girls in India", in *Population Studies* (London), 45: 203-219.

Braun, J. von; Kennedy, E. 1986. *Commercialization of subsistence agriculture*. Washington, DC, IFPRI.

Braun, J. von, et al. 1989. *Irrigation technology and the commercialization of rice in the Gambia: Effects on income and nutrition*. Research Report 75. Washington DC, IFPRI.

Buvinić, M. 1993. *The feminization of poverty? Research and policy needs*. Paper presented to the symposium on "Poverty: New approaches to analysis and policy", 22-24 November. Geneva, IILS.

Cain, M.T. 1991. "The activities of the rural elderly in Bangladesh", in *Population Studies* (London), 45, 2: 189-202.

Chambers, R. et al. (eds.) 1981. *Seasonal dimensions to rural poverty*. London, Pinter.

Chaudhri, D. 1979. *Education, innovations and agricultural development*. London, Croom Helm.

Chayanov, A. V. 1966. *Theory of peasant economy*. Ed. D. Thorner. Homewood, Irwin.

Chen, L. et al. 1981. "Sex bias in the family allocation of food and health care in rural Bangladesh", in *Population and Development Review* (New York), 17, 1.

Chenery, H.; Srinivasan, T.N. (eds.). 1988. *Handbook of development economics*, Vol. 1. Amsterdam, North Holland.

Collier, P. S. et al. 1986. *Labour and poverty in rural Tanzania*. Oxford, Oxford University Press.

Coulombe H.; Mckay, A. 1991. *The causes of poverty: A study based on the Mauritania Living Standards Survey 1989-90*. Working Paper, Washington DC, World Bank

D'Souza, S.; Chen, L.C. 1980. "Sex differentials in mortality in rural Bangladesh", in *Population and Development Review* (New York), 6, 2.

Dasgupta, B. 1977. *Village society and labour use*. Delhi, Oxford University Press.

DasGupta, M. 1987. "Punjab: selective discrimination against female children in India", in *Population and Development Review* (New York), 13, 1.

Dasgupta, P. 1993. *An inquiry into well-being and destitution*. Oxford, Clarendon.

Datta G.; Meerman, J. 1980. *Household income and household income per head in welfare comparisons*. Staff Working Paper No. 378. Washington, DC, World Bank.

de Janvry, A.; Sadoulet, E. 1987. "Agricultural price policy in general equilibrium models", in *American Journal of Agricultural Economics* (Ames), 69, 2.

de Soto, H. 1989. *The other path: The invisible revolution in the Third World*. London, I.B. Tauris.

Deaton, A.; Muellbauer, J. 1980. *Economics and consumer behaviour*. Cambridge, Cambridge University Press.

Deaton, A.; Paxson, C.H. 1991. *Patterns of ageing in Thailand and Côte d'Ivoire*. Working Paper No. 81, LSMS, Washington DC, World Bank.

Delgado, C. et al. 1991. "Coping with household-level food insecurity in drought affected areas of Burkina Faso", in *World Development* (New York), 16, 9.

Dev, S. M. 1991. "Non-agricultural employment in rural India: evidence at a disaggregate level", in *Economic and Political Weekly* (Bombay), 25, 28.

Dev, S. M. et al. 1991. *Rural poverty in India: Incidence, issues and policies*, Discussion Paper No. 55. Ahemedabad, Indira Gandhi Institute for Development Research.

Dickens, C. 1849-50. *David Copperfield*. London, Chapman and Hall.

Drèze, J. 1990. "Widows in rural India". DEP No. 26, Development Economics Research Programme, London, London School of Economics.

Drèze J.; Sen. A. K. (eds.). 1991. *The political economy of hunger*. Oxford, Clarendon Press.

Dubos, R. 1965. *Man adapting*. New York, Yale University Press.

Edmundson, W. C.; Sukhatme, P. V. 1990. "Food and work: Poverty and hunger", in *Economic Development and Cultural Change* (Chicago), 38 (2), Jan., pp. 263-280.

Eveleth, P.; Tanner, J. 1976. *Worldwide variation in human growth*. Cambridge, Cambridge University Press.

Ferro-Luzzi, A. 1992. Work-in-progress seminar, IFPRI, Washington, DC.

Foster, C. et al. 1984. "A class of decomposable poverty measures", in *Econometrica*, 52: 761-765.

Gaiha, R. 1989. "Poverty, agricultural production and price fluctuations in rural India: a reformulation", in *Cambridge Journal of Economics* (Cambridge), 13, 2.

Gaiha, R.; Kazmi, S. 1982. *Aspects of poverty in rural India*. Working Paper, Delhi, Faculty of Management Studies.

Gaiha, R.; Spinedi, M. 1992. "Agricultural wages, population and technology in Asian countries", in *Asian Survey*, 32, 5.

Garcia, M. 1991. "Impact of female sources of income on food demand among rural households in the Philippines", in *Quarterly Journal of International Agriculture* (Frankfurt-am-Main), 30, 2.

Garcia, M.; Mason, J. 1992. *Second report on the world nutrition situation*, Administrative Committee on Co-ordination - Sub-committee on Nutrition. Geneva, United Nations.

Glewwe, P. 1990. "Investigating the determinants of household welfare in Côte d'Ivoire". LSMS Working Paper No. 71. Washington DC. World Bank.

—. 1992. "Targeting assistance to the poor: efficient allocation of transfers when household income is not observed", in *Journal of Development Studies* (London), 38, 2: 297-321, April.

Greenhalgh, S. 1985. "Sexual stratification: The other side of 'growth with equity' in East Asia", in *Population and Development Review* (New York), 11, 2.

Greer J.; Thorbecke, E. 1986. *Food poverty and consumption patterns in Kenya*. Geneva, ILO.

Guhan, S.; Bharathan, K. 1984. *Dusi: a re-survey*. Working Paper No. 52, Madras, Madras Institute of Development Studies.

Haddad, L. 1991. "Gender and Poverty in Ghana", in *IDS Bulletin* (Brighton), 22, 1.

Hagenaars A.J.M.; Van Praag, B. 1985. "A synthesis of poverty line definitions", in *Review of Income and Wealthy* (New Haven), 139-154.

Hajnal, J. 1982. "Two kinds of pre-industrial household formation system", in *Population and Development Review* (New York), 8, 3.

Hansen, B. 1969. *Economic development in Egypt*, Memorandum RM-5961-FF, Santa Monica, Rand Corporation.

Hanson, J.A.; Lieberman, S.S. 1989. *India: Poverty, employment and social services*. Washington DC, World Bank.

Harriss, B. 1986. "The intra-family distribution of hunger in South Asia". In Drèze and Sen (eds.), 1991.

Harriss, J. 1993. "What is happening in rural West Bengal? Agrarian reform, growth and distribution", in *Economic and Political Weekly* (Bombay), June 12.

Hart, G. 1986. "Exclusionary labour arrangements: interpreting evidence on employment trends in rural Java", in *Journal of Development Studies*, (London) 22, 4.

Hassan, R.; Babu, C. 1991. "Measurement and determinants of rural poverty: Household consumption patterns and food poverty in rural Sudan", in *Food Policy* (Guildford), 16, 6: 451-60.

Hayami, Y.; Ruttan, V. 1985. *Agricultural development: An international perspective*. Baltimore, Johns Hopkins.

Hayami, Y. et al. 1990. *Towards an alternative land reform paradigm: A Philippine perspective*. Manila, Ateneo de Manila University Press.

Hazell, P.; Ramaswamy, C. (eds.). 1992. *The green revolution reconsidered*. Baltimore, Johns Hopkins.

Helmsing, A. 1991. *Small-scale rural industries in Zimbabwe: an overview*. Working Paper No. 17, Harare, Zimbabwe Experimental Research Organization.

Hill, P. 1982. *Dry grain farming families*. Cambridge, Cambridge University Press.

Hoff, K. et al. (eds.) 1992. *The economics of rural organisation: Theory, practice and policy*. New York, Oxford University Press.

Hopper, D. 1955. "Seasonal labour cycles in an Eastern Uttar Pradesh village", in *The Eastern Anthropologist, VIII*, 3-4

Howes M. 1982. "The creation and appropriation of value in irrigated agriculture: a comparison of the deep tubewell and the handpump in rural Bangladesh". In Howes M. and M. Greeley (eds.), *Rural Technology, Rural Institutions and the Rural Poorest*. Dhaka, CIRDAP/IDS.

Jackson J.C.; Collier, P. 1988. *Incomes, poverty and food security in the communal lands of Zimbabwe*. Occ. Paper 10, Dept. of Rural and Urban Planning. Harare, University of Zimbabwe.

Jamison. D.; Lau, L. 1982. *Farmer education and farm efficiency*. Baltimore, Johns Hopkins University Press.

JASPA (Jobs and Skills Programme for Africa). 1990. *Strategies for employment creation in Africa*. Addis Ababa, JASPA.

Jodha, N.S. 1986. "Common property resources and rural poor in dry regions of India", in *Economic and Political Weekly* (Bombay), 21: 1169-1181.

—. 1988. "Poverty debate in India: A minority view", in *Economic and Political Weekly* (Bombay), 23: 45-47.

Kakwani, N. 1993. "Measuring poverty: definitions and significance tests with application to Côte d'Ivoire". In Lipton and van der Gaag (eds.), 1993.

Keller, W.; Fillmore, C. 1983. 'Prevalence of protein-energy malnutrition", in *World Health Statistics Quarterly*, 36: 129-167.

Kennedy, E.; Peters, P. 1992. "Household food security and child nutrition: the interaction of income and gender of household head", in *World Development* (New York), 20 (8).

Klitgaard, R. 1991. *Adjusting to reality: Beyond the market and the State*. San Francisco, Institute for Contemporary Studies.

Krishnaji, N. 1984. "Family size, levels of living and differential mortality in rural India: some paradoxes", in *Economic and Political Weekly* (Bombay), 9 (6).

—. 1987. "Poverty and sex ratio: some data and speculations", in *Economic and Political Weekly* (Bombay), 22, 23.

—. 1989. "The size and structure of agricultural labour households in India". In Rodgers, G. (ed.), 1989.

Krishnamurthy, J. 1988. "Unemployment in India: The broad magnitudes and characteristics". In Srinivasan and Bardhan (eds.), 1988.

Kumar, S. 1977. *Role of the household economy in determining child nutrition at low income levels: a case study of Kerala*, Occasional Paper No. 95, Division of Nutritional Sciences. Ithaca, N.Y., Cornell University.

Lal, D. 1988. "Trends in real wages in rural India 1880-1980". In Srinivasan and Bardhan (eds.), 1988.

Lalwani, M. 1991. "Technological change: scale biases in the distribution of output and employment gains in India's dairy farming sector", in *Social Action* (New Delhi), 41 (1).

Lanjouw, P.; Stern, N. 1991. "Poverty in Palanpur", in *World Bank Economic Review* (Washington), 5, 1: 23-55.

Lanjouw, P.; Ravallion, M. 1994. *Poverty and household size*, Policy Research Working Paper WPS1332. Washington DC, World Bank.

Lazear, E.; Michael, R. 1980. "Family size and the distribution of per capita income", in *American Economic Review* (Nashville), 70, 1.

Lecaillon, J.; Paukert, F. et al. 1984. *Income distribution and economic development: An analytical survey*. Geneva, International Labour Office.

Levinson, 1974. *Morinda: An economic analysis of malnutrition amoung young children in rural India*. International Nutrition Policy Series. Cambridge, Mass., Cornell University and Massachusetts Institute of Technology.

Lewis, W.A. 1954. "Economic development with unlimited supplies of labor", in *Manchester School*.

Lipton, M. 1977. *Why poor people stay poor: Urban bias and world development*. London, Temple Smith.

—. 1983. *Labour and poverty*. Staff Working Paper No. 616. Washington DC, World Bank.

—. 1983a. *Demography and poverty*. Staff Working Paper No. 623. Washington DC, World Bank.

—. 1983b. *Poverty, undernutrition and hunger.* Staff Working Paper No. 597. Washington DC, World Bank.

—. 1984. "Urban bias revisited". In J. Harriss and M.P. Moore (eds.), *Development and the rural-urban divide.* London, Cass.

—. 1985. *Land assets and rural poverty.* Staff Working Paper No. 744. Washington DC, World Bank.

—. 1985a. "A problem in poverty measurement", in *Mathematical Social Sciences*, 10: 91-97.

—. 1989. "Attacking undernutrition and hunger: some issues of adaptation and sustainability". Pew Lecture series. Ithaca, Cornell University

—. 1990. "State compression: friend or foe of agricultural liberalization?", in Indian Society of Agricultural Economics, *Agricultural development policy: Adjustments and reorientation.* New Delhi, Oxford University Press.

—. 1991. "Responses to rural population growth: Malthus and the moderns". In McNicoll, G. and M. Cain (eds,), *Rural development and population: Institutions and policy,* New York, Oxford University Press.

—. 1992. "Forces for change in dryland agriculture", mimeo, Rome, IFAD.

—. 1993. "Land reform as commenced business: the evidence against stopping", in *World Development,* 21, 4: 641-657.

Lipton, M.; Ravallion, M. 1994. "Poverty and policy". In Behrman and Srinivasan (eds.), 1994.

Lipton, M.; de Kadt, E. 1988. *Agriculture-health linkages.* Geneva, WHO.

Lipton, M. with Longhurst, R. 1989. *New seeds and poor people.* London, Unwin Hyman.

Lipton, M.; van der Gaag, J. (eds.). 1993. *Including the poor.* Regional and Sectoral Studies. Washington DC, World Bank.

Lloyd, C.B.; Brandon, A.J. 1991. *Women's role in maintaining households: Poverty and gender inequality in Ghana.* Washington DC, International Center for Research on Women.

Malthus, T.R. 1798/1803/1960. *Essay on the principle of population* (ed. as *On population* by G. Himmelfarb). New York, Modern Library.

Martorell, E. 1985. "Child growth retardation: A discussion of its causes and its relationship to health". In Blaxter, K. and Waterlow, J.C. (eds.). *Nutritional adaptation in man.* London, Libbey

Maxwell S.; Fernando, A. 1989. "Cash crops in developing countries: the issues, the facts and the policies". in *World Development* (New York), 17, 11: 1677-1709.

Meesook, O. 1979. *Income, consumption, and poverty in Thailand,* Working Paper No. 364. Washington DC, World Bank.

Mitra, A. 1978. *India's population: Aspects of quality and control (Vol 1).* New Delhi, Abhinav, for Family Planning Association /ICSSR.

Moore M.; Harriss, J. (eds.). 1984. *Development and the rural-urban divide.* London, Frank Cass.

Morris, M.D. 1979. *Measuring the condition of the world's poor: The PQLI index.* Oxford, Pergamon.

Mueller, E.; Short, K. 1982. *Income and wealth as they affect the demand for children in developing countries.* Research Report No. 82-35. Ann Arbor, University of Michigan, Poplulation Studies Centre.

Muhuvi, D.K.; Preston, S.H. 1991. "Effects of family composition on mortality differentials by sex among children in Matlab Thana, Bangladesh", in *Population and Development Review* (New York), 17, 3.

Musgrove, P. 1980. "Household size and composition, employment and poverty in urban Latin America", in *Economic Development and Cultural Change* (Chicago), 28, 2.

Myrdal, G. 1968. *Asian drama.* New York, Pantheon.

Nakamura, C. 1986. *Subjective equilibrium theory of the farm household.* Amsterdam, Elsevier.

Nordhaus, W.; Tobin, J. 1972. *Is growth obsolete?* National Bureau of Economic Research: 50th Anniversary Colloquium. New York, Columbia University Press.

Paddock, W.; Paddock, P. 1967. *Famine - 1975! America's decision: who will survive?* New York, Little Brown.

Pathak R. et al. 1977. "Shifts in patterns of asset holding of rural households, 1961-62 to 1971-72". in *Economic and Political Weekly* (Bombay), VIII, 12.

Payne, P.R.; Lipton, M. 1994. *How Third World households adapt to dietary energy stress,* Washington DC, IFPRI, Food Policy Review No. 2.

Pelletier, D. 1991. *Relationships between child anthropometry and mortality in developing countries: Implications for policy, programs and future research.* Ithaca, Cornell Food and Nutrition Policy Program Monograph 12.

Poleman, T.; Edirisinghe, N. 1983. "Behavioural thresholds as indicators of perceived dietary inadequacy". International Agricultural Study No. 17, Ithaca, Cornell University.

Quibria, M.G.; Srinivasan, T.N. 1991. "Rural poverty in Asia: priority issues and policy options". Manila, Asian Development Bank, mimeo.

Ratha, D.K.; Sharma, A. 1992. "Price subsidies and irrigation investment in India: Macro implications", in *Economic and Political Weekly* (Bombay), 26 Sep.

Raut, L.K. 1993. "Per capita income growth, social expenditures and living standards: evidence from rural India", in *Journal of Asian Economics* (Greenwich), 4, 1.

Ravallion, M. 1990. "On the coverage of public employment schemes for poverty alleviation", in *Journal of Development Economics* (Amsterdam), 34, 1/2: 57-79.

Ravallion, M.; Sen, B. 1992. *Impact on rural poverty of land-contingent targeting with and without productivity effects.* Washington DC, World Bank, Working Paper.

Reddy, P. 1991. "Family structure and age at marriage: evidence from a South Indian village", in *Journal of Asian and African Studies* (Leiden), 26, 3-4.

Robbins, L. 1930. "On the elasticity of demand for income in terms of effort", in *Economica* (London), No. 28, 123-129.

Rodgers, G. (ed.). 1989. *Population growth and poverty in South Asia.* New Delhi, Sage.

Rosenhouse, S. 1989. *Identifying the poor: Is headship a useful concept?* LSMS Working Paper No. 58. Washington DC, World Bank.

Rosenzweig, M.R.; Schultz, T.P. 1982. *Market opportunities, genetic endowments, and the intra-family distribution of resources: Child survival in rural India.* New Haven, Yale University Economic Growth Center Discussion Paper No. 347.

Rowntree, B.S. 1901. *Poverty: a study of town life.* London, Macmillan.

Runciman W.G. 1966. *Relative deprivation and social justice.* London, Routledge.

Ryan, J.G.; Walker, R.S. 1990. *Village and household economies in India's semi-arid tropics.* Baltimore, Johns Hopkins.

Safilios-Rothschild, C. 1991. "Gender and rural poverty in Asia: implications for agricultural projects", in *Asia Pacific Journal of Rural Development,* 1, 1.

Sahn, D. (ed.). 1989. *Seasonal variability in Third World agriculture.* Baltimore, Johns Hopkins.

Sambrani, S.; Pichholiya, K. 1975. *An enquiry into rural poverty and unemployment.* Ahmedabad, Indian Institute of Managment.

Sanyal, S. 1988. "Trends in poverty in rural India". In Srinivasan and Bardhan (eds.), 1988.

Scheigel, A. 1976. *Sexual stratification: A cross-cultural view.* New York, Columbia University.

Schofield, S. 1979. *Development and the problems of village nutrition.* London, Croom Helm.

Schofield, S. 1974. "Seasonal factors affecting nutrition in different age-groups", in *Journal of Development Studies,* 11, 2: 24-47.

Schultz, P. 1981. *Economics of population.* Reading, Mass., Addison Wesley.

—. 1988. "Education investments and returns". In Chenery and Srinivasan (eds.), 1988.

Schutjer, W.; Stokes, C. (eds.). 1984. *Rural development and human fertility.* New York, Macmillan.

Seabright, P. 1991. "Identifying investment opportunities for the poor: evidence from the livestock market in South India", in *Journal of Development Studies* (London), 28, 1: 53-73.

Sen, A.K. 1975. *Employment, technology and development.* Oxford, Clarendon.

—. 1980. *Levels of poverty: Policy and change.* Staff Working Paper No. 401, Washington, DC, World Bank.

—. 1981. *Poverty and famines: An essay on entitlement and deprivation*. Oxford, Oxford University Press.

—. 1985. *Commodities and capabilities*. Amsterdam, North-Holland.

Shankar, K. 1992. "Water market in Eastern U.P.", in *Economic and Political Weekly* (Bombay), May 2.

—. 1993. "Agricultural labourers in Eastern U.P.", in *Economic and Political Weekly* (Bombay), June 12.

Shapiro, D. 1990. "Farm size, household size and composition, and women's contribution to agricultural production: evidence from Zaïre", in *Journal of Development Studies* (London), 27, 1: 1-21.

Simon, J. 1981. *The ultimate resource*. Princeton, Princeton University Press.

—. 1986. *Theory of population and economic growth*. Oxford, Blackwell.

Singh, I.J. 1990. *The great ascent: The rural poor in South Asia*. Baltimore, Johns Hopkins.

Singh, R.P.; Richard, J. 1989. "Socio-economic and demographic correlates of the age of marriage", in *Demography*, 18, 1-2.

Srinivasan, T.; Bardhan, P. K. (eds.). 1988. *Rural Poverty in South Asia*. New York, Columbia University Press.

Standing, H. 1985. "Women's employment and the household: some findings from Calcutta". in *Economic and Political Weekly*, 20, 17.

Standing, G. 1985. *Labour force participation and development*. Geneva, ILO.

Stephenson, L. et al. 1986. *Schistosomiasis and malnutrition*. International Nutrition Monograph No. 16. Ithaca, Cornell University.

Stiglitz, J. 1988. "Economic organization, information and development". In Chenery et al. (eds.), 1988.

Stiglitz J.; Weiss, A. 1981. "Credit rationing in markets with imperfect information", in *American Economic Review*, 71, 3: 393-410

Stoeckel, J.; Chowdhury, A. 1980. "Fertility and socio-economic status in rural Bangladesh", in *Population Studies*, 3.

Sukhatme, P.; Margen, S. 1982. "Autoregulatory homeostatic nature of energy balance", *American Journal of Clinical Nutrition*, 35: 355-367.

Sundaram, K.; Tendulkar, S. D. 1988. "Towards an explanation of interregional variations in poverty and unemployment in India". In Srinivasan and Bardhan (eds.), 1988.

Svedberg , P. 1990. "Under-nutrition in sub-Saharan Africa: is there a gender bias?", *Journal of Development Studies* (London), 26, 3.

Taylor, C. et al. 1978. "The Narangwal experiment on interactions of nutrition and infections: 1. Project design and effects upon growth", in *Indian Journal of Medical Research*, 68 (Supplement).

Thomas, D. et al. 1992. *Public policy and anthropometric outcomes in Côte d'Ivoire*, LSMS working paper No. 89, Washington DC, World Bank.

Udall, A.; Sinclair, S. 1982. "The luxury unemployment hypothesis: a review of evidence", in *World Development*, 10, 2.

Unni, J. 1991. "Regional variations in rural non-agricultural employment: an exploratary analysis", in *Economic and Political Weekly* (Bombay), 26, 3: 109-22.

Vandemoortele, J. 1991. *Employment issues in sub-Saharan Africa*. African Economic Research Consortium, Special Paper No. 14. Nairobi, UNDP.

Varshney, A. (ed.). 1993. *Beyond urban bias*. London, Frank Cass.

Visaria, P. 1980. *Poverty and living standards in Asia: An overview of the main results and lessons of selected household surveys*. Working Paper No. 2, Living Standards Measurement Study. Washington DC, World Bank.

—. 1977. *Living standards, employment and education in Western India*. Working Paper No. 1, ESCAP/IBRD project on Asian Income Distribution Data. Washington DC, World Bank.

—. 1981. "Poverty and unemployment in India: an analysis of of recent evidence", in *World Development*, 9.

Visaria, P. ; Minhas, B. S. 1991. *Evolving an employment policy for the 1990s: What do the data tell us?* Ahmedabad, Gujarat Institute of Area Planning, Annual Conference of the Indian Association for the Study of Population, Udaipur, 1990.

Watanabe, B.; Mueller, E. 1982. *A poverty profile for rural Botswana*, mimeo.

Weiner, M. 1991. *The Child and the State in India*. Princeton, Princeton University Press.

World Bank. 1984. *World Development Report 1984*. Washington DC, World Bank.

—. 1990. *World Development Report 1990: Poverty*. New York, Oxford University Press.

Zeitlin, M.F. et al. 1987. "Positive deviance in nutrition: an approach to health whose time has come". In Jelliffe (ed.), in *Advances in international maternal and child health*, Vol. 7. Oxford, Clarendon.

5 Towards a strategy for action against poverty: Proposals and debates

The sweeping political, economic and social changes that are under way world-wide have had a serious impact on the incidence of poverty and unemployment. The capital-intensive bias of industrialization has limited the demand for labour and contributed to both unemployment and under-employment. The growing flexibilization of labour use is resulting in the casualization and informalization of work, a growth in job insecurity and pressure to lower wages. Poverty is now perceived as a global issue, and in the developed countries is once again being regarded as a structural problem and not a residual one. The problem is aggravated by policies which aim to control inflation at the expense of employment. In many developing countries, the persistent poverty crisis has been deepened by structural adjustment programmes which have involved reductions in social expenditures, cut-backs in public sector employment, the lowering of real wages and the emergence of less secure forms of employment. There are many reasons for these trends, but they underline the need for new thinking about the mechanisms, policies and strategies at the national, regional and global levels which can deal effectively with the problem of poverty.

This was the basis for a concluding debate in the symposium, which tried to identify some key elements for future ILO action against poverty.[1]

---

[1] The panellists in the debate were Luis Anderson, General Secretary, Inter-American Regional Organization of Workers, Mexico; Jean-Jacques Oechslin, International Organization of Employers, Geneva; Dharam Ghai, Director, United Nations Institute for Social Development; Victor Tokman, Director, Latin American Regional Department, ILO; Juhani Lönnroth, Director, Employment and Development Department, ILO; Colin Gillion, Director, Social Security Department, ILO. Their comments, together with the ensuing discussion, are the basis for this summary. However, diverse views are reflected here and the panellists do not necessarily subscribe to statements and comments in the following pages.

There is no simple solution, but there emerged during the discussions a clear consensus on the need for a coordinated and integrated approach to action against poverty. Decades of experience show that partial solutions are not enough. Recalling the ideas expressed in Section IV of *The framework of ILO action against poverty*, reproduced above, such an approach, at both the international and national level, calls for the design of systematic policy prescriptions with a strong anti-poverty orientation. It was recognized that the international community and leading groups in civil society have important roles to play in ensuring that poverty issues remain at the forefront of any development agenda. The links between poverty and unemployment were underlined, together with the consequent need for a focus on employment policy, labour markets, human resource development and labour institutions in any attempt at poverty eradication. Many participants noted that the ILO had an important contribution to make to combating poverty on the basis of its traditional instruments and unique structure. The ILO's normative actions — international labour standards — can contribute to action against poverty through protection of workers and their rights; through its research and technical cooperation activities it can have an impact on many anti-poverty policies, especially the creation of employment opportunities; taking advantage of its tripartite structure, it can act as a forum for dialogue among its constituents, and between the social partners and members of the international and academic communities and grass-roots groups.

I. Keeping poverty on the policy agenda

Much debate in the symposium revolved around the question "why is poverty still with us?" For this question to be rendered obsolete, there is a need to maintain poverty on the policy agenda at all times, at both national and international levels. Given that poverty today is increasingly seen as a one-world problem, it is necessary for policy-makers from rich and poor countries alike to cooperate in addressing the problem from a global perspective. This also requires a philosophical and conceptual reorientation to produce the kind of analysis that would assist policy-makers in the design of future anti-poverty policy, for effective anti-poverty strategy is increasingly dependent on its consistency with the imperatives of global markets. In both developed and developing countries, to link growth with employment and equity requires new thinking about the ways the latter objectives may be obtained, about the linkage between investment promotion, human resource development and competitiveness in a framework which combines these with a concern for equity.

Developing countries where "trickle-down" has failed require the design and implementation of macro-economic policies that contain the long-term objective of poverty eradication. To further this end, targeted interventions at the micro-level must be linked more closely with the policies upstream, if they are to have a sustainable effect on the causes and structure of poverty. This is as true in the industrialized countries, faced with persistent unemployment and social exclusion, as in lower-income countries. It was also recognized that in order to create the conditions for equitable growth, meso-level policies — particularly labour market interventions — must be linked to institution-building at the intermediate level. The provision of social security and other forms of social protection, the development of human resources and labour market regulations all affect economic incentives, and so have both a direct and an indirect bearing on poverty eradication strategies: but all require the creation and development of relevant institutions to ensure their effective implementation. The role of such middle-level institutions becomes all the more crucial as political and economic changes at the global level have weakened the ability of the State to effectively tackle poverty directly. Regulatory structures are also important to underpin the meso-level policies that create institutions and set their mandates and agendas. Thus, institutional policies are necessary in order to facilitate the actions of emerging social actors. This extends to creating the political space to enable the poor to organize and articulate their own perceptions and demands.

When re-examining the poverty debate, importance must be given to a social policy that underscores the need to protect the vulnerable and the unemployed. Resources are always scarce, but the priorities according to which they are allocated need to be investigated and evaluated, and public support mobilized for the provision of appropriate social services. This illustrates the need to harmonize economic and social policy objectives, and to fully understand the relationship between the two in the context of poverty eradication. An important example concerns the way in which gender-based discrimination contributes to the growing feminization of poverty. The vulnerability of female-headed households, and the fact that women constitute an increasing share of the workforce, disproportionately in the informal sector, poses a specific challenge in the efforts to combine economic and social objectives within an effective anti-poverty programme.

A view was expressed that the successful eradication of poverty requires the development of micro-level research activities[2] that can be adapted to each national context. The economic consequences of policies to protect rights or raise the living standards of the poor are often ill understood. Systematic analyses of these issues within a consistent conceptual framework would allow national policy-makers to better evaluate the specific impact of a set of anti-poverty policies. The construction of a *poverty profile*, whereby a country's poverty status can be clearly identified and analysed, would be important for this purpose. However, the consensus was that the *statistical information* necessary to develop such a profile and support anti-poverty measures is often lacking or of poor quality. Better data collection and the corresponding accounting frameworks would contribute greatly to the efficient management of measures for poverty eradication.

There was strong support for the view that the international community must support the creation of a new dialogue on development, particularly in generating the political support for an anti-poverty strategy. The promotion of *social and national dialogue* is fundamental, because it creates the conditions for generating proposals which are acceptable to the various social actors concerned by their implementation. Such an effort should be aimed at reaching consensus on development projects which can simultaneously promote economic growth and increase social welfare. Some participants felt that the exclusion of important social and political actors has often seriously hampered or distorted the process of structural adjustment. This argument applies with particular force to the tripartite actors of the ILO — workers, employers, and governments. But for successful, broad-based dialogue it would be imperative to also reach out to new social actors such as those in the informal sector, and to many other associations and action groups. In this sense, social dialogue is closely related to decentralization of policy against poverty, another idea which was widely supported in the symposium.

II. Challenge for the ILO

There was consensus that the profound economic and social changes in the global environment require that the ILO engage in some serious reflection and introspection. Many of the ILO's objectives and assumptions

---

[2] Along the lines discussed in the article by Professor Lipton in this book.

are under challenge. The ILO seeks full employment, but unemployment and underemployment remain widespread. ILO action is built around regular, protected employment but there seems to be a growth of precarious jobs. ILO standards are challenged by philosophies of deregulation. Social security is no longer seen as universal and effective. Trade unions find their legitimacy questioned in many countries. For effective action against poverty, the ILO needs to reappraise its instruments, constituencies and strategies, and explore new ways of reaching its basic objectives.

In terms of the ILO's concerns, the main issues were identified as the promotion of full, productive, secure and remunerative employment; the formulation, promotion and implementation of labour standards aimed at welfare and security for all workers; enabling the poor to organize themselves better; the promotion of a more constructive dialogue between trade unions, employers' organizations and governments, at the national, regional and global levels; the changing role and functions of the State; and the development of a coordinated effort at the international level.

The relationship between *international labour standards* and poverty was referred to by almost all the speakers, spotlighting the need to reflect on the contribution of many of the Conventions and Recommendations of the ILO to the aim of poverty eradication. It was noted that the regulatory framework should not have a negative impact on employment creation. It was emphasized, however, that competition among nations and regions based on reducing labour costs through non-compliance with international labour standards can only lead to social dumping in the developing countries and a growth of insecure and ill-paid employment in the industrialized world. Indeed, the logic of a global economic system should lead more forcefully than before to the universal application of labour standards, and to the realization that the eradication of poverty, economic growth and social protection are not contradictory objectives but can and should complement each other.

However, the ways in which labour standards can be applied in practice to the circumstances of different groups in different countries remains a vital issue which requires serious attention and analysis in the context of action against poverty. It was emphasized that the nature of employment varies between countries and the poor are faced with forms of exploitation that often run entirely contrary to any form of existing legislation. The problem is not with the standards, but with the fact that many groups remain unprotected because of their economic situation or because the law remains unenforced. Questions of enactment, enforcement, and inspection require further investigation in order to identify where the problems arise and to find the appropriate course of action to rectify them.

In this context, a suggestion was made that the ILO become more actively involved in the protection of rights of marginal workers in both the formal and informal sectors — child labour, domestic workers, workers in free-trade zones and home-based workers.

It is imperative to promote universal coverage of at least a minimum set of protections, such as, for example, those ILO Conventions that relate to primary legislation in the area of child labour, discrimination and occupational safety. In the context of poverty eradication, a clear focus must emerge on what and how to regulate, and how to maximize the potential contribution of this domain to strategies against poverty. It was suggested that the ILO should undertake a study of the actual and potential effects on poverty of the universal application of existing Conventions and Recommendations in order to evaluate the trade-offs that may occur in terms of demand for labour, productivity, social protection and exclusion.

The problems associated with *social protection* are aggravated by the need to adapt to the contemporary labour market, increasingly character-ized by high levels of mobility and flexibility. Traditionally, minimum levels of protection have been provided to people in secure and permanent employment, leaving those who are mobile unprotected and vulnerable. The reduction of permanent and secure employment, the growth of part-time work and the increasing casualization of jobs highlights the need to look into new ways to protect workers who have to constantly change jobs, sectors, and working time arrangements. New structures and mechanisms that can be created for this purpose also have to be identified.

In addition, it is necessary to analyse the impact of wage policies on employment generation and how best to use such policies to achieve equity, particularly given the changing nature of the labour market. An increasing informalization of production and employment has resulted in the lowering of real incomes and higher wage differentials between workers in different sectors. It was suggested that particular attention be paid to the contribution of minimum wages policy to action against poverty; a realistic and sustainable minimum wage policy covering a large proportion of all workers was required.

In many countries undergoing rapid economic and political trans-formation, the altered role and functions of the State pose a serious threat to the maintenance of *social security and related measures* that traditionally provided a degree of protection for the poor. As such, it was recognized that the problems of social security and welfare, in both developed and developing countries, had to be looked at in a much wider context. It was emphasized that it was necessary to identify and analyse methods by which adequate resources can be mobilized and allocated for social expenditures.

These may include the reallocation of existing public expenditure, for instance through reductions in defence budgets; new forms of taxation; and the potential contribution of the private sector.

There was consensus that poverty had to be investigated in relation to emerging trends in the organization of work, particularly in the *informal sector*. The expanding informal sector constitutes a major source of employment and income generation, and is therefore important in any anti-poverty strategy. In particular, the question was raised as to how informal and small-sector enterprises could be made complementary to large-scale firms; and how government policies pertaining to incentives, infrastructure, training and research, and legislation on the terms and conditions of work, need to be adapted to the specific circumstances of both small and large. Furthermore, the globalization of production, together with the free movement of capital, has resulted in the development of enterprises which organize production in new ways, and create new kinds of employment relationships in different parts of the world. The implications for global unemployment and poverty of these new patterns in the international division of labour are not easy to analyse, but it seems likely that they will be considerable.

It was recognized that the *skill levels* of a country's workforce have a fundamental role to play in increasing productivity and competitiveness, but also that lack of skills is an important correlate of poverty, notably affecting labour market access and earning capacity. Training is therefore all the more essential to counter the growth of informal and precarious jobs. Furthermore, specific programmes, adapted to regional and national needs, and which take into account technological developments, must be designed and implemented to protect against unemployment and the resultant poverty. It was also recognized that education policies, in general, and not just vocational training, must be more closely related to labour market needs. Grass-roots education was given special emphasis because it reaches the poor more directly.

III. Options for the ILO

The ILO, with its wide knowledge and experience, skills and research capabilities, is well placed to play a significant and authoritative role in all the areas identified above. Moreover, its unique tripartite structure facilitates a constructive dialogue among relevant actors, while its international profile and reach would enable it to function effectively in the coordination of appropriate global action. How can it use these advantages to further the cause of poverty reduction?

One objective, it was suggested, would be to determine the preconditions for equitable and poverty-reducing growth, in contrast to some of the structural adjustment packages which have been adopted in recent years. This implies a need for coherent national strategies, involving both macro and micro elements. Within the ILO, the WEP comprehensive employment missions of the 1970s provide an example of what could be done.

The WEP was seen to contain some of the elements, such as research-related technical cooperation, tripartite involvement and a "people-centred" perspective, that had been identified as necessary for an integrated approach to poverty eradication. It was noted that, in today's context, the success of such an approach would require that it be coordinated not only with the work of the rest of the ILO but also with the poverty eradication and development assistance work of other organizations.

It was clear from the discussions in the symposium that, while some elements of anti-poverty strategies are reasonably well understood, others are not. A significant research effort, which the ILO could promote, was required in several domains, including:

(a) the relationships between labour standards, labour institutions and poverty, including the analysis of many labour market interventions, as noted above;

(b) the need to effectively capture the "informal" constituency; how could their representation be assured and their bargaining power increased? Might an expansion of the cooperative movement help, by creating conditions for poverty eradication through participative democracy?

(c) the need to better understand the social and economic forces which exclude some and include others, with respect to representation, to labour market access, to assets, to many public goods;

(d) the ways in which enterprises could contribute to strategies against poverty through their role in the community and their response to social concerns.

Beyond the issue of information and understanding, it was argued that the ILO needs to deal with the political economy issues. This task is primarily institutional. In today's context, the political economy of an international poverty eradication programme requires that the parameters of the debate be widened and the range of actors participating in it increased. This highlights the importance of *alliance building*, involving in particular a search for the common interest of the trade unions, the employers and other groups within civil society. New groups entering the labour market need to be organized and represented, dialogue needs to be established with the associations, action groups and local communities which often represent substantial segments of the poor. To this end, a greater commitment is required, particularly on the part of the trade unions, to recognize this need and support these efforts. Employers and their organizations have an equally important role. With their participation, the debate on social policies could even be extended to include the more contentious issue of business ethics and practices. The question still remains, however, as to whether the social partners can really reach out to the poor any better than the machinery of the State. The ILO, by providing both groups with a forum in which to exchange views and information, can enhance their joint capacities to contribute to the eradication of poverty.

A second role for the ILO here is one of advocacy and monitoring. Tracking trends in poverty, their relationship with labour market trends, and the effectiveness and intensity of policy efforts, can provide powerful support to international action. At the same time, an advocacy role remains crucial, convincing governments, the social partners and other groups in civil society of the need to act against poverty in their own self-interest and in the interest of the community as a whole.

Institutional change within the ILO is also on the agenda. The decentralization and reorganization of ILO activities, along the lines of the new "Active Partnership Policy", allow the organization to work more closely at the country level with the national actors. These actors are also concerned with the problem of poverty eradication, and need to be brought into broad-based policy interventions. The potential role of the ILO in co-ordinating international action against poverty was also discussed, particularly in relation to organizations such as the World Bank, the International Monetary Fund and regional level institutions. It was cautioned that a clear but collaborative division of labour between the international organizations was needed, in order to enhance their combined effectiveness in action against poverty.

In conclusion, it was argued that the symposium had shown that much was being done and that much could be done. But a dispersion of activities across the different domains of the ILO reduced the potential for mutual reinforcement. An integrated strategy, bringing together into a common framework the different aspects of ILO work on poverty, could contribute significantly to the effectiveness of action in each separate field.

6 The ILO's approach to poverty: A bibliographical review

Maryse Gaudier[1]

This chapter provides a summary review of the ILO's approach to poverty as seen through a chronological selection of texts and publications. The choice, in no way exhaustive, includes material in three categories: official (basic or normative texts, reports of the Director-General, solemn declarations); conceptual (clarifying the problem); or strategic (fixing objectives, proposing policies or activities). Six major periods have been selected, taking into account the historical context and the evolution of the Organization itself: 1919-43; 1944-47; 1948-68; 1969-75; 1976-79; 1980 onwards.

1919-1943: This period starts with the setting up of the ILO and the drawing up of its Constitution. The external context is dominated by the economic crisis of the 1930s and the two world wars. Poverty is addressed through the notion of social injustice, and the ILO's action is oriented above all to the fight against unemployment and the protection of workers. The activities of the organization are essentially normative, but also include support to the creation and development of social security systems in Europe and the Americas.

Major documents:

1919
Constitution of the ILO

Conventions and Recommendations
  C. concerning unemployment (No. 2)
  C. concerning minimum age (industry) (No. 5)
  R. concerning unemployment (No. 1)
  R. concerning reciprocity of treatment (No. 2)

---

[1] International Institute for Labour Studies, Geneva.

1921

Conventions and Recommendations
    C. concerning minimum age (agriculture) (No. 10)
    R. concerning unemployment (agriculture) (No. 11)
    R. concerning social insurance (agriculture) (No. 17)

1927

Conventions and Recommendations
    C. concerning sickness insurance (Nos. 14, 25)
    R. concerning sickness insurance (No. 29)

"Social work and social legislation." By G. A. Johnson. *International Labour Review*, 16, Oct., pp. 449-471.

1928

Conventions and Recommendations
    C. concerning minimum wage-fixing machinery (No. 26)
    R. concerning minimum wage-fixing machinery (No. 30)

1931

"Social effects of the economic depression in North America." By H.B. Butler. *International Labour Review*, 23, Mar., pp. 301-323.

1933

Conventions and Recommendations
    C. concerning old-age insurance (Nos. 35, 36)
    C. concerning invalidity insurance (Nos. 37, 38)
    C. concerning survivors' insurance (Nos. 39, 40)
    R. concerning employment agencies (No. 42)
    R. concerning invalidity, old age and survivors' insurance (No. 43)

Unemployment insurance and various forms of relief for the unemployed. 2 v. (ILC, 17th session, Geneva, Report III)

1934

Conventions and Recommendations
    C. concerning unemployment provision (No. 44)
    R. concerning unemployment provision (No. 44)

1935

Conventions and Recommendations
    C. concerning maintenance of migrants' pension rights (No. 48)
    R. concerning unemployment (young persons) (No. 45)

1936

The social consequences of the economic depression. By W. Woytinsky. 364 p. (Studies and reports, No. 21)

1938

The worker's standard of living. 101 p. (Studies and reports, No. 30)

1939

Conventions and Recommendations
    C. concerning migration for employment (No. 66)
    R. concerning migration for employment (No. 61)

1940

"The compensation of war victims; general principles." *International Labour Review*, 41, Apr.-May, pp. 371-386, 506-516.

1943

"Minimum welfare standards as a post-war objective." By E.R. Walker. *International Labour Review*, 48, Oct., pp. 417-433.

1944-1947: This period is dominated by the historic 26th Session of the ILO Conference in Philadelphia, which adopted the revised objectives of the Organization as enshrined in the Declaration of Philadelphia. The poverty problem is explicit in the Declaration: poverty is inadmissible not only in itself but also because it constitutes an obstacle to development. The aim is to permit all humans to pursue their material and spiritual progress, in economic security and with equal chances. The policies which are proposed go beyond those of the 1920s and 1930s. They encompass the promotion of full employment and the raising of living standards, especially through increasing productivity and the extension of social security measures.

Major documents:

1944

Conventions and Recommendations
    R. concerning income security (No. 67)
    R. concerning social policy in dependent territories (No. 70)
    R. concerning employment (No. 71)
    R. concerning employment service (No. 72)

Declaration concerning the aims and purposes of the International Labour Organisation. (ILC, 26th session, Philadelphia).

Minimum standard of social policy in dependent territories. vii, 107 p. (ILC, 26th session, Philadelphia)

Social policy in dependent territories. vi, 185 p. (Studies and reports, N.S. 38)

Social security, principles and problems arising out of the war. 2 vols. (ILC, 26th session, Philadelphia, report IV)

1945

Maintenance of high levels of employment during the period of industrial rehabilitation and reconversion. iv, 181 p. (ILC, 27th session, Paris, report III)

Protection of children and young workers. iii, 192 p. (ILC, 27th, Paris, report III)

1947

Conventions and Recommendations
    C. concerning social policy (non-metropolitan territories) (No. 82)

Economic background of social policy, including problems of industrialisation. New Delhi, iv, 221 p. (Preparatory Asian Regional Conference, report IV)

Problems of social security. New Delhi, iii, 123 p. (Preparatory Asian Regional Conference, report IV)

1948-68: This period is dominated by the process of decolonization and the broadening of the membership of the Organization to cover the majority of countries of Africa, Asia and Latin America. The problem of poverty takes on a universal character. The objective is to permit the workers of the world as a whole to achieve a minimum standard of living. The policies proposed include the modernization of economic structures, growth in both employment and productivity. The objective is to reinforce the social institutions which can underpin the attainment of a minimum standard of living, including the reinforcement of social security systems. The main new instrument lies in programmes of technical cooperation, concentrated on projects to increase the production of goods and services in the newly-independent countries of the Third World.

Major documents:

1948

Conventions and Recommendations
    C. concerning employment service (No. 88)
    R. concerning employment service (No. 83)

International social policy. By Albert Thomas. Geneva. 162 p.

1949

Conventions and Recommendations
    C. concerning protection of wages (No. 95)
    R. concerning protection of wages (No. 85)
    R. concerning migration for employment (No. 86)

"Post-war trends in social security, income security." I-II. *International Labour Review*, 59, June, pp. 668-683; 60, Jul., pp. 28-47.

1950

Action against unemployment. Geneva, iv, 260 p. (Studies and reports, N.S., 20)

1951

Conventions and Recommendations
C. concerning minimum wage-fixing machinery (agriculture) (No. 99)
C. concerning equal remuneration (No. 100)
R. concerning minimum wage-fixing machinery (No. 89)
R. concerning equal remuneration (No. 90)

Objectives and minimum standards of social security. (ILC, 34th session, Geneva, report IV)

1952

Conventions and Recommendations
C. concerning social security (minimum standards) (No. 102)

"The I.L.O. and technical assistance." *International Labour Review*, 66, Nov.-Dec., pp. 391-418.

"Social policy." *In: Report of the Director-General.* pp. 32-46. (ILC, 35th session, Geneva, report I)

Social security, achievements and future policy. Geneva, iv, 108 p. (Labour Conference of American States, 5th, Rio de Janeiro, report II)

1953

Indigenous people, living and working conditions of aboriginal populations in independent countries. Geneva, xviii, 628 p. (Studies and reports, N.S., 35).

"Population growth and living standards." By C. Clark. *International Labour Review*, 68, Aug., pp. 99-117.

1954

"Action against discrimination in employment." *International Labour Review*, 70, Jul., pp. 67-83.

Minimum wages in Latin America. Geneva, vi, 184 p. (Studies and reports, N.S., 34)

"Population growth, socio-economic development and living standards." *International Labour Review*, 70, Nov., pp. 442-449.

1955

Conventions and Recommendations
R. concerning protection of migrant workers (No. 100)

"Colombo (The) Plan." *International Labour Review*, 71, May, pp. 498-515.

1957

Protection and integration of indigenous and other tribal and semi-tribal populations in independent countries. (ILC, 40th session, Geneva, report VI)

1958

Conventions and Recommendations
    C. concerning discrimination (employment and occupation) (No. 111)
    R. concerning discrimination (employment and occupation) (No. 111)

Social security; a workers' education manual. Geneva, vi, 131 p.

1959

The ILO and women. Geneva, 32 p.

1960

Contribution of the ILO to the raising of incomes and living conditions in rural communities with particular reference to countries in process of development. Geneva, ii, 31 p. (Permanent Agricultural Committee, 6th session, report III(3))

"Sharing the benefits of productivity." *International Labour Review*, 82, Jul., pp. 1-25.

Youth and work. Report of the Director-General. Geneva, v, 119 p. (ILC, 44th session, report I)

1961

"Andean (The) Programme." By J. Rens. *International Labour Review*, 84, Dec., pp. 423-461

Economic growth and social policy. Report of the Director-General. Geneva, iv, 163 p. (Conference of American States, 7th, Buenos Aires, report I)

Employment objectives in economic development. Report of a meeting of experts. Geneva, xi, 255 p. (Studies and reports, N.S., 62)

Role of the ILO in the promotion of economic expansion and social progress in developing countries. iv, 69 p. (ILC, 45th session, Geneva, report X)

1962

Conventions and Recommendations
    C. concerning social policy (basic aims and standards) (No. 117)
    C. concerning equality of treatment (social security) (No. 118)

Some labour and social aspects of economic development. Report of the Director-General. Geneva, vi, 156 p. (Asian Regional Conference, 5th session, Melbourne, report I)

Unemployment and structural change. Geneva, v, 206 p. (Studies and reports, N.S., 65)

1963

Hunger and social policy. Geneva, vi, 66 p. (Freedom from Hunger Campaign. Basic study, 14)

Social and labour aspects of economic development: the ILO's approach. Geneva, 80 p.

1964

Conventions and Recommendations
    C. concerning employment policy (No. 122)
    R. concerning employment policy (No. 122)

Employment and economic growth. Geneva, vi, 217 p. (Studies and reports, N.S., 67)

Women workers in a changing world. (ILC, 48th session, Geneva, report VI)

1965

Conventions and Recommendations
    R. concerning employment (women with family responsibilities) (No. 123)

"The distribution of gains from economic development." *International Labour Review*, 91(5), May.

1967

Conventions and Recommendations
    C. concerning invalidity, old-age and survivors' benefits (No. 128)
    R. concerning invalidity, old-age and survivors' benefits (No. 131)

"The concept and measurement of minimum living standards." By N.N. Franklin. *International Labour Review*, 95(4), Apr.

1968

Minimum wage fixing and economic development. Geneva. (Studies and reports, N.S., 72)

1969-75: This period is marked by the launching of the World Employment Programme. The problem of poverty is set within a renewal of an approach to development oriented towards social and human factors. The living standards of the majority of workers cannot increase unless there is a growth in productive employment. Employment becomes the central element of the strategy against poverty and inequality. The policies proposed are wide ranging, and cover not only the development of human resources but the reorientation of development strategy as a whole towards labour-intensive growth. The activities include comprehensive employment strategy missions to a number of countries, a broad-based research programme covering income distribution, labour market and other issues, and the development of policy advice, especially through the establishment of regional employment teams in Asia, Africa and Latin America and Caribbean.

Major documents:

1969
Conventions and Recommendations
    C. concerning medical care and sickness benefits (No. 130)
    R. concerning medical care and sickness benefits (No. 130)

World Employment Programme. Report of the Director-General. 145 p. (ILC, 53rd session, Geneva, report I)

1970
Conventions and Recommendations
    C. concerning minimum wage fixing (No. 131)
    R. concerning minimum wage fixing (No. 135)

Poverty and minimum living standards; the role of the ILO. Report of the Director-General. 122 p. (ILC, 54th session, Geneva, report I.)

Towards full employment: a programme for Colombia. Geneva, viii, 471 p.

1971
Matching employment opportunities and expectations; a programme of action for Ceylon. Geneva, vi, 251 p.

1972
Employment, incomes and equality; a strategy for increasing productive employment in Kenya. Geneva, xx, 600 p.

1973
Conventions and Recommendations
    C. concerning minimum age (No. 138)
    R. concerning minimum age (No. 146)

Prosperity for welfare: social purpose in economic growth and change. Report of the Director-General. 63 p. (ILC, 58th session, Geneva, report I)

1974
Income security in Europe in the light of structural changes. Geneva, ii, 111 p. (European Regional Conference, 2nd, Report III)

Sharing in development: a programme of employment, equity and growth for the Philippines. Geneva, xxvii, 687 p.

1975

Basic needs, growth and redistribution; a quantitative approach. By M.J.D. Hopkins and others. Geneva. (Population and employment working paper, 29.)

Conventions and Recommendations
   C. concerning rural workers' organisations (No. 141)
   C. concerning human resources development (No. 142)
   R. concerning rural workers' organisation (No. 149)
   R. concerning human resources development (No. 150)
   R. concerning migrant workers (No. 151)

1976-1979: This is the period of the World Employment Conference, which coincided with the end of the period of stable growth in the world economy. The problem of poverty is re-conceptualized in terms of the satisfaction of basic needs, including basic consumption of goods and access to public services. The notion of basic needs includes both decent jobs and participation by the poor in the decisions affecting their lives. The aim is to achieve the satisfaction of basic needs for all, and the policies proposed include the reorientation of investment towards the production of basic needs goods, asset redistribution, organization of the rural poor, a more equitable distribution of access to public services and international solidarity. The activities undertaken include an intensification of the research effort and of the diffusion of its results.

Major documents:

1976

Employment, growth and basic needs: a one-world problem; the "international basic needs strategy" against chronic poverty, and the decisions of the 1976 World Employment Conference. New York, Praeger. xi, 223 p.

Rural and urban income inequalities in Indonesia, Mexico, Pakistan, Tanzania and Tunisia. By W. van Ginneken. Geneva, 67 p.

Social policy in a changing world: the ILO response. Selected speeches by W. Jenks. Geneva, 270 p.

1977

A basic needs strategy for Africa. Report of the Director-General. Geneva, iv, 92 p. (African Regional Conference, 5th, Abidjan, part I)

Basic-needs approach to development; some issues regarding concepts and methodology. Geneva, v, 113 p.

Inventory of ILO research in rural development with an anti-poverty component. Geneva, 1 vol. (ILO D.3.1977)

Meeting basic needs: strategies for eradicating mass poverty and unemployment; conclusions of the World Employment Conference 1976. Geneva, 60 p.

Pobreza urbana y empleo en América latina: lineas de acción. Por V.E. Tokman. Santiago, 36 p. (PREALC)

Poverty: measurement and analysis. By R.J. Szal. Geneva, 42 p. (ILO-WEP 2-23/WP.60)

Poverty and landlessness in rural Asia. Geneva, 228 p.

1978

Children and work; an ILO policy framework for the International Year of the Child, 1979. Geneva, 13 p.

Empleo, distribución del ingreso y necesidades básicos en América latina. Santiago, 1 vol. (PREALC)

Five essays on the basic needs approach. By J. Mouly and S.A. Kuzmin. Geneva, iii, 54 p. (ILO-WEP 2-32/WP.11)

Popular participation in decision-making and the basic needs approach to development: methods, issues and experiences. By D. Curtis and others. Geneva, viii, 160 p. (ILO-WEP 2-32/WP. 12)

Three notes on the concept of poverty. By A. Sen. Geneva, 40 p. (ILO-WEP 2-23/WP.65)

1979

Approaches to the analysis of poverty. By G. Rodgers. Geneva, 51 p. (Population and employment working paper, 71)

Asalariados de bajos ingresos y salarios minimos en América latina. Por H. Szretter. Lima, 126 p. (PREALC)

Growth, employment and basic needs in Latin America and the Caribbean. Report of the Director-General. Geneva, 88 p. (Conference of American States Members of the ILO, 11th, report I)

Poverty and basic needs. By G. Standing and R. Szal. Geneva.

Poverty and employment in rural areas of the developing countries. Geneva, 55 p. (Advisory Committee on Rural Development, 9th session)

Poverty and the impact of income maintenance programmes; case studies of Australia, Belgium, Norway and Great Britain. By W. Beckerman et al. Geneva, ix, 85 p.

Rural poverty in the third world: trends, causes and policy reorientations. By D. Ghai, E. Lee and S. Radwan. Geneva, ii, 70 p. (ILO-WEP 10-6/WP. 23)

1980 onwards: During this period, the external context of recession and structural adjustment dominates. Within the ILO, the notion of basic needs is pursued less vigorously, but the elimination of poverty and unemployment are reaffirmed as central objectives. The need to protect workers from the consequences of economic crisis are seen as urgent, and research programmes investigate the means to limit the adverse effects on poverty of structural adjustment. The policy priorities shift towards a widening of social protection and the reinforcement of social legislation. Activities focus on technical assistance programmes, covering issues such as social security and the formulation of social institutions; the development of employment policy; and the promotion of employment in the informal sector.

Major documents:

1980

Challenge (The) of rural poverty; a progress report on research and advisory services with special reference to rural employment, agrarian institutions and policies. Geneva.

"Changing approaches to rural development." By E. Lee. *International Labour Review*, 119(1), pp. 99-114.

ILO in participatory research. By A. Rahman. Geneva, 8 p.

Research and action programme for least developed countries: some tentative proposals. B. Norbyo Odk. Geneva, iii, 38 p.

1981

Besoins de base et niveaux de satisfaction dans la Communauté Economique de l'Afrique de l'Ouest; essai de synthèse globale. Addis Ababa, xi, 481 p. (JASPA)

Child work, poverty and underdevelopment. By G. Rodgers and G. Standing. Geneva, xii, 310 p.

Conventions and Recommendations
     C. concerning workers with family responsibilities (No. 156)
     R. concerning workers with family responsibilities (No. 165)

Income distribution, structure of economy and employment: the Philippines, Iran, the Republic of Korea and Malaysia. By F. Paukert et al. London, C. Helm, 170 p.

Monitoring the condition of the poor in the third world: some aspects of measurement. By N. Fergany. Geneva, iv, 35 p. (ILO-WEP 10-6/WP.52)

Poverty and famines: an essay on entitlement and deprivation. By A. Sen. Oxford, Clarendon Press. ix, 257 p.

Urban informal sector in developing countries: employment, poverty and environment. By S.V. Sethuraman. Geneva, xii, 225 p.

1982
Conventions and Recommendations
    C. concerning maintenance of social security rights (No. 159)
    R. concerning maintenance of social security rights (No. 167)

1983
Agrarian policies and rural poverty. By D. Ghai and S. Radwan. 311 p.

Basic needs in development planning. By M. Hopkins and R. van der Hoeven. Aldershot, Gower, xvii, 184 p.

Conventions and Recommendations
    C. concerning vocational rehabilitation and employment (disabled) (No. 159)
    R. concerning vocational rehabilitation and employment (disabled) (No. 168)

Promotion of employment and incomes for the rural poor, including rural women, through non-farm activities. Geneva, 131 p. (Advisory Committee on Rural Development, 10th session, report III)

Répartition du revenu et développement économique; un essai de synthèse. By J. Lecaillon et al. Geneva, ix, 208 p.

Social aspects of development in Africa: the role of social institutions. Report of the Director-General. Geneva, vi, 72 p. (African Regional Conference, 6th, Tunis, report I)

1984
Basic needs and the urban poor: the provision of communal services. By P. Richards and A.M. Thomson. London, C. Helm, 276 p.

Into the twenty-first century: the development of social security. Geneva, xi, 115p.

Participatory organisations of the rural poor; introduction to an ILO programme. By A. Rahman. Geneva, 30 p.

Poverty and population; approaches and evidence. By G. Rodgers. Geneva, 213 p.

Poverty in rural Asia. Ed. by A.R. Khan and E. Lee. Bangkok, xii, 276 p. (ARTEP)

Recession, employment and poverty in the developing countries of Asia. By R. Islam. Bangkok, 58 p. (ARTEP)

Rural urban gap and income distribution: a comparative sub-regional study; synthesis report of seventeen African countries. Addis Ababa, x, 67 p. (JASPA)

1985

Crisis in the North and the South: the impact of the world recession on employment and poverty in developing countries. Geneva, x, 181 p. (ILO-WEP 2-32/WP.59)

Employment and poverty in a troubled world; report of a meeting of high-level experts on employment. Geneva, 55 p.

Impact of recession in African countries; effects on the poor; synthesis report. By K.M. Gozo and A.A. Aboagye. Addis Ababa, 1 vol. (JASPA)

Operationalizing concepts and measurement of poverty and basic needs. By L. Barreiros. Santiago, 46 p. (PREALC)

Popular participation in planning for basic needs: concepts, methods and practice. By F. Lisk. Aldershot, Gower. ix, 277 p.

Strategies for alleviating poverty in rural Asia. Ed. by R. Islam. Bangkok, xii, 315 p. (ARTEP)

1986

Buscando la equilidad: planificación por la satisfacción de la necesidades básicas. Santiago, xiii, 205 p. (PREALC)

Challenge (The) of employment and basic needs in Africa. Nairobi, Oxford University Press, xii, 379 p. (JASPA)

Fighting poverty: Asia's major challenge. New Delhi, 40 p. (ARTEP)

International employment policies: stabilisation, adjustment and poverty. Geneva, vi, 171 p. (ILO-WEP 2-46/WP.1)

Sex inequalities in urban employment in the Third World. By R. Anker and C. Hein. London, Macmillan, xx, 378 p.

"Unemployment and poverty." *In: Report of the Director-General.* (ILC, 72th session, Geneva, report I)

World recession and global interdependance: effects on employment, poverty and policy formation in developing countries. Geneva, 139 p.

1987

Background document. High-level meeting on employment and structural adjustment. Geneva, 55 p.

Beyond the crisis. Santiago. (PREALC)

Pobreza y mercado de trabajo en cuadro paises: Costa Rica, Venezuela, Chile y Peru. Santiago, 118 p. (PREALC)

Protección social de los desocupados en América latina. Por J. Rodriguez. Santiago. (PREALC)

Theoretical and methodological questions in the promotion of people's participation in rural development. By M.A. Rahman. Geneva, 1 vol.

World recession and global interdependence: effects on employment, poverty and policy formation in developing countries. Ed. by R. van der Hoeven and P.J. Richards. Geneva, xi, 139 p.

1988

Conventions and Recommendations

C. concerning employment promotion and protection against unemployment (No. 168)

R. concerning employment promotion and protection against unemployment (No. 176)

Meeting the social debt. Santiago, PREALC, xiii, 124 p.

Recent trends in employment, equity and poverty in African countries. International Conference on "The Human Dimensions of Africa's Economic Recovery and Development", Khartoum. Addis Ababa, 33 p. (JASPA)

1989

From pyramid to pillar: population change and social security in Europe. Geneva, viii, 187 p.

"Rural labour markets and poverty in developing countries." Ed. by S. Radwan. *International Labour Review*, 128(6). (Special issue)

Strategies for growth and employment in Asia: learning from within. By G. Edgren and M. Muqtada. New Delhi. (ARTEP)

Urban poverty and the labour market: access to jobs and incomes in Asian and Latin American cities. By G. Rodgers. Geneva, xv, 257 p.

Urbanisation, poverty and employment: the large metropolis in the third world. By A. Singh. Geneva, 42 p. (Population and Labour Policies Programme. Working paper, 165)

1990

A review of institutional linkages for assistance to the urban informal sector. By R.G. Sison. New Delhi. (ARTEP)

Employment challenges for the 1990s. New Delhi, 147 p. (ARTEP)

Labour laws and the working poor. Bangkok. (ARPLA)

Structural adjustment and its socio-economic effects in rural areas. Geneva, 52 p. (Advisory Committee on Rural Development, 11th session, report II)

Women and social security: progress towards equality of treatment. By A.-M. Brocas et al. Geneva, viii, 116 p.

1991

"Deprivation and the labour market: research issues and priorities." By G. Rodgers and F. Wilkinson. *Labour and society,* 16(2), pp. 219-229.

Dilemma (The) of the informal sector. Report of the Director-General. iii, 65 p. (ILC, 78th session, Geneva, report I)

Monitoring poverty and employment trends: an index for social debt. Paper presented at an international workshop on poverty monitoring in international agencies organized by ILO/PREALC/UNICEF, Santiago.

Poverty monitoring in the rural sector. By H. Tabatabai. Geneva, viii, 42 p. (Rural Employment Policy Research Programme. Working paper, 107.)

"Savings, credit and the poor: what has the ILO to do with the financial sector?" *International Labour Review,* 130(5-6), pp. 645-655.

1992

"Fighting poverty by promoting employment and socio-economic rights at the grass-roots level." By Ph. Garnier and J. Majeres. *International Labour Review,* 131(1), pp. 63-76.

ILO (The) and the elderly; activities and services the International Labour Office can offer to improve the situation of the elderly. Geneva, viii, 80 p.

Monitoring poverty and employment trends: an index for social debt. By R. Infante and V. Tokman. Santiago, 22 p. (PREALC. Working paper, 22)

"Productive employment for the poor." Ed. by J. Gaude and S. Miller. *International Labour Review,* 131(1), 1992. (Special issue)

1993

Incidence of poverty in developing countries: an ILO compendium of data. By H. Tabatabai and M. Fouad. Geneva, 105 p.

Links between structural adjustment and poverty: causal or remedial? By J.J. Thomas. 39 p. (PREALC. Working paper, 373)

Poverty, inequality, exclusion: New approaches to theory and practice. By M. Gaudier. Geneva, xiv, 208 p. (IILS. Bibliographical series, 17)

Poverty monitoring: an international concern. Ed. by R. van der Hoeven and R. Anker. London, Macmillan.

Structural adjustment and income distribution: issues and experience. By A. Rahman Khan. Geneva, ILO, iv, 80 p.

1994

The employment challenge — An agenda for global action, paper prepared for the UNDP Round Table on "Global Change" (Stockholm, 22-25 July), Geneva, 26 p.

"The employment problem and the international economy." By L. Emmerij. *International Labour Review*, 133(4), pp. 449-466.

Overcoming exclusion: Livelihood and rights in economic and social development. By G. Rodgers, with contributions from J. B. de Figueiredo, C. Gore, F. Lapeyre and H. Silver. Geneva, vi, 53 p. (IILS. DP/72)

Social debt: the challenge of equity, Ed. by R. Infante. (PREALC) Santiago, p. 227.

Towards full employment. ILO paper submitted to the Preparatory Committee for the World Summit on Social Development. Geneva. 23 p.

This bibliographical review shows that the poverty issue has consistently affected, and at some times dominated the work of the ILO. In this, the ILO has responded to external events as well as to its own internal dynamics. But it is interesting to note that there do not appear to have been systematic evaluations of the effectiveness of its actions at various periods of its history — assessments of how the problem of poverty has been taken into account by its tripartite constituency, evaluations of the extent to which the various policies proposed have achieved their objectives, or assessments of the impact of ILO thinking on the international community.

Annex

Agenda of the Symposium

Monday, 22 November

11.30 - 12.30: Opening session

- Address by the Director General of the ILO
- The Symposium's objectives and expected outcomes, by Padmanabha Gopinath, Director, International Institute for Labour Studies
- An introduction to the ILO background papers, by Gerry Rodgers, International Institute for Labour Studies

14.00 - 18.00: Session I: The framework of ILO research and action on poverty: A review and panel discussion

Three ILO papers provided the background to this session: A framework paper reviewing the main ILO views on and policy approaches to poverty; a paper summarizing the global situation; and a bibliography of recent writings on poverty.

Introduction: An analytical review of ILO research and action on poverty, by Paul Streeten

Panel discussion:
- Susil Sirivardana, Commissioner, Janasaviya (Poverty Alleviation) Programme, Colombo
- Rodney Bickerstaffe, Associate General Secretary, Unison, the Public Service Union, London
- Nora Lustig, Brookings Institution, Washington
- Jean-Jacques Oechslin, International Organization of Employers, Geneva.
- Jan Bremen, Centre for Asian Studies, University of Amsterdam
- Vremudia Diejomaoh, Director, ILO East Africa Multidisciplinary Advisory Team, Addis-Ababa

General debate

Tuesday, 23 November

09.30 - 13.00:   Session II: Recent trends and new options
in the analysis of poverty

This session explored recent developments in the theoretical and empirical literature on poverty, including new approaches to analysing the sources of poverty and the social and economic mechanisms on which policy against poverty might operate. There was a particular focus on institutional change and economic transformation, and the consequences for deprivation of labour market structure, status and access.

09.30 - 10.45:   1. Key advances in recent work on poverty

Reviewed by Michael Lipton, Institute of Development Studies, University of Sussex

Discussant: Eddy Lee, ILO, Geneva

11.00 - 13.00:   2. Poverty, institutions and labour market outcomes:
Issues and research findings

"Poverty and the operation of urban labour markets in developing countries", by Gerry Rodgers, Jean-Pierre Lachaud and José B. Figueiredo, International Institute for Labour Studies

"Labour market, urban poverty and adjustment: new challenges and policy options", by Ricardo Infante, PREALC, Santiago de Chile

"Rural institutions and rural poverty", by Rizwanul Islam, ARTEP, New Delhi

Discussant: Rosemary Vargas-Lundius, UNDP, New York

"Labour market marginalization and deprivation in Europe, East and West", by Peter Townsend, University of Bristol

"Gender, poverty and the labour market", by Mayra Buvinic, International Centre for Research on Women, Washington

"The new analytics of poverty processes in Africa", by Vali Jamal, Employment and Development Department, ILO

Discussant: John Micklewright, European University Institute, Florence.

14.30 - 18.00: Session III: Poverty and social policy

This session focused on the actual and potential impacts on poverty of a range of social policy instruments, stressing new approaches or new instruments.

14.30 - 16.00: Policy session A: Macro-economic and sectoral policies in strategies against poverty

This session explored how the global, economy-wide and sectoral policy environments affect poverty and modify the effectiveness of action against poverty, taking into account the experiences of the ILO and of other organizations, notably the World Bank. It reviewed development policy at the macro- and sectoral levels, social sector policies and more generally the degree to which the poor benefit from policy interventions to promote economic development.

"The design of macro-economic policy to reduce the adverse effects on poverty of structural adjustment", by Rolph van der Hoeven, ILO, Geneva; "Lessons from the structural adjustment processes of Costa Rica, Chile and Mexico", by Norberto García, PREALC, Santiago de Chile

"The World Bank's strategy to reduce poverty", by Emmanuel Jimenez, Chief, Policy Research Department, Poverty and Human Resources Division, World Bank, Washington

"Adjustment and poverty in Latin America: Government responses", by Nora Lustig, Brookings Institution, Washington

Discussant: Anna Tibaijuka, University of Dar es Salaam

16.30 - 18.00: Policy session B: Poverty and labour market policy

This session reviewed the experience of particular labour market interventions in action against poverty. It was built around papers which reflect different aspects of the ILO's work.

"Labour market policy and poverty", by José-Marcio Camargo, Catholic University of Rio de Janeiro

"Minimum wages and their impact on poverty", by Zafar Shaheed, ILO, Geneva

"Labour market policy for vulnerable groups", by Richard Anker, ILO, Geneva

Discussant: Frank Wilkinson, Department of Applied Economics,
University of Cambridge

Wednesday, 24 November

09.30 - 11.10:   Policy session C: Exclusion, poverty and social integration

This session considered the phenomenon of social exclusion, its
relationship to poverty, and the effectiveness of policy to promote social
integration. Policy approaches covered included transfers, social security
and related "safety-net" policies, and the social protection of labour; the
relationship between poverty, legal systems, values and standards were also
explored. The focus was on policy innovations and their success, and on
how to overcome the mechanisms which lead to the exclusion of particular
groups from coverage and access. The session also examined the concept
of exclusion and its usefulness for the analysis of and action against
poverty in ILO contexts.

"The design of policy against exclusion", by Jean-Baptiste de Foucauld,
Commissaire au Plan, Paris

"Some paradoxes of social exclusion", by Marshall Wolfe, former Head,
Social Policy Division, ECLAC, Santiago de Chile

"Poverty and income security in developing countries: formal and informal
systems and policy options", by S. Guhan, Madras Institute of
Development Studies

Discussants: Hilary Silver, Brown University, Providence, R.I.; Peter
Scherer, OECD, Paris.

11.30-13.00:   Policy session D: The organization and representation
of the poor

This session studied the representation and organization of the poor,
both as a means of directly promoting the interests of the poor, and as a
support to other policies against poverty. It looked at questions such as:
how could one correct the lack of, or the insufficient organization and
representation of deprived population groups; what new forms of organiza-
tion/representation are needed, what new coalitions might be formed; how
could conventional forms of representation be adapted and extended
(notably looking at trade union and employer strategies to represent the
poor); is it possible to improve representation through the ILO's tripartite
constituency?

Panel discussion:
- Luis Quiñones, Programa Economia del Trabajo, Santiago de Chile
- Jimi Adesina, University of Ibadan
- V. Ramachandran, Director, Rajiv Gandhi Foundation, New Delhi
- Ibarra Malonzo, President, National Federation of Labour,
  the Philippines
- A. Redegeld, ATD Quart Monde, Belgium
- Will Hutton, Economics Editor, The Guardian, London

14.00 - 16.00:   Session IV: Where do we go from here?
                  A panel discussion and general debate

This session aimed to produce the elements for an ILO research and policy agenda, taking into account changes in the methods of the office, notably the formulation of regional multidisciplinary teams.

Panellists and commentators:
- Luis Anderson, General Secretary, Inter-American Regional
  Organization of Workers, Mexico
- Jean-Jacques Oechslin, International Organization of Employers,
  Geneva
- Dharam Ghai, Director, U.N. Institute for Social Development
- Víctor Tokman, Director, ILO Regional Office, Lima
- Juhani Lönnroth, Director, Employment and Development
  Department, ILO
- Colin Gillion, Director, Social Security Department, ILO

Followed by a general discussion

List of participants

(This list does not include ILO Staff members from Geneva,
of whom many participated in the symposium)

Mr. Jimi Adesina
Department of Sociology
Faculty of Social Sciences
University of Ibadan
(Nigeria)

Mr. Tatsuru Akimoto
ILO Regional Office for Asia
and the Pacific
Bangkok
(Thailand)

Mr. Luis Anderson
General Secretary
Inter-American Regional
Organization of Workers (ORIT)
Mexico

Mr. Mongi Bedoui
Agence tunisienne de l'Emploi
Ministère de la Formation
professionnelle et de l'Emploi
Tunis
(Tunisia)

Mr. Rodney Bickerstaffe
Associate General Secretary
UNISON
London
(United Kingdom)

Mr. Jan Breman
Centre for Asian Studies
Amsterdam
(The Netherlands)

Mrs. Mayra Buvinić
International Center for Research
on Women
Washington, DC
(United States)

Mr. J.M. Camargo
Professor
Departmento de Economía
PUC
Rio de Janeiro
(Brazil)

Mr. Vremudia Diejomaoh
Director MDT
ILO Office
Addis-Ababa
(Ethiopia)

Mr. Jean-Baptiste de Foucauld
Commissaire au Plan
Paris
(France)

Mr. Norberto García
PREALC
Santiago
(Chile)

Mr. Dharam Ghai
Director
United Nations Research Institute
Geneva
(Switzerland)

Mr. S. Guhan
Madras Institute of Development
Studies
Madras
(India)

Mrs. Mouna Hashem
New York
(United States)

Mr. Ricardo Infante
PREALC
Santiago
(Chile)

Mr. Rizwanul Islam
ILO/ARTEP
New Delhi
(India)

Mr. Emmanuel Jimenez
Chief, Policy Research Dept.
Poverty & Human Resources
Division, World Bank
Washington
(United States)

Mr. Bjorn Jonzon
Deputy Assistant Under Secretary
Ministry of Labour
Stockholm
(Sweden)

Mr. Jean-Pierre Lachaud
Professor
Université de Bordeaux
Pessac
(France)

Mr. Michael Lipton
Institute of Development Studies
University of Sussex
Brighton
(United Kingdom)

Mrs. Nora Lustig
Senior Fellow
The Brookings Institution
Foreign Policy Studies Program
Washington
(United States)

Mr. Negatu Makonnen
Department of Economics
Gothenburg School of Economics
& Commercial Law
Gothenburg
(Sweden)

Mr. Ibarra Malonzo
President
National Federation of Labour
Metro/Manila
(Philippines)

Mr. John Micklewright
Professor, European University
Institute, Department
of Economics, San Domenico
Difiesole/Florence
(Italy)

Mr. Jean Jacques Oechslin
President
International Organization of
Employers
Geneva
(Switzerland)

Mr. G. Pennisi
Director, ILO Office
Rome
(Italy)

Mr. L. Quinones
Coordinator
Area Economía Popular
Programa de Economía y Trabajo
Santiago
(Chile)

Mr. V. Ramachandran
Director
Rajiv Gandhi Foundation
New Delhi
(India)

Mr. A. Redegeld
Mouvement international ATD
Quart Monde
Cergy-Pontoise
(France)

Mr. P. Robineau
United Nations Conference
on Trade and Development
(UNCTAD)
Geneva
(Switzerland)

Mrs. Françoise Rutherford
Commission of the European
Communities
Brussels
(Belgium)

Mr. Peter Scherer
Organisation for Economic
Co-operation and Development
Paris
(France)

Mrs. Hilary Silver
Department of Sociology
and Urban Studies
Brown University
Providence
(United States)

Mr. Susil Sirivardana
Commissioner
Janasaviya (Poverty Alleviation)
Programme
Colombo
(Sri Lanka)

Mr. Paul Streeten
Spencertown
(United States)

Mrs. Natalia Tchernina
Institute of Economics
and Industrial Engineering
Novosibirsk
(Russian Federation)

Mrs. Anna Tibaijuka
Economic Research Bureau
University of Dar-es-Salaam
Dar-es-Salaam
(Tanzania)

Mr. Victor Tokman
Regional Director a.i. for ILO
activities in Latin America
and the Caribbean
Santiago
(Chile)

Mrs. Rosemary Vargas-Lundius
Policy Analysis Officer
Bureau for Programme Policy
and Evaluation, UNDP
New York
(United States)

Mr. Frank Wilkinson
Department of Applied Economics
University of Cambridge
Cambridge
(United Kingdom)

Mr. Marshall Wolfe
East Arlington
(United States)

Ms. Isabel Yépez
Institut d'Etudes des Pays
en Développement
Université catholique de Louvain
Louvain-la-Neuve (Belgium)